D1382077

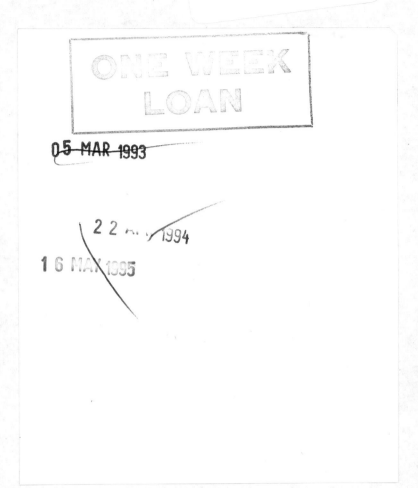

ONE WEEK
LOAN

05 MAR 1993

2 2 ~ ~ 1994

1 6 MAY 1995

SAFE AS HOUSES

Chris Hamnett is a senior lecturer in geography and Director of the Urban and Regional Research Unit at The Open University. He has held visiting appointments at the University of British Columbia, Australian National University and George Washington University, among others. He has written widely on housing. His latest book, *Cities, Housing and Profits*, was published by Hutchinson (London) in 1988.

Michael Harmer is Research Officer for Tai Cymru/Housing for Wales. Previously he worked at the Open University and the Universities of Birmingham and Lancaster. He has undertaken research and published in a number of key areas including housing inheritance, housing subsidies, building-society history and home ownership.

Peter Williams is Professor of Housing Management at the University of Wales, College of Cardiff, and Director of the Centre for Housing Management and Development. Previously he was a deputy director of the Institute of Housing and has worked at universities in Australia, Canada and the UK. He has published extensively in the housing field, in particular on home ownership, gentrification, the home and housing management.

SAFE AS HOUSES

Housing Inheritance in Britain

CHRIS HAMNETT
MICHAEL HARMER
and
PETER WILLIAMS

P·C·P
Paul Chapman
Publishing Ltd

Copyright © 1991 Chris Hamnett Michael Harmer and Peter Williams

Paul Chapman Publishing Ltd
144 Liverpool Road
London
N1 1LA

British Library Cataloguing in Publication Data

Hamnett, Chris
  Safe as houses : housing inheritance in Britain
1. Great Britain. Residences. Inheritance
I. Title II. Harmer, Michael III. Williams, Peter
333.338

ISBN 1–85396–105–1

Typeset by Burns & Smith Ltd, Derby

Printed by St Edmundsbury Press, bound by W.M. Ware

ABCDEFG 6543210

CONTENTS

Acknowledgements   vii
Glossary   ix

1.   Introduction   1
2.   House Prices and House - Price Inflation   11
3.   Housing, Wealth and Equity Extraction   39
4.   Demographic Trends and Future Housing Inheritance   65
5.   Patterns of Bequeathing   76
6.   A Nation of Inheritors?   95
7.   Housing Inheritance: Uses and Impacts   112
8.   Beneficiaries of Inherited Wealth: Case Studies   127
9.   Inheritance and Taxation   140
10. The Future of Housing Inheritance   150

References and Bibliography   163
Index   169

ACKNOWLEDGEMENTS

In undertaking this study and preparing the book we would like to acknowledge the invaluable help of Dr Ian Bracken in the Department of City and Regional Planning at the University of Wales, College of Cardiff. He wrote the forecasting model used in Chapter 4 and, with Dr Lawrence Moore, assisted in preparing the forecast. We would wish to thank Mrs Susan Hodgkinson of the same department for her unfailing assistance and courtesies in getting together a final manuscript. Our thanks also go to the Inland Revenue for kindly preparing data on estates in England, Wales, Scotland and Northern Ireland; the staff at Probate Registry, Somerset House, for assistance with wills; Professor Colin Harbury for early advice; and last (but not least) the individual beneficiaries who shared with us their inheritance experiences. Finally, we would wish to acknowledge the Economic and Social Research Council and the Housing Research Foundation for their joint funding of the research. We remain responsible for any errors of fact or interpretation.

ACKNOWLEDGEMENTS

GLOSSARY

Beneficiary   One who benefits from the provisions of a will.

Housing Equity   The value of a house less any outstanding mortgages or loans secured on the property.

Personalty   Personalty (our personal property) consists of 'movable' assets, such as stocks and shares and money, and personal effects, such as clothing and furniture. It excludes freehold estates and interests in land (see *realty*).

Probate   Probate is a certificate issued by the Family Division of the High Court on the application of the executors named by will. It establishes that the will is valid and that the executors are authorized to act. Probate is not needed for the transfer of jointly owned property, such as a house, for property covered by the Administration of Estates (Small Payments) Act 1965 worth less than £1,500 and for several less significant types of property.

Realty   Realty, or real property, consists mainly of land and houses. It is, broadly speaking, property that is 'immovable'.

Testator   A testator is a person who has made a valid last will and testament to regulate the rights of others over the testator's property or family after his or her death. About half of the population in Britain die having made no will, i.e. intestate.

Trust   A legal arrangement whereby property is transferred to one or more trustees to hold for the benefit of one or more persons who are entitled to enforce the provisions of the trust by court action if necessary. The setting up of trusts is a common way of avoiding inheritance tax.

Will   A document by which a person appoints executors to administer his or her estate after death and directs the manner in which it is to be distributed to the beneficiaries he or she specifies.

1

INTRODUCTION

This is a book about wealth and its creation and distribution through home ownership. The book presents an analysis of an issue increasingly recognized to have major significance for the shape and direction of British society. By means of a wide-ranging study, including a uniquely detailed survey of property inheritance, we present an examination of the processes by which individuals accumulate wealth through housing. In so doing we address a series of important and topical questions, such as how significant is wealth inheritance through the bequest of an individually owned home? How many people inherit such property and what do they do with it? What are the likely impacts on the housing and finance markets and what are the broader implications for British society? We consider the experience of individual households and social groups and look at likely patterns of inheritance well into the twenty-first century. We begin here by sketching out the context within which the housing-inheritance question has arisen.

In the twentieth century Britain has witnessed a revolution in the way people are housed, with home ownership replacing renting as the dominant tenure. As the market has grown and expectations changed, so the conditions for substantial wealth accumulation and release by the ever wider spectrum of home owners have been gradually established. For most, property ownership has increasingly been associated with capital gains. Houses and flats have been perceived as stores of wealth – although over optimistically in some cases. Moreover, it seems that the promotion of ownership as a means of gaining freedom from landlords may have been overtaken by an emphasis on its investment value. Potentially, profits from housing can substantially overtake savings from lifetime waged earnings: a reality that has not escaped the attention of many including a number of politicians. Amongst the latter is Peter Walker, until recently the Secretary of State for Wales and a former Environment Minister. Perhaps unusually he has been alert to the wealth-making potential of home ownership for some years. In 1972 he suggested that council dwellings should be given away (Cooper, 1985) and, more recently, speaking in the Westminster Lecture series on the British Economy in the 1990s, he (1989, pp. 15–16) remarked:

We need to see that the country discontinues to be divided between the two thirds of the nation with a home of their own and one third of the nation who are permanent tenants of the state. We have now had 19 years of Conservative Government with but one four year gap of a Labour Government and yet with all of our efforts 80% who were council house tenants remain permanent tenants of the state. People who in the main are families who pass nothing on to generations in comparison with the two thirds in their towns who now convey substantial sums to their children and grandchildren. We need to pursue even more dynamic policies to see this spread so that we do become the capital owning democracy that Iain Macleod contemplated in the late 1960's.

Despite the realization that the growth of home ownership carried with it profound implications regarding wealth and life chances, it is strikingly apparent that there has, until recently, been a notable lack of interest in this issue. In part this is because the growth of home ownership has been gradual and only in the last few years has it been perceived as the dominant and 'natural' tenure. With poorer regions and income groups lagging well behind the national averages, most attention has focused on the promotion of ownership rather than on any consequences this expansion in the individual ownership of property may have. Furthermore, it is only with the most recent sustained boom in prices (from 1982 until 1989) that the inheritance implications of mass home ownership were really widely grasped.

For Peter Walker, Margaret Thatcher and others, home ownership has a range of virtues but key among them is the matter of something to pass on to one's children. As Mrs Thatcher commented in 1979 with respect to the sale of council houses, 'It will give more of our people ... that prospect of handing something on to their children and grandchildren which owner occupation provides'. Not only does inheritance carry with it a sense of continuity and stability but it also creates, through enhanced wealth, the potential for the exercise of greater choice by the beneficiaries. The Conservative government has become well aware of the potential this may have for private schooling, health care, and the like, and the long-term impacts of such choices. The housing market in general and home ownership in particular thus become, through the mechanism of inheritance, a potent force in the political process. But such benefits do, of course, have their costs. Endowing the tenure with these virtues, the government of the day is then obliged to work hard to maintain the conditions whereby property can be acquired and profits realized. In Britain this has proven difficult in 1989 and 1990. The high-interest regime introduced in the late 1980s to protect the pound, to prop up Britain's economy and to curb the 1982–9 house-price boom has undermined confidence in property ownership and halted further growth (in the short term at least) of the inheritance value of property. Conflicting pressures now exist to reduce interest rates, not least because it is felt this could simply result in a new surge in house prices. The situation is complex and it has created the opportunity for more attractive investment goods to emerge to compete with property. The 1970s and 1980s may have been the golden era for home ownership.

In the final analysis, therefore, the inheritance potential of housing is linked to prices and the demand for and cost of purchase. Late in the most recent house-price boom period, the inheritance factor began to attract a great deal of attention. Among a number of analyses published by banks and finance houses the 1987 Morgan Grenfell report, 'Housing inheritance and wealth', attracted considerable interest. Morgan Grenfell estimated the total value of former owner-occupied houses in estates in 1987 to be £6.5 billion and that, with certain assumptions regarding inflation, this would rise to £24.3 billion by the turn of the century. Inheritance through house property in 1987 was thus greater than the value of mortgage tax relief or housing benefit in that year and, like those two subsidies, it was a benefit enjoyed by a specific group – in this case, mainly the relatives of deceased owner-occupiers. As we show later in the book, property inheritance is highly clustered and, as a consequence, it has important implications for patterns of inequality. Given the expansion of home ownership in the recent past, it is evident that considerable potential for inheritance through the housing market now exists.

We have thus gone from a situation where ownership was valued for the assumed benefits it carried regarding thrift, independence and stability, to a position where more emphasis is placed on the investment/inheritance value the dwelling represents. Clearly it is possible that this is a short-term factor and, as prices rise and fall, so such attitudes to ownership may change. Survey evidence shows considerable stability in the reasons for buying property and, although investment is one reason, other factors – such as changes in family size or job moves – tend to dominate (see, for example, Saunders, 1990). House prices have risen sharply in recent years and a substantial industry has been built up around the buying and selling of property that has a considerable interest in rising prices. This, of course, brings home an important issue we develop later: the extent to which housing wealth is real or fictitious. Much of the promotional commentary surrounding property prices pays no regard to inflation or the extent to which capital is put into a dwelling to improve it. Price in year X is simply compared with price in year X plus 10 and the change noted. Just like returns from any investment, the nominal increase can look staggering but the reality can be sharply different.

Despite such qualifications and the very evident uncertainties of the housing market, it is apparent that the focus on the investment value of home ownership can and is contributing to the residualization of other tenures, notably public housing and a corrosive marginalization of the non-owner in British society. The stress on the virtues of ownership help to create a climate where other tenures are measured against it. What positive features they may possess are held for nought by the popular commentaries against the supposedly certain benefits of home ownership – namely capital gains. Public housing in particular has suffered in recent years from this comparison. In the 1930s the comparison was with the private rented sector and building societies and others were not slow to point out the virtues of ownership. As the private rented sector declined under the dual assault from home ownership and public renting, so the focus has shifted to the latter – with all the negative consequences we are aware of. Even though in the UK we still have a public sector of some 5 million dwellings (25 per cent of all households) the imagery associated with it has become that of a residual sector – to be maintained only until something better comes along. Within this apparently 'residual' sector live a large number of what is an increasingly marginal population: households dependent on state benefits and with little or no access to life beyond continuing poverty. For them the wealth-creating potential of home ownership is not only a distant reality but it also acts to exacerbate their own position. As those who own accumulate, they increasingly move along a trajectory that separates them from the non-owners. In analysing wealth, inheritance and home ownership we cannot disregard the negative consequences of this process.

Housing wealth and inheritance

Britain's middle classes, so long demoralised and impoverished, are about to grow rich once more. ... The generation of Britons now reaching retirement age was the first to put a big proportion of its savings into home ownership. Houses have proved a wonderful investment, thanks to a tax system which smiles on owner occupiers, the virtual disappearance of private rented accommodation, and a big growth in the number of households. At the end of the second world war, a quarter of Britons were home owners. Now almost 60% are. Today 50% of pensioner households are home owners. ... These pensioners often caricatured as poor are really growing rich, but their riches are tied up in roofs over their heads. Only when they die, bequeathing their property to their children, can this most popular form of British investment be cashed in.

So the bequest, that staple of Victorian melodrama, is about to make a dramatic comeback.

The Economist, 1988a. p. 13)

The above quote from *The Economist* is indicative of contemporary comment on inheritance. It reflects a growing public awareness of an issue that, for a number of factors, has been developing in significance over a number of years and has become pronounced recently because of a particular combination of circumstances. There are perhaps four factors that account for the rise in significance of housing wealth. These are the growth of home ownership and trends in house prices that have led, in turn, to a growing volume of housing equity and shifts in the pattern of personal wealth holdings. Alongside these factors have been a series of demographic changes that have had important effects on the wealth-realization process.

Home ownership has emerged from being the tenure of a tiny minority of the population at the turn of the century to being the dominant tenure today. It has risen from well under 10 per cent in 1900 to over 65 per cent in 1990. Moreover it has become the most mixed tenure in terms of the socioeconomic characteristics of households, thus losing, in part, its élite image. At the same time, in becoming more widespread, ownership is now more varied in terms of the size, quality and price of dwellings, and in the income and characteristics of the occupants (see Forrest, Murie and Williams, 1990). The differences between regions and groups suggest that, in some areas, ownership might still expand rapidly given favourable circumstances, whereas in others future growth may be quite limited. Surveys of tenure preference indicate that most households would prefer to be owners but a substantial minority either expect to rent (because they cannot afford to own) or wish to rent (because they do not want the responsibilities of ownership). Ownership levels are much higher amongst the younger age-groups reflecting the growth of this tenure in recent years. Thus the likelihood of beneficiaries in each successive generation already being home owners is getting greater all the time. There is a suggestion that because of the recession of the early to mid-1980s, ownership levels may ultimately be lower in households now forming, but the evidence is weak.

House prices have also risen relative to wages. They have gone up by over 1,000 per cent since 1970, while average earnings have gone up by around 700 per cent. In relation to inflation in general, housing has performed relatively well. Out of the 20 years, 1970–89, house prices increased faster than the rate of inflation in 13 of those years. In 1990 mortgage interest rates moved to record high levels (15.5 per cent), inflation increased to over 8 per cent and national average price increases fell to around 0 per cent.

The Halifax Building Society (Halifax Building Societ 1989, p. 3) commented that 'because general inflation is much lower than was the case from 1974–1976, we not only expect real falls in house prices (general inflation higher than house-price inflation), this time they will be accompanied by a noticeable fall in average nominal (cash) house prices'. As is shown in Chapter 2, although house prices have risen overall there has been a pattern of considerable fluctuation. This reflects changes in incomes and interest rates and the supply of property and mortgages. The ratio of house prices to income has risen sharply in recent years and has moved well above the historic 3.5 average. Indeed, in late 1988 the ratio exceeded 5 in the South and this (in conjunction with rising interest rates) lead to the very rapid cessation of the house-price boom in that region (Amex Bank Review, 1990). One of the features of the 1980s was the divergence in regional house-price trends. The gap between the highest-priced English region (London) and the lowest priced (Northern) was 185 per cent in 1988 (*Nationwide Anglia Bulletin*, Q.3, 1988). Subsequently they have narrowed again suggesting a cyclical pattern of variation. Price differentials are likely to remain, however, reflecting the different economic fortunes of the regions.

The growth of home ownership and rising house prices has meant that more people have accumulated equity in property – in other words, the property has a value greater than the outstanding mortgage. As the level of equity in housing has risen, so people have become more aware of the possibilities of releasing it through cash withdrawal by trading down: not reinvesting the full proceeds of a previous sale and, most importantly, last-time sales that arise because of death, changes of tenure or emigration. Ignoring the cash put into moves and improvement by owners, equity withdrawal in 1984 was estimated at £10.4 billion, around £4.5 billion of which were sales of houses by or on behalf of elderly people (Holmans, 1986a). Clearly not all of these will be due to death, but the great proportion will be, suggesting that around 40 per cent of the equity withdrawn from the owner occupied market in any year will be because of death and inheritance.

The value of housing has played a key role in patterns of personal wealth holding. In 1968, dwellings net of mortgage debt accounted for 17 per cent of net personal wealth. With the rise of house prices over the intervening years, by 1974 dwellings accounted for 37 per cent of net personal wealth (excluding pension rights). By 1985 it had risen to 48 per cent, reflecting continuing house-price rises. It should be noted, however, that the calculation of overall personal wealth by the Inland Revenue is based on samples of estates at death. Actual wealth distribution amongst the population as a whole may be quite different, not least in our case due to the 1 million council houses sold between 1979 and 1989. Whatever the present figure for net personal wealth across the entire population, it is apparent that housing is now very significant. The growth of ownership has brought greater wealth to many households and, with inflating house prices, the differentials between them and non-owning households have grown much greater.

In 1986 the UK's estimated population stood at 56.7 million, an increase of some 13 per cent over the 1951 population (OPCS, 1987). It has been projected to rise a further 4 per cent by the year 2000 giving, a population close to 59 million. Households are also expected to increase, from 21.1 million in 1989 to 23.9 million by the turn of the century, although the rate of household formation is forecast to decline. In England and Wales the net increase in the number of households is expected to fall from 180,000 a year in the 1980s to 95,000 a year at the end of the 1990s. These changes are significant because they will influence the actual demand for housing in the future. However, with respect to inheritance and wealth, in the short term they are overshadowed by two other critical factors – first, the growth in the number of home owners of pensionable age in recent decades and continued growth in the future and, second, the reductions in mortality rates.

Households headed by retired males and females in England and Wales will rise from 5.3 million in 1985 to 5.8 million in 2001 and within that the number of very elderly households (80 years and over) will grow significantly. This increased longevity of individuals (and therefore households) will affect the inheritance rate by slowing the benefaction process and increasing the period in which people are reliant on pensions and savings. By the year 2024 in the UK, males will be expected to live an average of 75.2 years and females 80.3 years. Currently it is 72.0 and 77.7 respectively. Changes in longevity have had and will have the effect of postponing intergenerational inheritance, slowing the impact of the large numbers of people now entering or already in the retirement stage of their lives. Recognizing this, this analysis is further developed in Chapter 4 by projecting ahead these demographic changes and linking them to the inheritance process.

Realizing housing wealth

As argued above, there are a number of factors that have lead to the current preoccupation with the wealth potential of home ownership. This potential has been greatly enhanced by the circumstances prevailing in the UK in recent years – namely the inflation in house prices – but it is equally important to appreciate how this potential is translated into reality.

In the UK, home ownership has been treated relatively generously in taxation terms and, at root, it is taxation that influences the outcomes we are concerned with here (for a detailed discussion, see Chapter 9). Purchasers are given assistance through the taxation system, sellers are not taxed on the proceeds of selling their main residence and the deceased are given a substantial allowance (£128,000 in 1990) before inheritance tax is applied to their estates (typically among home owners it is the dwelling that makes up most of the estate). All of these factors do a great deal to enhance the attractiveness of home ownership and to endow it with favoured status in tenure terms. In reality this taxation treatment allows the generated wealth to be realized (it also adds to the pressures that generate that wealth). In other countries no tax relief is given on house-purchase costs, capital gains are taxed and more punitive inheritance taxes are imposed. Estimates of the value of this assistance vary considerably but one recent figure (H.M. Treasury 1990 pp. 107–9) for tax relief and capital gains exemption was £14 billion (estimated for 1988–9 at £7 billion for mortgage interest tax relief and £7 billion for capital gains exemption).

The taxation treatment accorded to housing by successive UK governments reflects a desire to promote and sustain this tenure and its wealth-transmitting potential, arguing that this accords with the wishes of the electorate. However, as Kay and King in their authoritative book, *The British Tax System*, (1986) suggest, house prices reflect the capitalized value of tax concessions and in that sense buyers pay for their tax concessions. 'The principal gainers', Kay and King argue (*ibid*, p. 56), 'have been those who have owned houses in the past – or rather their descendants. ... Perhaps if it had been understood that the main beneficiaries of the policy of tax concessions to owner-occupation were the dead, the policy might have been adopted somewhat less enthusiastically'. But as this book will make very clear the benefits are then transmitted from the dead to the living through the inheritance process. Of course, stored equity can be removed prior to death by trading down, remortgaging or changing tenure and it is estimated that about 60 per cent of housing equity is withdrawn through these different routes. The other 40 per cent is extracted by death and inheritance and this is the most important single route by which equity is extracted from housing.

Home ownership has been promoted through an electorally popular and favourable tax treatment and politicians judge it difficult to propose the complete and rapid withdrawal of these concessions in their election manifestos. In recent years there has been some moderation of this view even within the Conservative Party, with Mr Lawson, a previous Chancellor of the Exchequer, being known to favour the withdrawal of mortgage-interest tax relief. Most recently, the Bow Group has published a pamphlet arguing for its abolition (Atkinson, 1989). However the Prime Minister, Mrs Thatcher, has gone on record as saying there will be no change while she remains at No 10.

In essence the outcry whenever the issue has been raised is sufficient to deter reformers – and the high interest rates of 1990 made the debates about interest-rate relief even more sensitive. Since the increase to £30,000 in 1983, the Conservative government salved its conscience by making no further increases in the amount eligible for relief and seems content to erode but not remove the benefit (in 1989 mortgage-interest tax relief was restricted to £30,000 per property and improvement work ceased to be eligible). The taxing of capital gains has also been an electoral issue, not least because it is a tax applied to other assets. Home ownership has, however, retained its privileged status as an exempt asset and again appears unassailable. Indeed, unlike mortgage-interest rate relief, where – by keeping the eligible limit low the treatment becomes less generous year by year (even more so if the removal of higher-rate tax bands are considered) – inheritance tax has been uprated each year since 1980 (see Table 9.5). The lower limit below which tax is not levied has gone up from £50,000 in March 1980 to £128,000 in

March 1990, though it should be noted that since 1988 inheritances above this limit have been taxed at the one rate of 40 per cent. Overall, it has been a pattern of more generous treatment and it remains to be seen whether this uprating will continue.

The politics of the taxation of home ownership thus remain complex, even though there is little sign at present of radical change. As the inheritance factor grows in importance, so it may become easier to withdraw at least some of the privileges now in existence. However, it is evident that the Conservative government has identified housing wealth as one means by which the elderly might supplement their income during their own lifetime and thus reduce their dependence on the State. As the number of elderly in general and the number of elderly home owners in particular grows, so both the pressures and opportunities to do this intensify. If we do see a rise in the use of equity during the lifetime of the household then it will diminish the significance of the inheritance issue and, at the same time, maintain the pressure for tax reliefs on the use of that equity. We return to these issues later, but it is worth noting here that equity extraction during the owners' lifetime now has a well-established place in US social policy (see, for example, Wise, 1988 and Scholen and Chen, 1980).

Housing inheritance: its impact on British society

Alongside its concern to create a property owning democracy, the current government has been keen to increase the levels of home ownership in Britain in order to ensure that more households have something to pass on to succeeding generations. The government has enhanced the right-to-buy scheme for council and non-charitable housing association tenants on several occasions and, in 1990, it now provides for discounts up to a maximum of £50,000.

About 50 per cent of the growth in home ownership that has taken place in the 1980s has come through the right to buy. While it would be possible to develop the existing scheme further, the government has announced plans to fund transferrable discounts and to develop a 'rents into mortgages' scheme. At present the latter is being piloted in Scotland and Wales but there is every prospect that it will become a major manifesto commitment. The scheme allows households who are not on housing benefit to convert their rental payments into mortgage payments. This scheme has many parallels with the proposals put forward by Peter Walker in the early 1970s and subsequently by the Tory Reform Group in 1979 in the publication, *An End to the Council Landlord*.

Although those schemes indicate a continuing desire to expand home ownership it is also clear there is widespread recognition that there is an upper limit for ownership (see, for example, the interview with Mark Boleat in *Roof*, March 1990). If home ownership continues to convey wealth to successive generations, then governments are also accepting the continuance of a divide between those who inherit and those who do not. This divide may be blurred by the experience of those who, while inheriting property (or the cash proceeds), do not benefit a great deal because of shared estates and/or low-value property but, unless it is eradicated by other means, the property-inheritance process could be central to the maintenance of social divisions in Britain. The boundary may be moved over time with more households joining the 'haves' but not eliminated. As we go on to argue in this book, there is a possibility that the inheritance process becomes an assumed element in the life-cycle of a household with all the implications that has for those who have not inherited and will not do so. Equally, assumptions regarding the ownership of property and the equity stored within it are beginning to play a part in thinking about social provision for an ageing society. In a recent study, Mackintosh, Leather and Means (1990) conclude that home equity-release schemes will play an increasing part in the financing of care as policy is reshaped and moves from direct provision to support through the community.

As this book shows, the incidence of inheritance is not a random process but has a strong class and tenure bias, and this has a 'cumulative effect'. The children of owner-occupiers are more likely to be home owners themselves and the incidence of ownership is strongly class- and socioecomic-group related. In other words, the process will build upon existing inequalities even though home ownership is now more widely distributed than any other tenure. Over the last decade government policy has encouraged greater differentiation in the provision of a range of services (e.g. schooling, health and housing) by placing a growing emphasis on consumer choice and the capacity of the user to pay for such choices. Under this model, the capacity to pay becomes all important and this clearly links to the inheritance process. While substantial equity may be extracted and used during the benefactor's lifetime (not least because such assets will be accounted for in the provision of social care), it is likely that a significant asset will remain to be inherited and used for the consumption of goods and services or for investment. Beneficiaries will thus benefit in a variety of ways enhancing their life chances and the divisions between themselves and the non-inheritors.

Inheritance could thus lead to reduced 'dependence' on State provision by a very significant proportion of the population. This reduction could be a function both of choice by the individuals concerned and of necessity as expenditure is reduced in line with the rise in property-related wealth. At the same time, it is important to realize that such a reduction will come about as a consequence of the State creating the conditions in which the creation and extraction of property-related wealth come about and are maintained. In that sense reliance on the State is enhanced and, as with the pattern of housing expenditure in the 1980s, we will see a re-orientation of the role of the State rather than a reduction (Hamnett, 1989b).

Structure of this book

This book provides the first major study of the housing inheritance process in the UK and provides a timely contribution to what has emerged as major factor in debates about the shape of British society in the twenty-first century. In this Introduction we have sketched out the broad lineaments of the home ownership and inheritance process. As we have shown, property inheritance is a matter of considerable significance with important implications for individuals, government and society. In the next three chapters we examine the impact of house-price inflation on equity accumulation in housing; the nature and scale of equity release via inheritance; and the extent of that release in the next century in the light of a number of important demographic changes. In Chapters 5, 6, 7 and 8 we go on to look at patterns of bequeathing, who inherits property and what they do with their inheritance, with Chapter 8 giving details of a small number of individual case studies. Finally, in Chapters 9 and 10, we consider the taxation treatment of heritable wealth and seek to draw a series of conclusions as to the impact of property inheritance on British society and how the inheritance issue may develop in the future.

The research on which this book is based was undertaken over the period 1987–9. It was conducted using a variety of methods, namely, secondary analysis of published and unpublished data; primary analysis of the wills records held in Somerset House; interviews with individual beneficiaries; and, finally, a major random-sample survey of households using an NOP omnibus survey. The combination of these different sources and methods has provided the insights into the inheritance process we report on here. Perhaps inevitably in a study that has broken new ground, with hindsight we can now identify areas where our empirical work could have been further developed and this work is now in hand with support from the Joseph Rowntree Memorial Trust.

2

HOUSE PRICES AND HOUSE-PRICE INFLATION

Introduction

We suggested in the introduction that the growing importance of housing wealth and housing inheritance in Britain since the 1970s rests on two key factors. First, the years from 1945 have seen the rapid expansion of the owner occupied sector – from 3 million households (25 per cent) in 1945 to almost 15 million (66 per cent) in 1989. Over the same period the private rented sector contracted from 65 per cent of households to under 10 per cent. These trends are not unconnected. Millions of private rented houses were sold into home ownership since the war and, between 1945 and 1975, 40 per cent of the growth in the number of owner-occupied dwellings occurred as a result of sales from private renting. As a result, Britain has moved rapidly from being a nation of renters to a nation of home owners with ownership levels similar to those in Australia, Canada and the USA (Harris and Hamnett, 1987). Second, the average price of houses has increased very rapidly since the early 1960s – far faster than the general level of prices, and faster than the price of many other assets. As a result, housing is now a key element in personal wealth ownership. The scale of this transformation can be simply shown. In 1960 housing comprised 17 per cent of net personal wealth in Britain. By 1975 this had risen to 37 per cent (Royal Commission on the Distribution of Income and Wealth, 1977), and by 1987 it had reached no less than 48 per cent (Building Societies Association, 1987).

The rise in house prices in Britain over the last thirty years has been enormous. Accustomed to the inflated house prices of the 1970s and 1980s, the house prices a generation ago seem so unreal that they conjure up a vision of a pre-inflationary Eden. This is a rather unrealistic picture, of course, not least because incomes and prices have also risen considerably over the same period. But as we will show, house prices have risen much faster than prices in general (though not incomes), and houses now cost considerably more in real terms than they did 20 or 30 years ago. As a result, existing owners now own assets that are often worth considerably more in real terms than they were when they bought them. Houses have not just kept their value in real terms: they have increased greatly in value, and most existing owners have found that home ownership has been a very good investment as well as a desirable form of accommodation. Home ownership has functioned not just as a store of wealth and a hedge against inflation but also as a *source* of wealth. As Ray Pahl (1975, p. 291) has put it, 'A family may gain more from the housing market in a few years than would be possible in savings from a lifetime of earnings'. Downs (1981, p. 3) has argued that many people have effectively 'moved their savings under their own roof', and Sternlieb and Hughes (1978) has gone so far as to suggest that the USA is now a 'post-shelter society' where the investment role of housing is as, if not more, important as its traditional role of providing a roof over people's heads.

In the rest of this chapter we examine the evidence for these claims, and the views of critics such as Duncan (1989), who argue that, although the nominal gains from house-price inflation seem large, real gains have been much smaller than generally claimed. Nor have house prices and rates of price inflation been even over the country as a whole. The existence of a marked north–south house-price gap is well known, and we therefore look at regional differences in house prices, rates of house-price inflation, ease of access to home ownership and accumulation potential across the country. First, however, it is important to outline the national history of house-price changes over the last forty years.

House-price inflation: the national picture

The increase in national average house prices in Britain over the last thirty years has been quite massive, at least when measured in nominal terms – that is, at prevailing or current prices making no allowance for inflation in general. In 1956, the first year for which Building Society Association statistics are available (Table 2.1), the average house price was £2,230. House prices rose slowly through the second half of the 1950s to £2,480 in 1960. The rate of inflation increased more rapidly during the 1960s and, by 1969, on the eve of the first major house-price boom, the average price had doubled to just under £5,000 – an increase of 100 per cent.

The years 1971–3 were the first period of rapid house-price inflation in Britain. In 1972 and 1973 average prices rose by 35 per cent a year, and by 1973 the national average price stood at just over £11,000 – an increase of just over 100 per cent in three years. From 1974 to 1977 house prices rose much more slowly and, by 1977, the average price was £14,000. But 1978 marked the start of the second major period of house-price inflation and, by 1980, average house prices had risen to £24,300 – a rise of almost 75 per cent over three years. In 1981 and 1982, the second phase of stagnation, house prices remained stable, and even fell slightly in London. But in 1983, prices began to rise again, and continued rising ever more rapidly until August 1988, when the impact of the Budget abolition of multiple mortgage-interest tax relief on the same property, and rising interest rates, suddenly took the fire away from beneath an already very overheated market. House prices had risen far more rapidly than average incomes since 1983, and the ratio of national average house prices to national average incomes, which had been about 3.5 in 1983 and 1984, had risen to an unsustainable 4.5 – their highest level since 1973.

The second half of 1988 and 1989 saw price rises slowing down rapidly, particularly in London and the South East, where prices had risen most rapidly. In 1990 prices fell in London, the South East, South West and East Anglia by some 10–20 per cent according to the Halifax and Nationwide Anglia Building Societies. There is no doubt that 1989 marked the start of the third phase of price stagnation since the early 1970s. The last twenty years have therefore been characterized by a cyclical pattern of rapid boom followed by relative stagnation and price falls in real, if not in absolute, terms. But – and this is the key point – the average price of houses in 1988 was £55,000. This represents an increase in nominal terms of over 100 per cent from 1982, when the average price was £25,500. Each of the three booms have therefore seen average prices double and, over the long term, average prices have risen by exactly 1,000 per cent from 1970 (£5,000 to £55,000), and by 2,000 per cent from 1960. This is a remarkable increase, and those fortunate enough to have bought in 1970 have seen the price of their houses rise tenfold on average. And even those who bought in 1976, when the average price was £13,000, have seen the value of their houses rise by over 300 per cent. It is clear that, other things being equal, the longer people have owned, the greater the rise in the value of their homes.

These increases are purely nominal ones, of course, and they take no account of the general rate of inflation. This is of great importance for a rise of 1,000 per cent in the average price of houses when prices in general have risen by 1,000 per cent would mean that the real value of a house in terms of purchasing power over other goods and services is precisely the same. There would have been no real capital accumulation, although owners would have seen an increase in their equity as their mortgage was reduced. However, Figure 2.1 shows that, whereas the retail price index rose from a base of 100 in 1954 to 850 in 1984, national average house prices rose almost exactly twice as fast to 1,650 in 1984. Real house prices therefore doubled over this period and, given the doubling of nominal house prices from 1983 to 1988, real house prices in 1988 were almost two and a half times higher than in 1954. But this increase in the real price of houses has not been an even one. Figure 2.2 shows that real house prices have varied considerably during the 1970s and 1980s and, although the general trend has been an upwards one (with steep rises in each of the three major house-price booms), the real price of houses also fell sharply from 1974 to 1977 and again from 1981 to 1982. It is also clear that the real price of houses began to fall sharply in 1989 and 1990, particularly in the south of Britain. The rise in the real price of houses has therefore been very uneven, and those who bought at or near the peak of each boom probably saw the real value of their investment fall in subsequent years. Timing is of considerable importance, not just for capital gains but for their measurement.

House prices and incomes

National average house prices rose by 1,000 per cent in 1969–88 and by about 2.5 times in real terms. However, although many potential first-time buyers have experienced considerable difficulties in buying, particularly those on below-average incomes and at times of rapidly rising prices, it has not become 10 times as

Table 2.1 The relationship between house prices, retail prices and earnings, 1956–89

Period	Average price (all houses) (£)	Increase (%)	Average earnings (£)	Increase (%)	House price/earnings ratio	Increase in retail prices index (%)	Increase in real personal disposable income (RPDI) (%)	Increase in real house prices (%)
1956	2,230		697		3.19	4.9	2.6	
1957	2,280	2.2	731	4.9	3.12	3.7	1.6	−1.4
1958	2,360	2.6	756	3.4	3.10	3.1	1.5	−0.5
1959	2,360	0.9	793	4.9	2.98	0.5	5.1	0.4
1960	2,480	5.1	849	7.1	2.92	1.1	6.6	3.9
1961	2,710	9.3	896	5.5	3.03	3.4	4.1	5.7
1962	2,890	6.6	922	2.9	3.14	4.3	1.1	2.2
1963	3,100	7.3	966	4.8	3.21	1.9	4.6	5.3
1964	3,390	9.4	1,040	7.7	3.26	3.2	4.2	6.0
1965	3,740	10.3	1,114	7.1	3.36	4.8	2.1	5.2
1966	4,040	8.0	1,187	6.6	3.40	3.9	2.2	3.9
1967	4,270	5.7	1,230	3.6	3.47	2.5	1.5	3.1
1968	4,650	8.9	1,326	7.8	3.51	4.7	1.8	4.0
1969	4,850	4.3	1,430	7.8	3.39	5.4	0.9	1.0
1970	5,190	7.0	1,595	11.5	3.25	6.4	3.9	0.6
1971	6,130	18.1	1,752	9.8	3.50	9.4	1.3	8.0
1972	8,420	37.4	1,964	12.1	4.29	7.1	8.5	28.3
1973	11,120	32.1	2,249	14.5	4.95	9.2	6.8	20.8
1974	11,300	1.6	2,659	18.2	4.25	16.1	−0.8	−12.5
1975	12,119	7.2	3,320	24.9	3.65	24.2	0.3	−13.7
1976	12,999	7.3	3,823	15.2	3.40	16.5	−0.6	−7.9
1977	13,922	7.1	4,170	9.1	3.34	15.8	−1.1	−7.5
1978	16,297	17.1	4,749	13.9	3.43	8.2	6.9	8.2

1979	21,047	29.1	5,503	15.9	3.82	13.4	5.4	13.8
1980	24,307	15.5	6,725	22.2	3.61	18.0	1.4	-2.1
1981	24,810	2.1	7,497	11.5	3.31	11.9	-1.3	-8.8
1982	25,553	3.0	8,165	8.9	3.13	8.6	-0.1	-5.2
1983	28,593	11.9	8,693	6.5	3.29	4.6	2.2	7.0
1984	30,812	7.8	9,447	8.7	3.26	4.9	2.3	2.8
1985	33,188	7.7	10,069	6.6	3.30	6.1	2.3	1.5
1986	38,121	14.9	10,790	7.2	3.53	3.4	3.8	11.1
1987	44,220	16.0	11,648	7.9	3.80	4.1	3.2	7.2
1988	54,280	22.7	12,782	9.7	4.25	4.9	4.8	17.9
1989	62,135	14.5	13,932	9.0	4.50	7.7	4.1	6.3

Notes

1. From 1975 the average house-price figures are at the approval stage. Between 1966 and 1974 the figures are equal to new house prices at the approval stage multiplied by the ratio (in the following quarter) of completion-stage figures for all house prices to new house-price figures from the sample survey results. Prior to 1966 the figures are equal to 0.98 of the actual figures for new house prices at the mortgage-approval stage. The series for all prices is therefore far from perfect but it is the best available and is adequate for developing a relationship with average earnings.

2. As there are no officially published figures for average annual earnings, it is necessary to construct a series. The method of construction is as follows:

   (a) From 1976 onwards the *New Earnings Survey* figures referring to weekly earnings in April of each year for those male employees whose pay was not affected by absence are used. (The annual rate of pay in April is calculated by multiplying by 52.) Quarterly and annual figures are then calculated by application of the index of average earnings (new series, whole economy, seasonally adjusted) to the April base.

   (b) From 1970 to 1975 the *New Earnings Survey* figures are linked to the 'old' index of average earnings (production industries and some services).

   (c) From 1963 to 1970 a backwards projection is made by application of the index of average earnings to the first *New Earnings Survey*, which refers to April 1970.

   (d) Prior to 1963 the series is constructed by reference to the percentage increase in the twice-yearly (April and October) survey of average weekly earnings of manual workers in manufacturing industry, with the figures derived from (b) above for April 1963 used as a base.

3. The source for the retail prices index and real personal disposable incomes is *Economic Trends*.

4. Increases are over previous year or same period of previous year.

5. All figures for 1989 apart from average house prices are estimates.

(*Source*: Building Societies Association, *Housing Finance*, February, 1990)

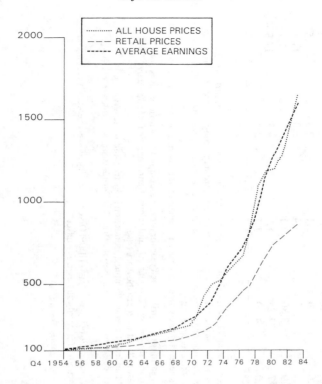

Figure 2.1   Indices of house prices, retail prices and average earnings, 1954–84 (Source: Nationwide Building Society, 1985)

difficult to buy since 1970. Looking at the growth of average earnings since 1954, Figure 2.1 shows that from a base of 100 they had risen to 1,590 by 1984, whereas national average house prices rose to 1,650 – a very similar rate of increase. As a result, the average house-price:earnings ratio 3.26 in 1984 was little more than the ratio of 1956 of 3.19. When measured over this period as a whole, houses did not become more expensive relative to incomes.

These changes are averages, of course, and like all averages they often conceal as much as they reveal. Figure 2.1 shows the relationship between changes in average earnings and house prices over time and it can be seen that the two have not risen in step. Instead, house prices rose slower than average earnings during the late 1950s, faster than earnings from 1961 to 1968 and slower in 1969 and 1970. They then rose much faster than earnings during the years 1971–3, slower than earnings from 1974 to 1977, faster from 1977 to 1979, slower from 1980 to 1983 and much faster from 1983 to 1988. The same pattern can be seen if we look at house-price:earnings ratios over the last thirty years (Table 2.1 and Figure 2.3). They fell from 3.19 in 1956 to a low of 2.92 in 1960, rose to 3.5 in 1968, fell to 3.25 in 1970 then rose rapidly to a high of 4.95 in 1973. They then fell to a 3.34 in 1977, rose to 3.82 in 1979, fell to 3.13 in 1982 and then rose rapidly to a peak of 4.50 in 1989. It can be argued that this ratio (like the high ratio in 1973) is temporary and unsustainable in

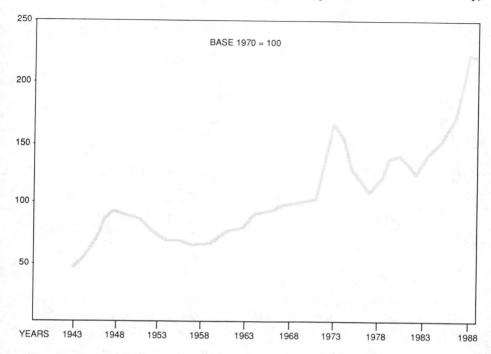

Figure 2.2   National average house prices in real terms, 1943–88 (Source: Holmans, 1990)

anything but the short term, and that the house-price falls in London and the South East in 1989 and 1990 mark the start of an adjustment process whereby house-price:income ratios will fall back, to something approaching their historical average. These ratios are national averages, and there are marked regional variations. London and the South East have the highest ratios, and the northern regions have the lowest (Figure 2.4). These differences have important implications for ease of access and affordability in that house purchase is, on average, easier in the north than it is the south, despite the lower average incomes in the north.

These cyclical changes in house prices and earnings suggest the existence of a process linking the two. The process is, we would suggest, quite simple. When earnings have run ahead of prices for a few years, and house-price:earnings ratios have fallen, it is easier to afford to buy a house. As more buyers enter the market, the relationship between the supply of and the demand for houses begins to shift, and house prices begin to rise rapidly. As house prices rise, new buyers are drawn into the market, worried (quite rightly) that if they do not buy now, they may not be able to. In this respect, the market for house buying is a very unusual one, in that price rises led to increasing demand, at least initially. As prices are bid up, the house-price:earning ratio rises to the point where demand is progressively choked off, and people become unable to buy. At this point, price rises peak and begin to slow down, earnings begin to rise faster than house prices and buyers are under less

Safe As Houses

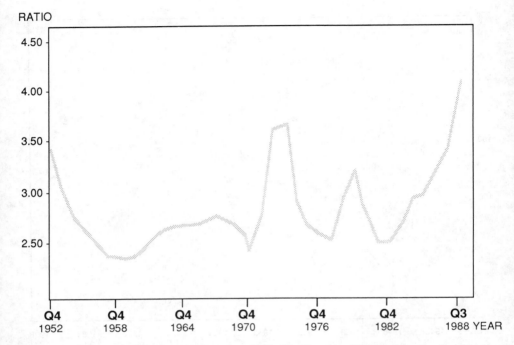

Figure 2.3   House-price:earnings ratio, 1952–88 (Source: Nationwide Anglia House Prices; DE Gazette)

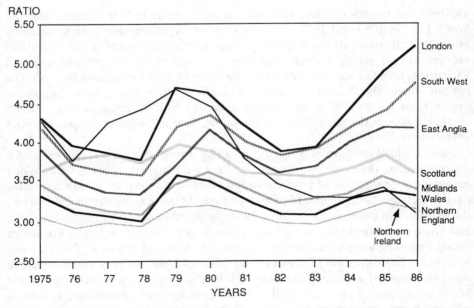

Figure 2.4   Ration of house prices to incomes – all households, QI 1987 –QI 1986 (Source: New Earnings Survey; Nationwide Building Society)

pressure to buy as prices are stable. As a result, sales slow down, and the market enters a period of relative calm until rising earnings and stable prices lead to the potential for new buyers to enter the market once more, at which point the cycle begins once more (Hamnett, 1989a).

Regional differences in house prices and rates of price inflation

We will consider the implications of house-price inflation for equity accumation shortly. First, however, it is very important to look behind national average prices to the marked variations in regional house prices and rates of house-price inflation. The existence of a marked north–south gap in the price of houses is well known and of long standing, but it became a subject of media interest and political concern from 1985 to 1988 when rapid house-price inflation in London and the South East combined with static prices in the Midlands and the North meant that the gap became larger than ever before. This led several commentators to suggest that the regional house-price gap will continue to grow. If they are right, this has major implications for housing access, interregional mobility and rates of equity accumulation between regions. A steadily widening gap suggests that the north–south divide in owner-occupied house prices will become more sharply defined, and that inequalities in housing access and accumulation will reinforce the divisions in regional employment and incomes.

This argument was made most forcefully by David Thorns (1982) in an important article in which he linked the changes in industrial restructuring and the labour and house property markets in Britain. He argued that the older industrial regions of the Midlands and the north were characterized both by high levels of job losses and by unemployment and by a depressed owner-occupied housing market in which prices and rates of house-price inflation were much lower than in the South East, and may even be falling. He argued that the owner-occupied market was reinforcing and reflecting labour-market conditions in the north and south and that a process of cumulative and progressive regional disadvantage was operating. This was opening up a growing gap between the affluent and depressed regions, providing jobs and equity accumulation in the south and locking residents of the depressed regions into a declining labour and housing market in which they were effectively trapped. As he put it (*ibid*. p. 759):

> The changes ... which have occurred since the early 1960s and have led to a considerable restructuring of the labour and property markets, have produced considerable wealth transfers. These transfers have been in the same direction and have given rise to a firmly entrenched 'middle class' group, increasingly regionally concentrated in the South East, regional centres, and new towns.

To assess the variations in regional house prices and rates of house-price inflation, we need a reliable source of regional house-price data. The best one available is the Building Societies Association/Department of the Environment (BSA/DoE) 5 per cent quarterly sample of building-society mortgage completions. This data series has been in existence since 1969 and, although it does not include bank mortgage lending (which has accounted for about a third of all mortgage lending since the early 1980s), it none the less provides the most comprehensive source of data. This information is supplemented by data provided by the Halifax and the Nationwide Anglia Building Societies, which is based on their own mortgage lending figures.

The basic data source (see Table 2. 2) shows the average price of houses and flats mortgaged to building societies by all the UK regions for each of the 21 years, 1969-89. The figures show that the average price of a London house (£81, 635) in the third quarter of 1989 was 2.0 times the average price of a house in the Northern region (£42,456). There is, of course, no such thing as an average house. The regional average house-price figures produced by the building societies are statistical artifacts that aggregate data on individual houses and flats of very different sizes, types and quality, the precise mix of which changes over time. Thus, a high proportion of the properties currently sold in London are flats, while the northern regions have a higher proportion of smaller, older terraced houses than in the Midlands and the South East. But the marked regional differences in average house prices are not simply a reflection of differences in the distribution of house types between regions. A similar gap shows up when like is compared with like, and the Halifax data on semi-detached houses shows that in the first quarter of 1990, the average ranged from £110,752 in London to £43,925 in South Yorkshire, £39,030 in Fife and £28,049 in County Down, Northern Ireland. Figure 2.5 shows the price differences for semi-detached houses by county for 1987, and it can be seen how prices fall away from the South East. Average regional prices also conceal the considerable differences that exist within regions. There are some northern towns and cities, such as Harrogate, York, Stockport, Glasgow and Edinburgh, where house prices are relatively high, just as there are some parts of the South East, such as Dover and Margate, where prices are much lower than the regional average. But the Halifax Building Society have produced figures for individual towns and house types that show that average prices in lower-priced towns in the South East are generally considerably higher than average prices in the high-priced northern cities.

The BSA/DoE regional-average figures are not easy to interpret in tabular form. However, a clearer picture is revealed when regional average prices for each year are shown as a percentage of the UK average for each year (Figure 2.6). It shows that there are marked and persistent differences between regions. At the top end, average prices in London and the South East have consistently been much higher than in other regions of the country, and have run between 25 and 60 per cent higher than the national average. The South West has run about 5–15 per cent above the UK average and East Anglia was 5–10 per cent below the UK average in the 1970s – though both have shown a general upward trend. East Anglia reached the average in 1985 and, by 1988, it was 15 per cent above. In all other regions, prices are below the UK average and at the bottom end, the Northern region and Yorkshire & Humberside, are about 70–80 per cent of the national average, with a general downward trend since the late 1970s to mid-1988, since when they have risen sharply as house-price inflation spread to the north. There is a distinct north–south divide in average house prices.

Given the wide variations in regional house prices, it is clear that the UK average is a rather artificial construct. Only London, the South East, the South West and

Table 2.2   Average regional house prices at mortgage completion stage, £

Period	Northern	Yorks. & Humber.	East Midlands	East Anglia	Greater London	South East (Excl. GLC)	South West	West Midlands	North West	Wales	Scotland	Northern Ireland	UK
1969	3,714	3,436	3,791	4,298	6,195	5,792	4,496	4,348	3,922	4,168	4,609	3,941	4,640
1970	3,942	3,634	3,966	4,515	6,882	6,223	4,879	4,490	4,184	4,434	5,002	4,387	4,975
1971	4,389	4,023	4,390	4,968	7,397	7,284	5,564	4,926	4,949	4,803	5,407	4,650	5,632
1972	5,413	4,880	5,621	7,031	11,113	9,914	7,771	6,232	5,742	5,935	6,233	4,934	7,734
1973	7,414	7,059	8,191	9,849	14,447	13,164	10,868	8,775	7,836	8,382	8,595	6,181	9,942
1974	8,444	8,289	9,191	10,996	14,857	13,946	11,606	10,252	8,890	9,401	9,775	8,710	10,990
1975	9,601	9,085	9,989	11,528	14,918	14,664	12,096	10,866	9,771	10,083	11,139	10,023	11,787
1976	10,453	9,995	10,646	11,850	15,566	15,548	13,003	11,621	10,500	11,129	12,974	12,860	12,704
1977	11,773	10,772	11,367	12,176	16,745	16,466	13,555	12,528	11,523	11,673	14,236	15,722	13,650
1978	13,044	12,099	12,810	13,968	19,160	18,915	15,503	14,342	13,410	13,373	16,147	18,395	15,594
1979	15,443	15,003	15,836	18,461	25,793	24,675	20,494	18,493	16,902	17,061	19,371	21,824	19,925
1980	17,710	17,689	18,928	22,808	30,968	29,832	25,293	21,663	20,092	19,363	21,754	23,656	23,596
1981	18,602	19,202	19,465	23,060	30,757	29,975	25,365	21,755	20,554	20,155	23,014	19,890	24,188
1982	18,071	18,180	19,487	23,358	30,712	29,676	25,514	20,992	20,744	19,662	22,522	20,177	23,644
1983	20,034	20,870	22,034	25,814	34,632	33,753	27,996	23,133	22,827	22,533	23,822	20,878	26,469
1984	22,604	22,356	24,377	28,296	39,346	37,334	30,612	24,989	24,410	23,665	25,865	21,455	29,106
1985	22,786	23,338	25,539	31,661	44,301	40,487	32,948	25,855	25,126	25,005	26,941	23,012	31,103
1986	24,333	25,607	28,483	36,061	54,863	48,544	38,536	28,437	27,503	27,354	28,242	25,743	36,276
1987	27,275	27,747	31,808	42,681	66,024	57,387	44,728	32,657	29,527	29,704	29,591	27,773	40,391
1988	30,193	32,685	40,521	57,295	77,697	72,561	58,457	41,700	34,074	34,244	31,479	29,875	49,355
1989	37,374	41,817	49,421	64,610	82,383	81,635	67,004	49,815	42,126	42,981	35,394	30,280	54,846

Notes
1. The figures are only based on a 5 per cent sample.
2. The figures are not adjusted to reflect changes in the mix of property mortgages to building societies.

(*Source: The Building Societies Association and Department of Environment: 5 per cent sample survey of building society mortgage completions.*)

Safe As Houses

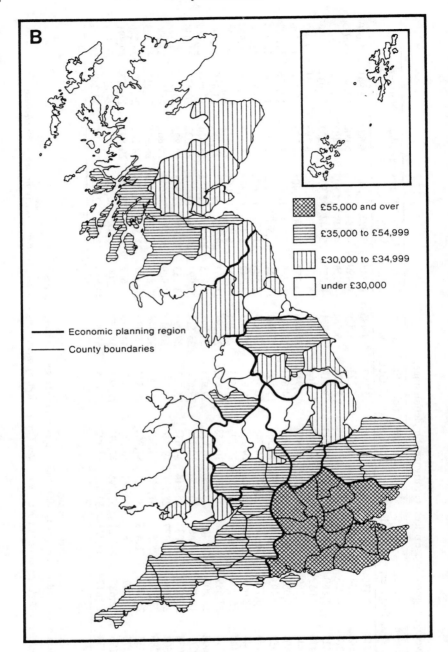

Figure 2.5   Mean price of semi-detached houses, by county, 1987 (Source: Lewis and Townsend (eds.) 1989)

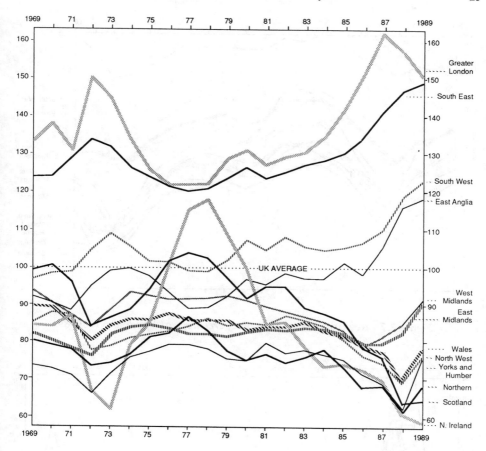

Figure 2.6 Regional average house prices as a percentage of the UK average, 1969–89

East Anglia are above the UK average, and London and the South East are so far above they pull up the national average. Because of this, and because it is the gap between these regions and the rest of the country that is the focus of concern, it is more effective to show regional house prices as a percentage of those in London. This is done in Figure 2.7, and it clearly shows the cyclical pattern of regional prices in relation to London. Average house prices in most regions fell sharply relative to London from 1969 to 1972, when the regional house-price gap reached its maximum. Average regional prices then rose consistently from 1972 to 1976 relative to London prices and the regional house-price gap was at its smallest. The gap then widened from 1978 to 1980, narrowed slightly from 1980 to 1982–3, widened from 1983 to 1987 and narrowed from 1988 onwards.

The differences in regional price movements relative to London and to the national average are a product of differential rates of regional house-price inflation. Table 2.3 and Figure 2.8 show that house-price inflation was led by the

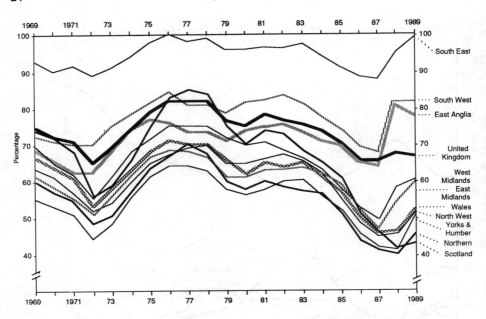

Figure 2.7 Regional house prices as a percentage of London's, 1969–89

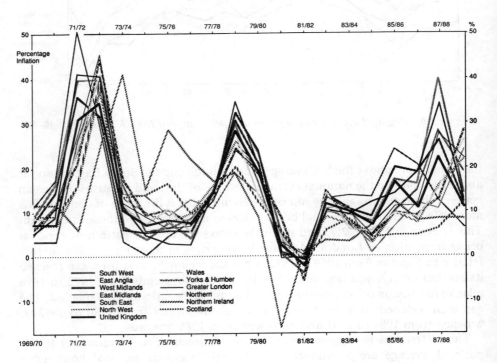

Figure 2.8 Regional house price inflation rates, 1969–79 to 1987–9

Table 2.3 Average regional rates of house-price inflation, 1970–87

Period	Northern	Yorks. & Humber.	East Midlands	East Anglia	Greater London	South East	South West	West Midlands	North West	Wales	Scotland	Northern Ireland	UK
1969–70	6.1	5.8	4.6	5.0	11.1	7.4	8.5	3.3	6.7	6.4	8.5	11.3	7.2
1970–1	11.3	10.7	10.7	7.5	17.0	14.0	14.0	3.3	6.7	6.4	8.5	11.3	7.2
1971–2	23.3	213.0	28.0	41.5	50.2	36.1	39.7	26.5	15.7	23.6	15.3	6.1	30.9
1972–3	37.0	44.6	45.7	40.7	30.0	32.8	39.8	40.8	36.9	41.2	37.9	25.3	34.8
1973–4	13.9	17.4	12.2	11.6	2.8	5.9	6.8	16.8	13.4	12.1	13.7	40.9	10.5
1974–5	13.7	9.3	8.7	4.8	0.4	5.1	4.2	6.0	9.9	7.2	13.9	15.0	7.2
1975–6	8.9	10.3	6.6	2.8	4.3	6.0	7.5	6.9	7.5	10.4	16.5	28.3	7.8
1976–7	12.6	7.3	6.8	2.7	7.6	5.9	4.2	7.8	9.7	4.9	9.7	22.2	7.4
1977–8	10.8	12.8	12.7	14.7	14.4	14.9	14.4	14.5	16.4	14.6	13.4	17.0	14.2
1978–9	18.4	24.0	23.6	32.2	34.6	30.4	32.2	28.9	26.0	27.6	20.0	18.6	27.9
1979–80	14.7	17.9	19.5	23.5	20.1	20.9	23.4	17.1	18.9	13.5	12.3	8.4	18.4
1980–1	5.0	8.5	2.8	1.1	-0.7	0.5	0.3	0.4	2.3	4.1	5.8	-15.9	2.5
1981–2	-2.8	-5.3	0.1	-1.3	-0.1	-1.0	-0.6	-3.5	1.1	-2.4	-2.1	1.4	-2.2
1982–3	10.8	14.8	13.0	10.6	12.8	13.8	9.7	10.2	7.9	14.7	5.3	3.4	11.9
1983–4	11.4	7.1	10.7	9.5	13.6	10.6	9.3	8.0	6.9	6.2	8.0	2.9	9.9
1984–5	0.8	4.4	4.8	11.9	12.6	8.4	7.6	3.5	2.9	5.6	4.2	7.3	6.9
1985–6	6.8	9.7	11.5	13.9	23.8	19.9	17.0	10.0	9.5	9.4	4.8	11.9	16.6
1986–7	12.1	8.4	11.7	18.4	20.3	18.2	16.1	14.8	7.4	8.6	4.8	7.9	11.3
1987–8	10.7	12.8	27.4	34.3	12.7	26.4	38.9	27.7	15.4	15.3	6.4	8.0	22.2
1988–9	23.8	27.9	22.0	12.8	6.0	12.5	14.6	19.5	23.6	25.5	12.4	8.0	11.1
1969–81	401.0	459.0	413.0	436.0	396.0	417.0	464.0	400.0	424.0	383.0	399.0	404.0	421.0
1969–87	634.0	707.0	739.0	893.0	966.0	891.0	895.0	651.0	653.0	613.0	542.0	605.0	770.0
1969–89	906.0	1,117.0	1,204.0	1,230.0	1,230.0	1,039.0	1,390.0	1,046.0	947.0	931.0	668.0	668.0	1,082.0

(*Source: Author's calculations from Building Society Association/Department of Environment 5% sample of mortgage completions.*)

southern regions during the 1970s and 1980s, particularly London and the South East. They were the first to rise, they rose most sharply and they were the first to fall back. Thus, the rise in house-price inflation that occurred in 1971–72 was most marked in Greater London where prices rose by 50 per cent, followed by East Anglia (41 per cent), the South West (40 per cent) and the South East (36 per cent). The North, Yorkshire & Humberside, the East and West Midlands and Wales experienced rates of inflation between 21 and 28 per cent, whilst the North West and Scotland had rates of just over 15 per cent. By 1972–3, inflation fell to just over 30 per cent in London and the South East, while all the other regions experienced rates of between 37 and 46 per cent. By 1973–4, inflation had virtually ceased in London, the South East and South West (3, 6 and 7 per cent respectively), while in other regions it varied between 12 and 17 per cent. These differentials persisted through 1975 and 1976 as the four southern regions all marked time, while the other regions caught up. A similar, though less marked, pattern characterized the late 1970s boom and the slump of 1980–2. In both periods, price movements in the non-southern regions were so lagged as to be partly counter-cyclical. If we measure the regional differences in house-price inflation over the period 1969–81, both dates when the regional house-price gap was narrow, regional house-price inflation rates ranged from 464 per cent in the South West and 459 per cent in Yorkshire & Humberside, to 417 per cent in the South East, 401 per cent in the North and 396 per cent in London. Although this is a 'trough-to-trough' measure, it is clear that house-price inflation in London and the South East was *not* higher than the rest of Britain during the 1970s.

The evidence of the 1970s and early 1980s does not support the thesis of a progressively widening regional house-price gap. But what of the mid-to-late 1980s? In 1983 and 1984 house prices began to rise rapidly in London and the South East, and they continued to rise until mid 1988. Meanwhile, house prices in the Midlands and the north remained sluggish. From 1982 to 1988 house prices rose by 40 per cent in Scotland and 67 per cent in the North but by 153 per cent in London: almost four times the rate in Scotland. As a result, some commentators suggested that the cyclical pattern of the 1970s may have disappeared to be replaced by a permanently wider and growing north–south price gap. The Building Societies Association (1987) suggested that, while long-term rates of house-price inflation had been similar between regions, this pattern may be coming to an end as a result of the differential impact of the recession and subsequent boom, lower levels of unemployment in the South East, the marked concentration of growth sectors of the economy in the South and the impact of prosperity brought to the region as a result of the M25 and other public expenditures. Foley (1986, p. 3) reached very similar conclusions:

> In previous cycles, prices in the rest of the country seem to have followed those in London and the south east. ... However, there is now more regional variation in economic performance than previously, so it is by no means certain that prices will respond in the typical fashion, although some pick up outside the South-East corner does seem probable.

Foley and the BSA were cautious in their interpretations, but Gail Counsell went further than most. She stated in *The Independent* in mid-1988 that there was no evidence of a return to the traditional pattern of cyclical variations:

> Such a reversal has yet to appear in this cycle. The current bout of house price inflation has proved so prolonged, and the north–south division so marked, that some are beginning to wonder whether we are now seeing a permanent change in the structure of the market – a Yorkshire property, for example, is now worth just 36 per cent of one in London. Even at their previous worst, in 1973–4, Yorkshire properties were still worth around 53 per cent of London ones.

What evidence is there to support such an interpretation? As we have seen, house-price inflation in London and the South East was far more rapid than in the Midlands and the North from 1983 to 1987, and by mid-1987 the gap between London and the South East and the northern regions was higher than ever. But the size of the gap was already beginning to narrow between London and some other southern regions as house-price inflation in London slowed down and increased in the other regions. As early as January 1987, the *Halifax House Price Index* for the fourth quarter of 1986 stated that

> there are signs that the rate of increase in Greater London and the South East have levelled off. ... The most noticeable feature of the fourth quarter was a relative recovery in house prices in the East and West Midlands regions, East Anglia and the South West as price inflation radiates out from the South East corner of the UK.

Subsequent Halifax and Nationwide quarterly reports confirmed this trend. As house-price inflation slowed down in London and the South East from 1987 onwards, it began to spread outwards. First to East Anglia and the South West, then in early 1988 in the East and West Midlands and Wales, and finally in late 1988 to Yorkshire & Humberside, the North, North West and Scotland. By early 1989, house-price inflation in London and the other southern regions had ground to a halt while house prices in the northern regions surged ahead. The differences became more marked in 1989. According to the Halifax Building Society, average prices in 1989 rose by 33 per cent in the North, 29 per cent in the North West, 24 per cent in Humberside and 17 per cent in Scotland while they *fell* by 8 per cent in London, 10 per cent in the South West, 11 per cent in the South East and by 16 per cent in East Anglia. The regional house-price gap therefore narrowed rapidly during 1989, and this process continued during 1990. It therefore appears that the 1980s have seen a continuation of the cyclical variations in regional house prices seen in 1970s.

Table 2.4 shows the ratio of regional house prices to those in London using Halifax quarterly data. It shows that the increases in house-price inflation moved progressively further outwards from London from early 1987 onwards while the rate of inflation began to decline in London and the South East. The pattern is akin to a wave radiating outwards from the centre like ripples in a pond. The gap between London and East Anglia, East and West Midlands and the South West reached its peak in autumn 1986 and has been declining ever since. The gap between London and the other regions reached a peak at various points in 1988 and has since declined. To take an example, in the third quarter of 1985, the average London price was 2.04 times that in the North. This subsequently rose to a

Table 2.4   The ratio of average London house prices to average regional prices

	East Anglia	East Midlands	West Midlands	South West	Wales	Yorks. & Humber.	North West	Northern Ireland	Scotland
Q.3 1985	1.47	1.83	1.79	1.38	1.93	2.07	1.89	2.04	1.64
Q.1 1986	1.57	2.03	1.99	1.51	2.16	2.32	2.02	2.32	1.92
Q.3 1986	1.61	2.12	2.06	1.54	2.17	2.42	2.13	2.42	2.02
Q.4 1986	1.53	2.08	1.95	1.52	2.18	2.43	2.07	2.41	2.02
Q.3 1987	1.48	2.05	1.97	1.49	2.29	2.51	2.19	2.44	2.09
Q.4 1987	1.41	2.01	1.94	1.45	2.31	2.53	2.20	2.49	2.13
Q.1 1988	1.36	2.00	1.93	1.45	2.37	2.61	2.31	2.59	2.20
Q.2 1988	1.28	1.97	1.81	1.41	2.31	2.63	2.29	2.65	2.24
Q.3 1988	1.29	1.85	1.74	1.34	2.34	2.57	2.42	2.80	2.36
Q.4 1988	1.20	1.80	1.66	1.35	2.25	2.40	2.34	2.76	2.28
Q.1 1989	1.28	1.80	1.62	1.35	2.09	2.20	2.18	2.53	2.27
Q.2 1989	1.40	1.74	1.62	1.40	1.93	1.99	1.98	2.28	2.12
Q.3 1989	1.43	1.67	1.58	1.34	1.83	1.81	1.79	2.07	1.89
Q.4 1989	1.48	1.66	1.56	1.37	1.82	1.78	1.74	1.98	1.82
Q.1 1990	1.60	1.72	1.62	1.44	1.91	1.83	1.77	1.99	1.89

Note
Underlining indicates date of maximum house-price gap; double underlining indicates date of minimum house-price gap.

(*Source: Quarterly Halifax Regional House Price Bulletins.*)

peak of 2.8 in the third quarter of 1988 before declining very rapidly to a low of 1.98 in the fourth quarter of 1989. This is similar to the patterns during the 1970s where the southern and Midlands regions followed London and the South East. While this pattern of price increases is unlikely to reduce price differences to the level of 1974–7, the regional price gap has stabilized and is narrowing once again as it did in the 1970s.

This does not mean, of course, that the regional house-price gap will keep narrowing. The economy of the South East is buoyant and the concentration of highly paid professional and managerial jobs in the region, the M25, the Channel Tunnel and the Green Belt are likely to continue to exert a strong upwards pressure on prices in the South East in the medium term. Indeed, Table 2.4 suggests that the gap between average house price in London and the other regions appears to have reached a minimum in the third quarter of 1989 and may already be slowly growing again.

This analysis shows that the regional house-price gap during the 1970s and 1980s was very variable, opening up rapidly during the early stages of a boom when prices rose fastest in the South East, and gradually closing during the later stages of the booms and during the 'slumps' when house prices outside the south gradually caught up. Depending on the stage of the cycle, it is possible to conclude that the regional house-price gap is either widening or narrowing. One consequence of the cyclical variations in regional house prices is that regional house-price inflation rates differ considerably depending on the time periods used for calculation. If we take the period 1969–87 when the house-price gap was at its greatest, Table 2.3 shows that the rates of house-price inflation ranged from 966 per cent in London, 895 per cent in the South West, 893 per cent in East Anglia and 891 per cent in the South East, to 634 per cent in the North and just 542 per cent in Scotland. But, as we have also seen, calculations based on the period 1969–81 (both years when the house-price gap was at its narrowest) show rates of inflation in London less than those of many other regions. Calculations over the period 1969–89 also show a smaller regional gap. Average house prices rose by 1,366 per cent in the South East, 1,293 per cent in London, 1,200 per cent in Yorkshire & Humberside, 1,083 per cent in the North West and 1,043 per cent in the North. It is clear that the rate of overall house-price inflation in London and the South East has *not* been consistently higher than in the northern regions.

Cyclical house-price inflation: towards an explanation

How can this consistent pattern of house-price increases moving outward from London and the South East in each of the three house booms be explained? We suggest a number of factors are involved. First, the proportion of high earners is greatest in London and the South East, and owner occupied housing is in relatively short supply in inner London (about 30 per cent of the housing stock) as a result of London's tenure structure and the Green Belt limiting development. Second, because of the large number of highly skilled young people who migrate to London for career reasons, the proportion of first-time buyers is greater in London than in other regions. Thus, it can be expected that when the house-price income ratio has fallen back and stabilized, rising incomes will cause any increase in demand for owner-occupied housing to take place first in London.

Because of the relative shortage of owner-occupied housing in London, prices will rise rapidly and will be reflected throughout the South East commuting area. Third, as prices rise in London and potential buyers are priced out of the market, some will begin to move out and look to other areas within commuting distance. This may help explain the fact that price rises in East Anglia and the South West have traditionally followed rises in London and the South East. It may also be that some existing owners in London decide to use their increased equity to move out to cheaper areas and increase their consumption of housing. Over a period of two to three years, enough owners or potential buyers may move out to push up prices in areas further from London where house-price:income ratios have been lower. As prices begin to rise in these areas, local buyers will also be drawn into the market in an attempt to buy before prices rise too far. By this stage, prices rises will have slowed or stabilized in London and the South East as the house-price:income ratio has reached its peak and prices have become unaffordable to all but a small number of buyers. The implications of the changes in regional house prices discussed above are outlined below.

Equity accumulation from the owner-occupied housing market

We noted earlier in the chapter that national average house prices increased by exactly 1,000 per cent between 1970 and 1988 – from £5,000 to £55,000. Although the rate of regional inflation has differed considerably, particularly during the 1980s, it is clear that virtually all existing home owners will have benefited from the rise in house prices, irrespective of where they live. Although a few commentators have argued that the gains from home ownership are illusory in that owners have to live somewhere, and cannot simply sell up and realize their paper profits, their case is based on totally invalid assumptions. As Ball (1976, p. 25) has pointed out: 'the correct comparison is between owning and non-owning at one point in time ... wealth is created for owners but not for non-owners. Whether this wealth is ever realised is immaterial. It still exists, even if it is used only as an inheritance for future generations'.

There is now a considerable body of support for the view that home ownership provides a major new source of wealth accumulation. Not only have house prices generally kept well ahead of the rate of retail price inflation, but mortgage finance has been available at relatively cheap and, until the 1980s, generally negative real rates of interest. Add on mortgage-interest tax relief, absence of capital gains tax on a main residence or a tax on imputed rent income, and house purchase becomes what Kit Mahon, Deputy Governor of the Bank of England, described as 'a cheap, almost risk-free method of financing an appreciating asset with a depreciating debt'. Whitehead (1979, p. 36) has said that 'Buying and living in one's own home has proved to be one of the most profitable investments, at least since 1945', and Saunders's (1978, p. 234), in a very influential article, has argued that 'owner occupation provides access to a highly significant accumulative form of property ownership'. Nor are such views confined to academics. Michael Hesseltine,

Secretary of State for the Environment, stated in 1979 (col, 407) that:

> in a way and on a scale that was quite unpredictable, ownership of property has brought financial gains of immense value to millions of our citizens. As house prices rose, the longer one had owned, the larger the gain became ... this dramatic change in property values has opened up a division in the nation between those who own their own homes and those who do not.

Such arguments about the financial potential of home ownership are at the heart of this book, but are they right and, if so, what is the scale of these gains? Measurement of achieved accumulation is complex. Are we concerned with absolute or relative gains, or with gains relative to other types of investment, and should they be measured in current prices or adjusted for the general rate of inflation to give a measure of real capital gains? And how far should we take the cost of housing into account? House prices can rise or fall over time in absolute terms, and even a fall in absolute prices from the time of purchase could leave owners with some capital as long as the value of the house exceeds the amount outstanding on the mortgage. Unlike non-owners, owners would still have a capital asset. But the term accumulation implies some degree of absolute price appreciation at very least. And the idea of real accumulation refers to assets that are appreciating not only in absolute terms but also at a rate over and above the rate of inflation. The rate of price appreciation can be compared with other commodities but this is more a measure of the relative accumulation potential of housing. We therefore need to define carefully what we mean by accumulation or capital gains and show how it can be measured. This is done in the next section.

The measurement of capital accumulation and rates of return

National average house prices in Britain may have increased by 1,000 per cent from 1969 to 1988 in nominal terms, but some critics are skeptical about the extent of real accumulation, particularly outside the South East. As Duncan (1989, p. 6) comments, 'it is easy to be mesmerised by large nominal figures, especially if they go up'. He argues that it is important to look at changes in real prices, and Badcock (1989, p. 72) states that 'changes in house prices need to be adjusted for inflation and expressed as a proportion of equity before anything meaningful can be said about real accumulation'. Duncan (1989) also argues that it is necessary to incorporate changes into the composition and quality of the stock. Comparing changes in the average price of houses over time is meaningless if we are comparing the price of old, poor quality, terraced houses to the average price of modern detached houses. This is correct, but the argument is less valid in the short term than in the long term. Duncan also argues that the cost of house improvements should be incorporated into the measurement of capital gains, as a paper gain of £10,000 could be accounted for by £5,000 spending on improvements and £5,000 in general inflation.

There are a number of different ways of attempting to measure achieved accumulation. The first, and simplest method, is simply to compare the buying- and selling-price house at two points in time. We can term this the *gross capital gain*, and a house that cost £5,000 and is now worth £55,000 has seen a gross capital gain of £50,000. But this excludes mortgages outstanding on the property, the original deposit, selling costs and the like, and if these are taken into account we get what Dupuis (1989) terms the owner's 'wealth increase' or what we term the net capital gain. In the example above, someone with a mortgage of £4,000 outstanding, who paid a £1,000 deposit, would have a net capital gain of £50,000 less transaction costs. Such a measure could also incorporate the cost of improvements. Finally, the *rate of return* is the annual average gross or net capital gain measured over a period of years. This is a difficult concept to measure because it largely depends on what basis the rate of return is measured. It can be argued, as Saunders (1990) does, that the best method of calculating relative rates of gain is not on the initial price of the house (as most of this is funded on borrowed money) but on the buyers' initial deposit, which represents the capital invested in the house. But, while this is technically correct, it leads to the paradox of an exponential inverse relationship between the size of deposit and the rate of gain on any given house. The smaller the deposit, the greater the rate of relative gain, and those buying with a 100 per cent mortgage will have had an infinite gain. The explanation for this paradox is that owners who buy entirely on borrowed money make capital gains on the entire value of the property. Such deposit-based measures lead Saunders to the bizarre conclusion that working-class and sitting-tenant council buyers who buy inexpensive houses with small deposits make larger rates of gain than middle-class owners who buy expensive houses with smaller deposits. This is nonsensical and, as buyers can make gains on both their own deposit and on borrowed money, we believe initial purchase price provides a more realistic base for calculation. It enables the comparison of houses of different prices in different regions irrespective of the size of the initial mortgage.

But these simple examples exclude the rate of price inflation over the period in question. If the general rate of inflation had been large, say 1,000 per cent, a house bought for £5,000 in 1970 and sold in 1988 for £55,000 would only be worth in real terms what the buyer had paid for it initially. If the rate of price inflation had been only 500 per cent, the house would be worth twice in real terms what the buyer initially paid for it. Using aggregate national data, Farmer and Barrell (1981) calculated that owner occupiers obtained annual real rates of return on their capital of between 12 and 16 per cent between 1965 and 1979, and the Nationwide Building Society (1986) *Housing as an Investment* showed that the net (after-tax) rate of return on a house bought on a 25-year mortgage in 1970 and sold in 1985 averaged 17 per cent per year. When notional-use values or imputed-rent payments were included, the rate of return rose to 25 per cent per year. This compared to pre-tax rates of return on other investments varying from 8 per cent on bank deposits and *The Financial Times* ordinary share index, 11 per cent on building-society deposits and 23 per cent on gold. If the calculations were repeated today they would show a much higher return on *The Financial Times* index even taking the 1987 crash into account, and much lower returns on gold. The returns on houses would also be higher until 1988.

This is not to suggest that home ownership in Britain has been a consistently good investment in all regions at all times. Rates of house-price inflation have varied considerably over time in different regions, and a study by Spencer (1987) argued that while the real rate of return on home ownership after mortgage interest rates and maintenance expenditure had been deducted was generally positive over the 1960s and 1970s, this was not true of the 1980s except in London and the South East where house-price inflation was much higher than the rest of the country – averaging 25 per cent in both 1986 and 1987 compared to only 5–6 per cent in the northern regions. But while this was true to 1987, and confirms what we have already shown about regional variations, house-price inflation subsequently rose rapidly outside the South East. If the calculations were repeated for the whole of the 1980s they would show a rather different result. It is also questionable whether mortgage interest rates should be included as such calculations as owners would have to pay rent if they did not own.

Relative rates of gain are important but, given our interest in interest in inheritance and wealth, it is more important to assess variations in absolute gains both over time and between different regions. A house that cost £3,000 in 1970 and that is now worth £33,000 has seen a relative rate of inflation of 1,000 per cent, and an absolute gross capital appreciation of some £30,000. But a house that cost £8,000 in 1970 and is now worth £88,000 has had the same relative rate of inflation but an absolute appreciation of £80,000 – 2.7 times that of the cheaper house. And a house that cost £10,000 in 1970 and is now worth £110,000 has shown an absolute appreciation of £100,000 – 3.3 times that of the cheaper house. Put more generally, for a common rate of price inflation, levels of absolute appreciation are directly proportional to the initial price difference of houses. A house three times more expensive than another will, over a given period of time, show an absolute gain of three times as much. It follows that for equal rates of price inflation, the more expensive the house owners can afford to buy, the greater their absolute capital gains. Thus, while Saunders (1990) argues that working-class buyers have often experienced very high relative rates of gain (because of their small initial deposit), their absolute gains will often be much smaller than buyers of more expensive houses.

Estimates of equity appreciation

Ideally, equity appreciation should be measured for individual properties. This would enable us to determine how long individuals have owned, the size of mortgages and the cost of improvements and the extent of any remortgaging through equity extraction or trading down. But given the almost complete absence of such data, apart from surveys (Saunders, 1990; Thorns, 1982), there is often no choice but to impute gains and rates of return from changes in aggregate house prices at a national, regional or urban level (Badcock, 1989). This has the disadvantage that composition of the housing stock changes over time, and new houses are generally more expensive than existing or demolished houses.

Given these problems, one extremely crude and indirect measure of the amount of achieved accumulation is given by BSA/DoE data for 1987 (Table 2.5), which shows average price paid for houses by existing owners in 1987, and average mortgage advance. The major disadvantage of these figures is that they take no account of the amount of equity that may have been injected or extracted in the move, or of the length of time that owners owned. Also, the data is for movers, who are generally younger and have accumulated less equity, than longer-term owners. But they provide an indication of the average equity of currently moving owners. They show that the national average implied equity was £20,500. But it varied from £10,800 in the North to £37,000 in London: a ratio of 3.4:1.

Given the caveats associated with this method, it is possibly better to construct tables showing the hypothetical average gross appreciation in different regions for different time periods. On the assumption that the mortgage debt outstanding is equal to the initial price of a house in year 1, we can simply subtract the average house price in year 1 from year $n + 1$ to get a measure of average capital appreciation. Thus, from the figures given in Table 2.2, we can calculate that between 1970 and the third quarter of 1988 average region capital appreciation varied from a low of £25,603 in Northern Ireland and £28,284 in the North to a high of £73,782 in London: a difference of almost threefold (Table 2.6). For houses purchased in 1981, average gross accumulation varied from £10,000 in Northern Ireland and £14,700 in the North and North West to £49,907 in London: a factor of 5 times in the former and 3.4 times in the latter (Table 2.7). Relative rates of capital gains varied by much less than the levels of absolute accumulation.

These figures are, of course, hypothetical, and assume that an average-priced house in 1970 was retained until 1988. They also include the price of all houses, including those bought by first-time buyers and existing owners. The latter are generally far more expensive, and the capital appreciation will be considerably more – but they do indicate the very considerable regional differences in potential equity accumulation over time. They have important implications both for existing owners who are able to move from an expensive to a cheaper region and release equity (and those who cannot make a reverse move) and for the beneficiaries of owners living in different regions. The beneficiaries of an owner living in an average price house in London stand to inherit two to three times more than the beneficiaries of an owner living in one of the cheaper regions.

As the figures given above, these are regional averages and some existing owners who bought expensive houses in London or the South East a few years ago may have seen their equity increase by hundreds of thousands of pounds. At the other end of the spectrum, buyers of cheaper houses in the northern regions in the last few years may have accumulated equity of only a few thousand pounds. Houses in Tregunter Road, Chelsea, selling for £70,000 (five times the London average price) in 1974 were selling in the 1980s for £1.4 million each – a relative inflation of 1,900 per cent and a capital appreciation of £1.3 million. The impact of these differentials on the geographical distribution of wealth is considerable. *The Economist* (1988b, p. 41) commented that 'The biggest regional reshuffling of wealth in Britain is occurring not through the work of the chancellor of the exchequer, but through the whim of the property market'. This view can be queried on the grounds that regional impacts of the Chancellor's economic policies and the cuts in income tax rates in the 1988 Budget have been very considerable and have benefited the South East more than other regions, but house-price inflation has clearly played a part in the regional redistribution of wealth.

Table 2.5 Implied equity: the difference between average dwelling price and average mortgage advance for former owners buying in 1987

Northern	Yorks. & Humber.	East Midlands	East Anglia	London	South East	South West	West Midlands	North West	Wales	Scotland	Northern Ireland
10,826	12,160	14,598	22,420	37,296	32,125	22,892	15,742	12,533	13,945	12,355	11,247

Source: Building Societies Association/Department of the Environment. 5% sample data

Table 2.6 Implied average regional equity appreciation, 1970–88

Northern	Yorks. & Humber.	East Midlands	East Anglia	London	South East	South West	West Midlands	North West	Wales	Northern Ireland
28,284	30,351	39,767	60,605	73,782	70,979	60,360	42,106	33,789	33,539	25,603

Source: Calculated from Table 2.2

Table 2.7 Implied average regional equity appreciation, 1981–8

Northern	Yorks. & Humber.	East Midlands	East Anglia	London	South East	South West	West Midlands	North West	Wales	Northern Ireland
14,624	14,783	24,268	42,060	49,907	42,227	39,874	24,699	17,232	17,818	10,000

Source: Calculated from Table 2.2

The key point, however, is that rapid house-price inflation since the early 1970s has led to substantial equity accumulation on the part of many home owners, and the earlier they bought and the more expensive the house, the greater the absolute accumulation. We can therefore agree with Saunders (1990) that home ownership has been a source of real accumulation, even in those regions where house prices and rates of inflation have been lower. But it is clear that the absolute level of accumulation has varied markedly from region to region, and between cheaper and more expensive houses. Generally speaking, owners of expensive houses in London and the South East have gained more in absolute terms than other owners.

The sources of capital accumulation

We have shown that home owners make substantial capital gains, but from where do these gains derive? Do they derive from other owners or from external sources or a mixture of the two? Saunders (1978) argues that there are *three* sources of capital gains. These are, *first*, interest rates that are only just above or below the rate of inflation, which allow owners to borrow at low or even negative real rates of interest; *second*, government tax subsidies, such as mortgage-interest tax relief and exemption from capital gains tax on main residences; and, *third*, gains made by existing owners at the expense of new buyers, or as a result of their own enforced savings, as they pay off the mortgage on the property. The relative importance of these sources of gain has changed over time. In the 1960s and 1970s, negative real interest rates meant that there was a substantial regressive redistribution of wealth away from building-society savers (the value of their savings fell in real terms) towards borrowers. But during the 1980s real rates of interest have been high, approaching 8 per cent in Britain and this source of gain has become much less important (Spencer, 1987).

The second source, government tax subsidies, is of continuing importance. Mortgage-interest tax relief (MINTR) was worth about £7 billion a year in 1988 (Inland Revenue, 1989) and the absence of a tax on home-owners capital gains is worth a similar amount. Although MINTR has existed for many years, it became important in 1974. Previously, interest on all borrowings was eligible for tax relief but when this was abolished in 1974 only borrowings for house purchase or home improvements were exempt. The value of this exemption has, however, been falling in real terms as house prices have risen. In 1974 tax relief was allowed on the first £30,000 of mortgages, which covered almost all mortgages. This was increased in 1983 to £35,000 but by the end of 1989 the average new mortgage advance in the UK was £38,000 and in London and the South East the figures were £61,000 and £53,000 respectively. As a result, a smaller proportion of new mortgages are eligible for tax relief and, as the basic rate of tax has been reduced from 31 to 25 per cent, the value of mortgage-interest tax relief has also fallen. Conversely, the value of capital-gains exemption has risen as house prices have increased. But it can be argued that whereas MINTR reduces the real cost of housing, and tax relief on capital gains reduces the tax on gains, neither provide a pre-tax source of gains. Indeed, it can be argued that both forms of relief are effectively capitalized into higher house prices than would otherwise obtain and do not reduce the real cost of housing.

We suggest that while tax relief and the ability to borrow at low or negative real rates of interest subsidize accumulation by reducing the real cost of mortgage payments, they do not comprise sources of accumulation *per se*. It should also be stressed that some owners pay cash for their homes and there are also millions of outright owners who have paid off their mortgage and who get no tax subsidies. Their homes have the same accumulation potential as owners buying their homes on a mortgage. MINTR is, therefore, not a direct *source* of accumulation.

The notion of enforced savings is an interesting one. Saunders (1978) illustrates it by taking the hypothetical example of an owner who buys a house for £5,000 using a £500 deposit from savings and a £4,500 mortgage. Assuming a 10-per-cent annual rate of inflation in house prices, wages and interest rates, in just over 7 years the money value of the house will have doubled to £10,000. If the house was sold, the owner would realize a capital gain of £5,500 – a real rate of gain on the deposit of 450 per cent. The entire increase in the money value of the house could be appropriated by the owner or invested in another house. He or she could buy an equivalent house for £10,000, take out a mortgage for £9,000 (an equivalent mortgage in real terms to the original one) with a £1,000 deposit and pocket £4,500. Alternatively, he or she could take out a £9,000 mortgage, put in the £5,500 equity and buy a house for £14,500 – almost half as much again as the original house. This, of course, is how people move up the housing ladder. Finally, he or she could keep the original mortgage, put in a £5,500 deposit and reduce the real cost of buying by half. In practice, it would simply be best to keep the original house, but the effect is the same. After 10 years the buyer is paying only half in real terms what it would cost to buy an equivalent house. The point, says Saunders (*ibid.* p. 244), is that 'when an individual sells his house at £10,000 he sells it at the same real value he paid for it; the buyer pays twice as much in money terms, but the same amount in real terms, given that wages have also doubled'. This gain, Saunders argues, represents enforced savings because, although the owner appropriates the increased value of the house, he or she pays for it by paying a rate of interest considerably higher than the inflation rate to compensate the lender for the erosion of the real value of the capital loaned. The owner 'appropriates the increased value of the house, but pays for it through increased interest charges – a case of robbing Peter to pay Peter' (*ibid.*).

This is an important argument but, as Saunders points out, his abstract example bears little resemblance to reality for the simple reason that house price have increased in real terms (over and above the rate of inflation) by 2 to 2.5 times over the last thirty years. As a result, the price paid for a house by a new buyer entering the market consistently increases in real terms, and the mortgage repayments made by existing owners generally fall in real terms except where interest rates rise rapidly as has happened in recent years. This would seem to support the argument that owners' capital gains are simply made at the expense of new buyers and do not represent a gain to the sector as a whole. But (and this is a crucial point), although the bulk of existing owners' capital gains are paid for by new buyers entering the market for the first time or by existing owners trading up and taking out a larger mortgage, this has not meant that new buyers have to pay a higher proportion of their incomes in the long term. In the short term, during the early 1970s and from 1983 to 1988, house prices rose much faster than incomes, and house price:income ratios rose but, in the long term, house prices have tended to increase at roughly the same rate as incomes and house price:income ratios have not increased. The recent fall in house prices will have the effect of bringing the ratio back into line. What this means in practice is that the rise in house prices in real terms and owners' capital gains are paid for out of rising real incomes. Saunders has recognized this fact, although he puts it in somewhat different terms. According to Saunders and Harris (1988, pp. 9–10), home owners:

> extract a portion of the growing real wealth of the society in which they live. ... The result is that home ownership has come to represent the equivalent of a certificate of entitlement to share the fruits of economic growth. It is, despite the critics claims to the contrary, literally a stake in the capitalist system.

But, although home ownership may be seen as the equivalent of a certificate of entitlement to share the fruits of economic growth, it is only a stake in the capitalist system to the extent that it is a result of rising real incomes – it does not represent a share in capitalist profits as such, except where some profits are applied to house purchase by share-holders, partners, directors and others. None the less, this is an important conclusion and it provides the key to understanding why house prices keep rising in real terms in the long run. They rise because incomes keep rising in real terms, and earners devote a high proportion of increases in incomes to expenditure on their homes. If, of course, incomes were to fall in real terms, it is to be expected that house prices would fall proportionately faster. The heat that keeps the house-price balloon rising would have been removed.

3

HOUSING, WEALTH AND EQUITY EXTRACTION

Introduction: the growth of housing wealth

Chapter 2 noted that home ownership in Britain has grown very rapidly since the 1950s. In addition, rapid house-price inflation since the early 1970s has greatly increased the average value of houses in Britain. As a result, most home owners today live in houses worth far more than they were when they bought them, although there are marked variations in gains depending on when, and where, people bought. The rapid growth of owner-occupation and house prices has meant that private housing is now a very important element in personal wealth. The most widely quoted measure of its importance is that housing accounted for 17 per cent of net personal wealth in 1960, and 37 per cent in 1975 (Royal Commission on the Distribution of Income and Wealth, 1977). This increase reflects both the growing number of owner-occupiers and, far more importantly, the impact of rapid house-price inflation that has increased the value of housing faster than other assets. Although the 1975 figure quoted in 1977 was probably inflated by the 1974 stock-market collapse, which reduced the value of stocks and shares by almost 50 per cent, the 1986 figure of 48 per cent includes the bull market in the early 1980s.

One major effect of the growth of housing wealth has been on the distribution of wealth. Prior to the advent of widespread home ownership, ownership of substantial assets was restricted to a relatively small number of wealth owners and housing wealth was limited largely to private landlords. But as Atkinson (1983) and other wealth economists have pointed out, wider home ownership has meant that wealth is now more widely spread than previously. This can be seen by comparing data on wealth distributions for various years. Table 3.1 shows that the wealth owned by the top 1 per cent of wealth holders has declined from 61 per cent in 1923 to 34 per cent in 1960 and 20 per cent in 1985. The share of the top 10 per cent of wealth owners has also declined from 89 per cent in 1923 to 54 per cent in 1985 and the share of the top 25 per cent declined though not by as much. It is noteworthy that the share of the top 50 per cent has hardly fallen at all. This suggests that the redistribution of wealth has been almost entirely within the top 50 per cent of wealth owners. The bottom 50 per cent (most of whom will not be home owners) have gained very little.

Safe As Houses

Table 3.1 The distribution of wealth among individuals in Britain, 1923–85

	1923	1938	1960	1971	1976	1980	1985
Top 1%	60.9	55.0	33.9	31.0	24	20	20
Next 4%	21.1	21.9	25.5	21.0	21	19	20
Next 5%	7.1	8.1	12.1	13.0	15	13	14
Top 10%	89.1	85.0	71.5	65.0	60	52	54
Next 10%	5.1	6.2	11.6	16.6	—	—	—
Next 15%	—	—	—	21.0	24	23	22
Top 25%	—	—	—	86.0	84	75	76
Top 50%	—	—	—	97.0	95	94	93

(*Source*: CSO, *Social Trends*, for figures from 1960.)

The importance of residential property in personal wealth-holdings is not evenly distributed, of course. At the top end of the wealth distribution the traditional assets of land and stocks and shares are still important. At the bottom end of the wealth distribution some 30 per cent of households are not home owners. They are also unlikely to own much other wealth. Unfortunately, because wealth ownership statistics are prepared by the Inland Revenue from data on 'estates passing at death' grossed up to the whole population, they reflect the asset composition of the dying population rather than the population as a whole. Also, the statistics are based on only the 40 per cent of the dying population whose estates need a grant of representation for legal purposes. This excludes estates passing between spouses by succession or those worth under £5,000.

What this means is that just over 50 per cent of individuals are excluded from the official wealth statistics on the grounds that they have no wealth over £5,000. Bearing this major caveat in mind, Figure 3.1 shows the relative importance of

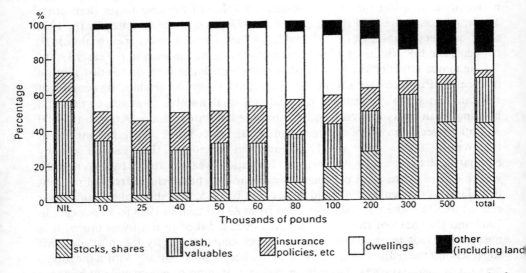

Figure 3.1 *Gross personal wealth 1985; asset composition by range (Source: Board of Inland Revenue 1987)*

various assets in different wealth bands in 1985. Residential property is most important in the bands from £10–80,000. Table 3.2 gives the preliminary figures for 1987. It shows that in the £10–100,000 bands, house property accounts for over 50 per cent of total personal wealth, rising to no less than 64 per cent in the £25–40,000 band. Put another way, residential property accounts for two thirds of net personal wealth in this wealth band. Given that 60 per cent of all wealth owners own residential property, there is a strong argument that home ownership and house-price inflation have together created a large new group of middle wealth owners in Britain since 1960.

Table 3.2   The differential importance of residential property in identified personal wealth, 1987

Range of net capital value of estate (£)	Residential Buildings		Total net capital value		Residential as % of total	
	Number (m.)	Value (£m.)	Number (m.)	Value (£m.)	Number (m.)	Value (£m.)
< 10,000	570	7,943	3,681	20,609	15.5	38.5
10,000–	1,907	35,806	3,653	63,757	52.2	56.2
25,000–	2,682	70,331	3,281	108,991	81.7	64.5
40,000–	1,066	34,370	1,291	59,033	82.6	58.2
50,000–	735	27,208	876	48,487	83.9	56.1
60,000–	1,439	64,142	1,648	115,178	87.3	55.7
80,000–	645	35,404	722	64,604	89.3	54.8
100,000–	948	62,444	1,143	148,728	82.9	42.0
200,000–	191	19,758	227	51,986	84.1	38.0
300,000–	96	12,767	121	43,139	79.3	29.6
500,000–	46	8,833	58	36,100	79.3	24.5
1 million–	10	4,126	13	18,694	76.9	22.1
> 2 million–	3	1,540	8	26,451	37.5	5.8
Total	10,338	384,670	16,724	805,757	61.8	47.7

(*Source*: Inland Revenue, 1989 – Table 10.3   Identified personal wealth of individuals in 1987.)

The limitations of these figures can be seen from the fact that only 10.34 million individuals out of a total of 16.7 million are shown as owning housing wealth in 1987–8. However, the number of owner-occupied houses alone exceeded 14.5 million in 1988 and the total adult population totalled 43.5 million. Under 40 per cent of the adult population were included in the statistics and, given that a large proportion of owner-occupied houses are owned jointly, it can reasonably be expected that at least 20 million people have some residential property wealth. As a result, the Inland Revenue estimate the value of residential property at only £385 billion. But the total value of wealth tied up in owner-occupied housing can be crudely estimated by multiplying the 14 million owner-occupied dwellings by £55,000 (the average price of houses sold in mid-1988) to give a total of £770 billion in 1988. It is, of course, necessary to deduct the value of outstanding mortgage debt from this sum, which totals over £170 billion, but even so the figure of £600 billion is substantially higher than the Inland Revenue estimate of £385 billion. Even if £55,000 is too high for older, poorly maintained houses owned by old people, which change hands less often (and figure less in the house-price sale statistics), this estimate is over 50 per cent higher than the Inland Revenue figure. We should therefore see the Inland Revenue figure as an estimate that measures only the wealthiest 40 per cent of the population because of its base in probate statistics. But the key question is not which estimate of housing wealth is more correct, but what happens to the accumulated equity?

What happens to home owners' accumulated equity?

A large proportion of accumulated equity remains locked up in people's houses. Were they all to attempt to sell simultaneously, the market would collapse. Fortunately they do not, but there is a constant flow of money into and out of the market as new buyers enter, existing owners move up or down market, and raise or lower their mortgages accordingly, as owners remortgage *in situ* and as property is sold on the owner's death. The home-ownership market can be compared to a barrel of value that is constantly replenished through monetary inflows but that has a tap through which equity is drawn off. It is also an expanding barrel. The flows into and out of the barrel are increasing, as is the volume of equity inside. The size of the home-ownership sector has increased rapidly, as have house prices. This means that far-larger mortgage flows are required to keep the market afloat. An indication is provided by the increase in building-society advances. In 1970 building societies lent £2 billion on 624,000 dwellings with an average advance of £3,100. In 1988 they lent £42 billion (20 times as much) on 1.23 million dwellings with an average advance of £35,000.

The increase in the volume of home owners' equity (the value of their houses less outstanding mortgages) also has to be released in some way. It cannot simply continue to accumulate indefinitely. While many existing owners undoubtedly feel wealthier, there is a question mark over how they can release their growing equity. For most people their capital gains have been purely paper ones. They may have made for satisfied dinner-party conversations by owners in London and the South East during the mid-to-late 1980s when house prices were rising rapidly but, for most owners, the gains are unrealized. They remain potential rather than actual. While some people do sell up and realize the gains or, more likely, move down market to a cheaper house or area (Muellbaeur and Murphy, 1988), this is not a feasible option for most owners who are tied to their local area by jobs, family and schools. For most owners the paper gains remain just that until it is possible to release them by remortgaging *in situ*, moving house and taking out a mortgage larger than necessary (thereby unlocking some of the accumulated equity), moving down market to a cheaper house or area, moving out of owner-occupation or by death and sale. In the rest of this chapter we examine the scale and importance of various forms of equity extraction before looking specifically at the rise of housing inheritance in Britain during the last twenty years.

Equity extraction from the housing market

Equity extraction from the housing market is not a new phenomenon. It has taken place for generations as private houses – both rented and owned – have been sold and the owners, or their beneficiaries, have pocketed the proceeds. The importance of housing inheritance as a source of wealth is clearly shown in such novels as Galsworthy's *Forsyte Saga* or Trollope's Barsetshire series and George Bernard Shaw's first play was entitled *Widowers' Houses*. In the nineteenth century, housing comprised a major source of wealth ownership for private landlords. What is new is the expansion of home ownership, the impact of house-price inflation on the size of the flows into and out of the private housing market and the emergence of what is termed 'premature equity extraction'. Put simply, a growing number of home owners are thought to be unlocking some of their accumulated equity by remortgaging their houses and using some of the surplus for general consumption rather than investing it in more expensive houses or home improvements or leaving it to their children and beneficiaries as in the past.

The 1980s house-price boom has been accompanied by a growing awareness among both home owners and financial institutions of the scale of equity tied up in owner-occupied housing (Figure 3.2) and its potential implications. This has been accompanied by changes in the structure of mortgage lending that have undermined the traditional dominance of the building societies. The banks first entered the domestic mortgage market in a major way in 1981 when lending restrictions were relaxed. This was partly to stop the inroads being made into bank lending by building societies and partly to take a share of a secure, growing and high-margin business. Hit by the growing problems of Third World debt, the banks were looking for a safe home for their surplus cash and mortgage lending in Britain seemed an answer. As a result, bank mortgage lending grew very rapidly from the early 1980s to take almost 40 per cent of the new-loan market by 1984. This has subsequently fallen back, but the banks now have a major presence in the mortgage market. They also pioneered development of the market for equity-withdrawal schemes in the late 1970s.

It was realized that a large amount of equity was locked up in owner-occupation. This was traditionally only released at the end of an individual's housing career through trading down or death and inheritance but it comprised good security for lending. In 1987, when the Treasury abolished mortgage-interest tax relief on loans for home improvements and allowed the banks to grant mortgages for anything on the security of a house, most banks set up so-called equity-release schemes and began to publicize actively the idea of home owners' equity and equity release as part of campaign to persuade owners to stop postponing gratification until tomorrow and release some of their equity today. The advertisements all stress the possibility of home owners increasing their current consumption and achieving a desired lifestyle by unlocking equity in their home. As the Bank of Scotland Equity Release Scheme put it,

> A trip to a local auction. A thumb through a classic car magazine. A browse round an antique shop. If you've an eye for a good investment, finding one isn't difficult. But finding the money to invest often is. To solve this problem we've introduced Equity Release. A unique scheme that allows you to get at the profit you've made on your house without selling up and moving out.

Until very recently, only those in the upper echelons of the social register ever inherited anything of any real worth. As the heirs of "well-to-do" families they knew what was coming to them, just as they knew what was expected of them.

This wealthy and worldly minority (perhaps 10% of the population) is now about to be superseded by a new, larger and more volatile band of inheritors: today's middle-aged, middle classes.

It is they who are set to become the "nouveau riche" of the 90's and beyond. And they will, in a very real sense, owe it all to their parents.

For it was the post-war generation who first enjoyed widespread home ownership. Now retiring in their millions, they will soon be conferring their wealth upon their already affluent 40 and 50 year old children.

A portentous event when one considers that even a modest estate can now be expected to top the £100,000 mark.

In fact, estimates predict that by 1997, parents passing away will pass on a staggering £24 billion a year. (240% up on current levels.)

Undeniably, the impact of this quiet, yet colossal transfer of wealth will be immense. It will affect

OVER THE NEXT 10 YEARS, MILLIONS OF PEOPLE WILL BE CONFRONTED WITH A UNIQUE PROBLEM.

companies big and small, old and new, progressive and old-fashioned alike. It will doubtless affect you and your company. After all, millions of dutiful sons and daughters will be presented with dauntingly large legacies.

But will they spend, spend, spend? Or will they use their vast discretionary wealth with discretion?

Will they, as some pundits predict, fritter their money away on the likes of fritto misto di pesce and moules à la crème; German fitted kitchens; Milanese designer furniture; winter holidays in St Lucia and summer jaunts to gîtes in the Camargue?

Or will they, as rival experts would have us believe, plough their considerable capital into the City's money markets?

As it is, 1 in 5 adults now hold stocks and shares of one sort or another. 1 in 3 have taken out their own private pension plan. 1 in 10 have decided to invest in private health care. These figures could advance dramatically given sufficient nouveaux inheritors with sufficient financial perspicacity. No area of finance would remain untouched.

Private education, for example, could become a realistic and popular option for legions of middle class families overnight.

Whilst an ever-decreasing retirement age and a less munificent welfare state could bring pension and private health care planning to the front of millions of minds.

The vagaries of luck and fate need not decide your company's eventual response to all this, though. You can start doing something about the matter today, just by thinking ahead.

For forward planning is the only answer. An answer that we at Ernst & Whinney have put into practice for companies of all sizes and complexions. In all probability, your company could benefit from contacting us. After all, without wishing to blow our own trumpet, we do have a wealth of experience.

EW Ernst & Whinney
Accountants, Advisers, Consultants.

Figure 3.2   Ernst & Whinney advertisement; Ernst & Whinney have merged with Arthur Young to form Ernst & Young

Or, as the Midland Bank said when it introduced Home Owner Reserve, 'If you're a home owner, it's more than likely that your house has gone up in value since you bought it. And that you're sitting on a comfortable profit. Until last year however, there was no easy way of releasing this money without selling up and moving out'.

The Trustee Savings Bank were equally explicit:

Why search for a loan when the money is right on your own doorstep? If you own a house, you could be sitting on a gold-mine. Your mortgage will have remained static, or may even have decreased, whilst the real value of your house will probably have risen steadily over the years. The only snag is you can't touch a single penny of it until you've actually sold up. But now things have changed. The new Equity Release scheme from TSB has finally solved this age-old financial dilemma and now make it possible to draw out money using your house as security.

There is also the Nat West Home Equity Loan, and Barclays Direct Loan to 'turn your home equity into ready cash' and a variety of others from less well-known or less reputable finance houses. All offer the same formulae: 'cash on the house'. As the Royal Bank of Scotland put it, 'Your House can now provide you with more than a roof over your head' (see also Chase de Vere, Figure 3.3).

The problem with all these schemes is that none of them offer equity release as such. What they offer is the equivalent of an overdraft, mortgage or personal loan secured on the equity of the house. Rather than releasing equity, they increase indebtedness. And the interest charges on the loans are more than conventional mortgages. The home owner really wanting to release equity rather than increase their borrowings and debt would be better advised to move down market to a cheaper house. Also lenders rarely, if ever, point out that borrowing against the security of the home has the risk of repossession if payments are in default. This is true of a conventional mortgage, of course, but the DTI is proposing to legislate to ensure that every advertisement for secured loans includes a financial health warning along the lines 'Your home is at risk if you do not make repayments on a secured loan'.

The so-called equity-release schemes are merely the latest and most explicit form of equity extraction from the home-ownership market. The importance of 'capital leakage' or the 'conversion into disposable income of capital invested in housing assets', as Kemeny and Thomas (1983, p. 13) defined it, was first identified as a problem in the 1970s when it was argued that owners were taking out larger mortgages than they needed to finance purchase of consumer goods. Subsequently it was argued by Kilroy (1979), Leigh Pemberton (1979), Downs (1981), Congdon (1982) and others, that lending for house purchase and equity release was diverting money away from industry and was contributing to inflation as consumer debt grew. Growing official concern about equity release was noted by Davis and Saville (1982) in the *Bank of England Quarterly Bulletin*:

not all mortgage lending is used to finance additions or improvements to the housing stock. It seems certain that a sizeable amount of new lending has gone indirectly to finance spending on goods or other real or financial assets, rather than additions or improvements to the owner-occupied housing stock.

(p. 395)

POTS AND POTS AND POTS OF THE STUFF.

Pots of money stacked in your larder?
Or maybe it's like Old Mother Hubbard's.
A little bare?

Never mind.

If you take a good look around your house you may be surprised at what you see.

Money!

Caught between each brick and stone; tied up in carpets and curtains; locked in bedroom, study and kitchen.

If you think we may be spreading it a bit thick then do remember that we are one of the most highly respected mortgage advisers in the UK. With all the expertise you need to release your capital *so you can use it now* when you need it. We'll defer your interest too, so you won't find yourself in a jam with rising rates.

You could pay off more expensive loans, settle all your credit card accounts, or just enjoy your money.

Then again, you might like to take advantage of a scheme which could lower and stabilise your monthly repayments for a significant period.

Whether you decide to spend or save, you can rest assured that you will always have the very best advice.

CHASE DE VERE HOME LOANS– MAKING PROVISIONS FOR YOUR FUTURE

For more details please contact us.

To: Chase De Vere Home Loans plc,
FREEPOST, 125 Pall Mall, London SW1Y 5EA

Name _____

Address _____

_____

Tailor Made Mortgages

Daytime Tel No. _____

CHASE DE VERE
HOME LOANS PLC

01•930 7242

AN APPOINTED REPRESENTATIVE OF SUN ALLIANCE LIFE MEMBER OF LAUTRO AND IMRO.
LICENSED CREDIT BROKERS AND MEMBERS OF THE CORPORATION INSURANCE AND FINANCIAL ADVISERS

Figure 3.3   Pots and pots of the stuff (Chase de Vere)

Concern about the possibility of direct withdrawal of equity from housing by borrowers obtaining more finance than required for house purchase, and its possible implications for credit and monetary aggregates, prompted a request to mortgage lenders by the Bank of England and the Treasury in January 1982 to limit this possibility.

(p. 396)

The scale of equity extraction from home ownership

In 1985, another paper in the *Bank of England Quarterly Bulletin* by Drayson pointed to the very rapid growth of what was termed 'net cash withdrawal' from the private-housing market. This was defined as net lending for house purchase that was not applied to either new private-sector housing or to improvement of existing privately owned houses. Net cash withdrawal thus includes lending for the purchase of houses previously in the privately rented or the council sectors, as well as remortgaging for non-housing uses moving down market, and the proceeds of inheritance from housing. The article suggested that the volume of net cash withdrawal had grown rapidly from £1.54 billion in 1979 to £5.74 billion in 1983 and £7.2 billion in 1984 when it accounted for 43 per cent of £16.6 billion of net new loans for house purchase. This is double the 1981 figure in real terms.

The major questions are how accurate are these estimates, and what happens to this money? Many commentators interpreted the figure of £7.2 billion as a measure of the money taken out for general consumption and, in an article in the *Guardian*, Martin Pawley (1985) suggested equity extraction was now the main motor of the British economy. We have, he suggested,

> found a way not only to get rich from our own houses, but perhaps even to live off them entirely in the future. ... The nation of homeowners has begun to play Monopoly in Reverse. ... Unlike the traditional board game, in which players start off with money and end up with property, today's Reverse Monopoly players start off with property and try to turn it into cash. ... The new style Monopoly player will begin to do consciously what he or she has done instinctively ever since they got a foot on the 'ladder' of home ownership. That is to increase the share of annual expenditure that is drawn from long-term housing credit, at the expense of the share drawn from earnings.

Pawley argued that, on the assumption that 50 per cent of housing credit leaks away into consumption, that £5.5 billion was diverted in this way in 1983. Dividing this by the 1.2 million people who took out mortgage loans in 1983, he suggested that an average of £4,583 was taken out for consumption and that this figure would increase to £6,500 in 1984 and £8,000 in 1985.

The argument is a fascinating one but, unfortunately for owners, home ownership is not a perpetual financial energy machine that produces money from nothing. This is no more than a contemporary version of the alchemist's dream of turning base metals into gold and it rests on a fundamental misunderstanding of the nature and origins of net cash withdrawal. As Davis and Saville pointed out in 1982 (p. 395), equity extraction from the housing market 'is inevitable; every chain in the secondhand housing market has an end: the final house comes onto the market because its owner-occupier has died, or ceased to own his house for other reasons, or because it is put on the market by its landlord after the tenant has left'. Each chain in the housing market also has a beginning, and equity extracted from the second-hand market is balanced by the deposits from first-time buyers, heavy mortgage repayments made by buyers in the early years of house purchase and by new mortgage finance. For each seller there is a buyer, and every pound extracted from the housing market is paid for directly or indirectly by a buyer. There is no free lunch in owner-occupation. Instead, there are intergenerational transfers of wealth from young to old and from tax-paying non-owners to mortgaged owners. All equity outflow is matched by an equivalent or greater equity inflow. This can be seen partly as the fruits of enforced savings, and partly as the results of a growth in real wages and house prices that enables home owners to share in the fruits of economic growth. The capital gains made by last-equity extractors are paid for by a generation of new buyers, paying a high proportion of incomes. But while house prices and equity increased rapidly in the mid-1980s and in previous booms, they have been broadly matched by rises in income, and house price:income ratios have not increased in the long term.

Pawley (1985) is also wrong in assuming that all the equity released is for consumption. Although the Bank of England (1985) commented that 'the excess lending has directly or indirectly been used for other purposes – to repay other borrowing, to finance interest payments on existing borrowing, to increase holdings of other assets (financial or real) or to sustain consumption', this is not the same as saying that all the money released has been diverted into consumption, or that all owners and buyers benefit equally from net cash withdrawal. In fact there is a strong case that much of the money released from the private housing market via housing inheritance goes back where it came from: into the financial system itself where it helps to sustain the increasing volume of new mortgage lending needed to support rising house prices. To assess this, we need to examine the various sources of net cash withdrawal.

Equity extraction: where does the money go?

The first attempt to measure the scale of capital leakage from owner-occupation was made by Kemeny and Thomas (1983). They noted that it posed considerable empirical problems as there is no data available on the purchase and selling price, and the present and previous mortgage for individual transactions. The result is that 'what is a relatively familiar financial restructuring for the individual becomes more difficult when considered at the macro level' (*ibid.* p. 16). They identified three methods of estimating the scale of leakage. The first compares the growth of mortgage lending with the rise in the number and value of owner-occupied houses. The difference between the two is the scale of capital leakage. The second method measured spending out of housing capital and the third the scale of capital release. While important, this work used data from the early 1980s and has been overtaken by other studies, the first by the Bank of England in 1985, the second by Holmans (1986a) and the third by Watson and Lowe (1989). We shall briefly consider each of these in turn.

The Bank of England defined net cash withdrawal as the difference between cash injections (both deposits and regular repayments of capital) and withdrawals from the private housing market including private rented housing. It examined five categories of transactor in the housing and mortgage markets in an attempt to pin down the cause of the rapid expansion of net cash withdrawal between 1982 and 1984. These were:

1. the owners of private rented dwellings;
2. first time buyers;
3. households leaving the owner-occupied sector;
4. non-moving owners; and
5. moving home owners.

They argued that house inheritance was a long-term trend and could not explain the rapid increase in net cash withdrawal they laid at the door of moving home owners taking out larger mortgages than they needed. Unfortunately, they gave no sources for their figures, and the basis of their conclusions was not shown in detail.

The most rigorous analysis of equity extraction to date is that of Holmans (1986a), despite its important definitional exclusions. He defined equity extraction (p. 5) as 'the sum of expenditure on house purchase by first-time purchasers, *plus* lending to moving owner-occupiers net of loans redeemed on the houses sold *plus* new money put in by moving owner-occupiers *less* purchase of new houses'. This definition (*ibid.*) 'includes the funds that become available when someone selling his present house and buying another has something left over after paying for the house being bought out of the proceeds of the previous sale without raising a mortgage'. In this respect the definition is broader than that used by the Bank of England, which related only to transactions where house-purchase loans were taken. But, in key respects, Holmans's definition is narrower than that of the Bank of England's.

First, it excludes money lent by building societies and other bodies for the improvement and alteration of owner-occupied homes. Building societies lent some £1.7 billion for this purpose in 1984 and this is a major omission. Second, it excludes the lending that occurs when a home owner with a mortgage pays off their present loan and replaces it with a new and larger loan, without moving house. This is unfortunate as 'remortgaging *in situ*' is a major source of equity extraction from the housing market, according to the Bank of England. Holmans accepts that, since the early 1980s, banks have been willing to remortgage houses and make larger loans than previously, but he argues that such increases in indebtedness do not represent lending for house purchase in the ordinary sense of the term and that they are not a qualifying purpose for tax relief. This is true but, as was shown earlier, this form of equity extraction has probably grown rapidly since 1987. Third, Holmans excludes regular repayments of mortgage principal by borrowers other than those associated with the sale of properties. Finally, it includes only the purchase and sale of owner occupied housing and excludes sales of housing-association property. He does, however, include estimates of the first three in his calculations, so it is possible to compare his results with those of the Bank of England.

As Holmans defines it, equity extraction relates to the four categories of

1. payments to 'last-time sellers', including the executors of deceased owners, elderly people who have gone to live with someone else or in a nursing home, owners who have sold and moved abroad or into rented accommodation and divorce-related sales;
2. payments to the owners of formerly private rented houses sold for owner-occupation;
3. borrowing by moving owner-occupiers in excess of what they would require if they made full use of the proceeds of selling their previous residence;
4. sums realized by owners who 'trade down' and pay less for the house being bought than they received from the house sold.

The results of Holmans analysis are shown in Table 3.3. It shows that the volume of equity extracted from owner-occupiers house-purchase transactions rose from £4.1 billion in 1977 to £8.8 billion in 1981. It then jumped sharply to £13.1 billion in 1982 and remained at this level in 1983 and 1984. The largest item in this definition of equity withdrawal were 'last-time sellers' who accounted for £7.36 billion (53 per cent of the total) in 1984. Of these, elderly dissolving households accounted for £4.55 billion (33 per cent). Purchases of privately rented and council houses accounted for a further £3.45 billion (25 per cent), and moving owner-occupiers for £3.02 billion or 22 per cent. According to his figures, increases in indebtedness through replacement of existing mortgages by larger ones without moving house accounted for a maximum of £300 million in 1982 falling to £45 million in 1984. This seems a remarkably low figure and should be treated with caution.

Table 3.3   Types of equity withdrawal from owner-occupiers house-purchase transactions (£m.)

	Last-time sellers		Private landlords	Public authorities	Moving owner-occupiers		Total
	Elderly households dissolved	Other			With mortgages	Without mortgages	
1977	1,425	830	710	100	725	325	4,115
1978	1,730	1,035	840	255	910	380	3,150
1979	2,145	1,250	980	415	960	455	6,205
1980	2,390	1,325	1,065	850	925	455	7,010
1981	2,850	1,540	1,205	1,255	1,490	470	8,810
1982	3,265	1,965	1,425	2,235	3,640	535	13,065
1983	3,695	2,135	1,590	1,780	2,990	530	12,720
1984	4,555	2,805	1,965	1,495	2,575	445	13,840

(*Source*: Holmans, 1986a, Table 4.)

Holmans's figures for equity withdrawal are substantially larger than the Bank of England's. This is primarily because Holmans excluded lending for home improvement (£3.4 billion in 1984) and the repayments of mortgage principal (£3.6 billion in 1984), which the Bank of England included. Holmans also included purchases from the private rented and council sector that the Bank of England deducted. As a result, Holmans's figure of £13.8 billion in 1984 is some £7 billion larger than the Bank of England's. But, when these differences are allowed for, the two sets of figures are in much closer agreement (Table 3.4) and both show a sharp jump in the level of equity extraction from 1981 to 1982 and the following years. On Holmans's data this was primarily the result of a £1 billion increase in the cash needed to finance sales of council houses (from £1.25 billion in 1981 to £2.23 billion in 1982), equity extracted by moving owners with mortgages that increased from £1.49 to £3.64 billion and payments to last-time sellers that increased from £5.83 to £7.36 billion.

Holmans also examined equity extraction in the narrower sense of equity withdrawal arising solely from the change of ownership of existing owner-occupied houses – that is, by last-time sellers and moving owner-occupiers. This excludes flows of funds associated with the sale of formerly privately rented and council dwellings for owner occupation. Table 3.5 shows that last-time sales by the elderly play an important part in equity withdrawal and account for about 43 per cent of total equity extraction on the narrow definition. Although the level of equity withdrawal accounted for by elderly last-time sellers has not grown as fast as some other categories, during the early 1980s it has consistently been the largest single component of equity extraction from the private housing market and Holmans's figures for this type of extraction are quite closely comparable to those produced by the Inland Revenue. This is a very important finding and justifies our focus on inheritance as a key element in equity extraction in Britain.

The most recent analysis by Lowe and Watson (1989) has reworked Holmans's calculations and suggest that in 1984 a total of £9.66 billion was released from the housing market on the narrow definition – excluding sales by private landlords and public authorities. Of this, they estimate that £3.826 billion (40 per cent) was released as a result of 'last-time' sales due to death of elderly households, £1.375 billion (14 per cent) from dissolution of elderly households for other reasons (such as moves into residential homes or to children), £1.492 billion 15.5 per cent from other last-time sales (owners going abroad or splitting-up, £2,414 billion (25 per cent) from movers with mortgages releasing equity via the move and £553 million (5 per cent) from movers without mortgages moving down market to a cheaper house. This work confirms that inheritance is the largest single source of equity extraction and accounts for 40 per cent of total equity extraction on the narrow definition used by Lowe and Watson. The remainder of the chapter examines the changing scale and value of housing inheritance in Britain during the 1970s and early 1980s and the importance of housing within inheritance as a whole.

The scale and importance of housing inheritance in Britain

Housing inheritance accounts for an estimated 40 per cent of the equity withdrawn from the owner-occupied housing market each year, but how widespread is inheritance, how fast has it grown, how much is it worth and how important is it within inheritance as a whole? To answer these questions we need to know how many estates are left each year containing house property, the value and location

Table 3.4 Comparisons between 'equity withdrawal' and 'net cash withdrawal'

	Equity withdrawal	Purchases from public authorities	Purchases from private landlords	Modified equity withdrawal	Injections by house-holds	Equity withdrawal net of injection	Net cash Withdraw
1977	4,115	100	710	3,305	1,085	2,220	1,420
1978	5,150	255	840	4,055	1,420	2,635	1,840
1979	6,205	415	980	4,180	1,380	3,430	1,540
1980	7,010	850	1,065	5,095	1,475	3,620	880
1981	8,810	1,255	1,205	6,350	1,930	4,420	2,360
1982	13,065	2,235	1,425	9,405	3,100	6,305	5,720
1983	12,720	1,780	1,590	9,350	3,450	5,900	5,740
1984	13,840	1,495	1,965	10,380	3,565	6,815	7,210

(*Source*: Holmans, 1986a, Table 7.)

Table 3.5   Equity withdrawal more narrowly defined

	(1) Elderly households dissolving	(2) Last-time sellers (total)	(3) Moving owners	(4) Equity withdrawal (narrowly defined)	(5) Own funds put in	(6) Balance (4) – (5)
1977	1,425	2,255	1,050	3,300	1,480	1,820
1978	1,730	2,765	1,290	4,055	1,950	2,105
1979	2,145	3,395	1,415	4,810	2,630	2,180
1980	2,390	3,715	1,380	5,095	3,050	2,045
1981	2,850	4,390	1,960	6,350	2,590	3,760
1982	3,265	5,230	4,175	9,405	2,720	6,685
1983	3,695	5,830	3,520	9,350	2,850	6,500
1984	4,555	7,360	3,020	10,380	3,140	7,240

(*Source*: Holmans, 1986a, Tables 4 and 8.)

of the property and the importance of other assets in estates of different size. We also need to know how the numbers and proportions have changed over time. The rest of this chapter examines these issues.

Data sources and methodology

There are two main methods of analysing the scale and value of housing inheritance. The first method, used by Morgan Grenfell (1987) in 'Housing inheritance and wealth', is the *indirect* one of applying age-specific death rates to home-ownership rates by age-group to produce estimates of the numbers of dying owners each year. These are then reduced to allow for the proportion of two-person households in the age-group where the survivor assumes ownership and continues to live in the property. The number of finally dissolving owning households each year is then multiplied by the average house price for the year to yield a total figure for the value of housing inheritance.

The second, and more direct method, uses the figures produced by the Inland Revenue on 'estates passing at death'. The information is collected for the purpose of taxation rather than the analysis of inheritance and the figures are based on a *stratified sample* of applications by executors for *grants of representation* or probate for deceased persons' estates. In 1985–6, the most recent year for which figures are available, there were 245,000 estates listed out of a total of about 600,000 deaths. The discrepancy is explained by the fact that only estates that require a 'grant of representation' for probate and other purposes are recorded by the Inland Revenue. Joint property passing to a surviving spouse by succession is excluded, as are smaller estates (valued at under £1,500 from 1965–83, and under £5,000 from 1984 onwards). No details are available of estates where these provisions apply (over 300,000 a year), even where wills have been made. This is not a major problem, however, as joint property passing between spouses does not constitute inheritance as usually defined, and estates worth less than the minimum are unlikely to contain house property. It should be stressed that the figures do not refer to estates liable for taxation. Only about 15 per cent all of estates are taxed.

Both methods have advantages and disadvantages. The advantage of the indirect method is that it can be used for making predictions of the future level of housing inheritance as the ownership rate in each age-group and the death rate is known. Its overwhelming disadvantage is that its accuracy is totally dependent on the validity of its assumptions and calculations. The Morgan Grenfell calculations include the following assumptions:

1. Owner-occupied property passes on death and not before.
2. Owners own only one house.
3. They do not own rented property.
4. The average value of houses bequeathed is equal to the mean value of all houses.
5. That no mortgages are outstanding on properties and that equity is not released before death.

The great advantage of the Inland Revenue statistics is that they provide reliable probate-based figures on the number of estates passing at death each year, which contain house property and its value, as well as data on the overall asset composition of estates, and the value of assets by size bands of estate. This information is not available from estimates. The disadvantage of Inland Revenue statistics is that future predictions can only be made by trend projection, which is unsatisfactory. Also, as we discuss below, the Revenue categories have changed over time. But these are relatively small problems, and in this analysis we draw mainly on Inland Revenue statistics.

The size distribution of estates passing at death

Before looking at the number of estates containing residential property and its value, it is first valuable to examine the size distribution of estates, which is very negatively skewed. In other words, there are far more small estates than large estates. Table 3.6 shows that in 1982–3, 36 per cent of estates were worth under £10,000, 28 per cent were worth £10–25,000 and 17 per cent were worth £25–40,000. Altogether no fewer than 80 per cent of estates were valued at under £40,000. Another 13 per cent were valued at between £40,000 and £60,000, and 5 per cent of estates at £60–£100,000. Just 1 per cent were valued at over £100,000 and 0.004 per cent over £1 million.

The distribution of estates by value is very different. At the bottom end, estates of under £10,000 accounted for over a third (36 per cent) of estates but only 5 per cent by value, and estates of under £25,000 accounted for almost two thirds (64 per cent) of all estates but only 22 per cent by value. At the other extreme, estates of over £100,000 comprised just 1 per cent of all estates, but 14 per cent by value. The 13 per cent of estates worth over £40,000 accounted for 50 per cent of value. The inequality in the distribution of wealth holdings at death is clear, particularly as a large, if unknown, number of estates are excluded from the Inland Revenue statistics as they are worth under £5,000. If they were included, the proportion of estates worth under £10,000 would rise substantially.

Table 3.6   The distribution of estates by net capital value (NVC), 1982-3

NCV of estate (£)	Number	%	Cumulative (%)	Value as % of total	Cumulative % value
0–	103,605	36.00	36.0	5.2	5.2
10,000–	80,265	28.00	64.0	17.0	22.2
25,000–	48,665	16.90	80.9	18.7	40.9
40,000–	17,345	6.00	86.9	9.5	50.4
50,000–	9,873	3.40	90.3	6.6	57.0
60,000–	10,932	3.80	94.1	9.0	66.0
80,000–	5,830	2.00	96.1	6.2	72.2
100,000–	8,481	2.90	99.0	13.7	85.9
200,000–	1,877	0.65	99.6	5.3	91.2
300,000–	849	0.30	99.9	3.7	94.9
500,000–	357	0.10	100.0	2.8	97.7
1m.–	85	0.03		1.3	99.0
>2m.	25	0.01		1.0	100.1
Total	288,189		100.0		100.0

(*Source*: Inland Revenue, 1987.)

The number of estates containing residential property

The Inland Revenue statistics only provide data on residential property in estates from 1968–9 onwards. Previously, the data was aggregated into a land-and-property category that was impossible to disaggregate. The categories of residential property employed in the Inland Revenue statistics have frequently been changed. In 1968–9, data was provided for all residential property in Britain. In 1972–3 it was split into freehold and leasehold property, and in 1974–5 the coverage was extended to the entire UK. From 1978–9 to 1980–1 it was split into owner-occupied and other residential property. Since 1980–1, the only category has been that of all UK residential property, but in 1984 the basis of the data was changed from that of estates recorded in a given year to a year-of-death basis. Accordingly, there are two sets of figures for 1980–1 and 1981–2 – all of which are given in Table 3.7 for purposes of comparison. Now that the new system of recording has settled down, the best basis for comparison over time is that of all residential property, which enables us to compare the early years to the most recent figures. In Table 3.7, figures for the number of estates containing freehold and leasehold property (1972–3 to 1977–8 inclusive) have been added together to give the total number of estates containing residential property. The same has been done for estates containing owner-occupied and the other residential category (1978–9 to 1980–1 inclusive). While the former addition is unlikely to inflate greatly the number of estates containing residential property, the addition of the number of estates containing owner-occupied and other residential property may well inflate the total as the owners of rented property are themselves likely to be owner-occupiers and their estates may count in both categories. This is confirmed by comparison of the data for 1980–1 using both classifications. The number of estates with owned or other property totalled 160,672, the number containing only

Table 3.7   The number of estates containing UK residential property

	Number of estates	Total no. estates	% of all estates	Value of residential property (£m.)	Total value (£m.)	% of Total
1968–9	125,085*	271,238	46.1	465	1.923	24.2 GB
1969–70	149,592*	287,239	52.1	501	1.948	25.7 GB
1970–1	142,473*	267,718	53.2	530	1.967	26.9 GB
1971–2	149,052*	288,796	51.6	638	2.275	28.0 GB
1972–3	138,489†	268,299	51.6	848	2.743	30.9 GB
1973–4	135,178†	294,405	45.9	1.065	3.127	34.1 GB
1974–5	136,086†	291,837	46.6	1.161	2.996	38.7 UK
1975–6	147,568†	310,472	47.5	1.367	3.442	39.7 UK
1976–7	146,945†	288,562	50.9	1.465	3.910	37.5 UK
1977–8	145,853‡	268,218	54.4	1.476	3.867	38.2 UK
1978–9	149,956‡	285,317	52.6	1.877	4.824	38.9 UK
1979–80	150,894‡	293,534	51.4	2.468	5.921	41.7 UK
1980–1	160,672‡	301,190	53.3	3.164	7.012	45.1 UK
1980–1	146,896§	301,190	48.8	3.164	7.012	45.1 UK
1981–2	142,646*	286,179	49.8	3.125	7.172	43.6 UK
1980–1	143,343‖	294,841	48.6	3.057	6.883	44.4 UK
1981–2	147,894‖	295,236	50.1	3.280	7.628	43.0 UK
1982–8	143,980‖	288,199	50.0	3.383	8.211	41.2 UK
1983–4	148,800‖	296,890	50.1	3.683	9.195	40.0 UK
1984–5	147,717‖	273,762	53.9	4.163	10.372	40.1 UK
1985–6	137,486‖	245,071	56.1	4.567	11.482	39.8 UK

Notes
* All (GB/UK) residential property.
† Freehold and leasehold estates.
‡ Owner-occupied and other residential.
§ Owner-occupied estates only.
‖ All UK residential property on year-of-death basis.

(*Source*: Annual Inland Revenue statistics, 1970 to 1989 inclusive.)

owner-occupied property was 146,896 and the number of estates containing residential property was 143,343 on the new basis of count. This suggests that the figures for the period 1977–8 to 1980–1, which add together the number of estates containing owner-occupied and the number containing other property, produces an inflated total. It also inflates the proportion of estates containing residential property. The addition is necessary, however, to yield total value of estates containing residential property.

The number of estates containing residential property has grown only slowly and erratically from 125,085 in 1968–9 to 148,800 in 1984–5 – an increase of 19 per cent (see Table 3.7). If 1969–70 is taken as the base year, the number of estates containing house property has not grown at all but has simply fluctuated between 142,000 and 149,000 estates a year. And while the 1985–6 figure of 137,500 is probably an anomaly, comparison of 1969–70 and 1985–6 would suggest a decline in the number of estates containing house property! These figures do not reveal the rapid growth of housing inheritance many pundits have suggested. And even if 1968–9 is taken as the base year and compared to 1984–5, a 19 per cent increase is small compared to the growth of owner-occupation over the last few decades. We have not yet experienced the enormous expansion of housing inheritance predicted by some commentators and Britain is not yet a nation of inheritors or an inheritance economy. But, as Chapter 4 shows, the post-war growth of home ownership will not feed through into housing inheritance for another twenty or thirty years. The Morgan Grenfell estimates for 1970 and 1987 were 120,000 and 155,000, which are quite close to the Inland Revenue figures. But the Inland Revenue figures include estates of both married and single persons and, in 1982–3, of a total of 288,200 estates, 87,400 or 30 per cent were married-couple estates, most of which will pass to spouses. This implies the Morgan Grenfell figures over-estimate the number of houses available for inheritance by 30 per cent.

The value of residential property in estates

The number of estates containing UK residential property rose erratically from 46 per cent in 1968–9 to 56 per cent in 1985–6. But the share of residential property as a proportion of the net capital value of estates increased rapidly from around 25 per cent in the late 1960s to 44 per cent in the early 1980s before falling back to 40 per cent in the years 1983–4 to 1985–6. This increase reflects inflation in the value of residential assets compared to other assets. The value of residential property in estates rose from £465 million in 1968–9 to £3.683 billion in 1983–4 – an increase of 692 per cent at current prices. By comparison, the total net capital value of estates grew by 378 per cent and that of non-residential assets by 278 per cent. The value of residential property in estates rose 2.5 times faster than the value of non-residential property. As the number of estates with residential property increased by only 19 per cent over this period at least 81 per cent of the rise in the value of residential property in estates occurred as a result of house-price inflation. If the calculation is done for the period 1968–9 to 1985–6, the value of residential property in estates rose to £4.567 billion – a rise of 882 per cent. This compares to an increase of 497 per cent for the total net value of estates and 374 per cent for the value of non-residential property. The value of residential property in estates therefore rose 2.36 times faster than the value of non-residential property over this period. As the number of estates containing residential property increased by only 10 per cent over this period, this suggests that price inflation accounted for over 90 per cent of the total increase in value. This can be simply demonstrated as follows:

1968–9   125,085 × Average property value (£3,719) = £465 million.
1985–6   137,486 × Average property value (£33,215) = £4,566.6 billion.
Increase in number of estates with house property = 12,401 = 9.9%.
Increase in value of house property = £4,101.6 billion = 882%.

If the number of estates had remained constant at 125,085, their value in 1985–6 would have been 125,085 × £33,215 = £4,154.7 billion or 91 per cent of the 1985–6 total. Therefore at least 91 per cent of the increase in value of residential property in estates has arisen from house-price inflation. As the average price of house property in the additional estates has also risen over time, the true figure will be in excess of 91 per cent.

These figures have important implications for the future growth of housing inheritance by value. Over the past 18 years this has been almost entirely a product of the rise in house prices rather than an increase in the number of estates containing residential property. The average value of residential property in estates in 1968–9 was £3,719. By 1983–4 it was £23,715 and by 1985–6 it was £33,215 – an increase of nearly 800 per cent.

Morgan Grenfell estimated that the total value of former owner-occupied houses in estates in 1987 was £6.5 billion by multiplying the estimated number of owner-occupied households finally dissolving through death by the national average house price. Given that the national average house price virtually doubled from 1983 to 1987, this is broadly compatible with projection of the Inland Revenue figures of £3.383 billion in 1982–3 and £4.567 billion in 1983–6, given that these values often relate to estates of people dying one or two preceding. But it should be stressed that continued rapid growth in the value of residential property in estates and, hence, the value of inheritance, is dependent on house-price inflation. Morgan Grenfell estimate that inherited house property would be worth £24.3 billion in the year 2000 assuming the continuation of past rates of house-price inflation or £8.9 billion with no inflation.

The assset composition of estates passing at death

How important is residential property within inheritance as a whole? Table 3.8 shows the relative importance of different asset categories within estates in 1985–6. Leaving aside cash and money in bank and building society deposits (present in 93 per cent of estates) and household goods (60 per cent), residential buildings were included in 56 per cent of all estates, just ahead of UK and municipal securities, such as National Savings certificates and Premium Bonds (53 per cent), and well ahead of insurance policies (39 per cent) and listed shares and company securities at 17 per cent. The proportion of estates containing UK residential property has grown from 46 per cent in 1982–3 to 50 per cent in 1982–3 and is currently 56 per cent.

The share of the total net value of estates taken by residential property rose rapidly from 24 per cent in 1968–9 to 44 per cent in the early 1980s before falling back to 40 per cent from 1983–4 onwards. It seems to have stabilized at this level and it comprises by far and away the most important single component of wealth at death. In 1985–6 it accounted for 39.8 per cent of the value of estates followed a long way behind by cash and interest-bearing deposits (26.3 per cent), UK listed securities (10.4 per cent), government and municipal securities (6.6 per cent) and land (3.2 per cent). None of the other types of asset exceeded 3.0 per cent of the total gross value of estates. This is an important finding that highlights the central role now played by housing in inheritance.

The figures given above are averages for all estates and ignore variations in the incidence and value of UK residential property by size of estate. Table 3.9 shows that only 9 per cent of estates valued at under £10,000 in 1985–6 contained

Table 3.8   The relative importance of different asset categories in estates passing at death, 1985–6

	Proportion of estates including asset	% gross value all estates	Average value (£) per estate including asset
UK residential buildings	56.1	39.8	33,215
Cash, bank and interest-bearing accounts	93.1	24.7	12,426
Listed UK company securities	21.3	14.4	31,716
UK government and municipal securities	52.8	7.0	6,199
UK land	3.1	3.0	45,497
Insurance policies	39.3	3.4	4,048
Household goods	60.1	2.6	1,993
Other personalty	47.0	3.6	3,592
Other UK buildings	1.7	1.0	28,162
Unlisted UK company securities	3.4	1.9	25,620
Trade assets and shares in partnerships	2.2	1.1	24,731
Overseas and foreign securities	1.6	0.5	13,951
Loans and mortgages owed to estate	3.5	0.7	9,293
Foreign immovables	0.4	0.1	18,421
	$n = 245,071$	100.0	46,850

(*Source*: Inland Revenue, 1990.)

Table 3.9   The proportion of estates containing residential property, and the average value of the property and its proportion of the net capital value of estates, by size of estate, 1985–6

Net value of estates	% of estates containing residential property	Average value of property (£000)	UK residential property as % of the total value
< £10,000	9.3	8.1	15.5
£10–25,000	53.6	15.2	46.3
£25–40,000	74.2	25.5	59.6
£40–50,000	75.8	31.9	54.4
£50–60,000	76.7	36.3	51.7
£60–80,000	76.8	42.5	48.7
£80–100,000	76.5	48.2	43.2
£100–200,000	74.1	59.4	34.2
£200–300,000	72.0	78.0	24.9
£300–500,000	69.0	106.5	20.8
£500,000–1 million	67.6	164.4	18.5
£1–2 million	63.4	215.5	11.8
> £2 million	51.2	404.5	6.9
Average	56.0	33.2	39.8

(*Source*: Inland Revenue, 1990.)

residential property. This is hardly surprising given that national average house prices in 1985 were £32,673. The proportion of estates containing house property rose sharply to 56 per cent in the 10–25,000 range and an average of 75 per cent of estates worth from £25,000 to £300,000. When the 21 per cent of estates under £10,000 are excluded, 69 per cent of estates include house property.

Not surprisingly, the value of residential property increases proportionately with the total value of the estate. In estates of under £10,000 (Table 3.9), the average value of residential property in estates containing such property was £8,100. In estates valued at £10–25,000 it was £15,200, and in estates of £25–40,000 it was £25,500 rising to £215,000 in estates of £1–2 million. In estates worth over £2 million the value of residential property increased dramatically to £404,000. This suggests the presence of large country houses, expensive houses in central London or both, and possibly several houses scattered across the country. It is likely that estates under £25,000 containing residential property are concentrated in northern areas where house prices are lower.

The value of UK residential buildings as a proportion of the total capital value of the estates in each size range also varied considerably, from 9 per cent of estates valued at under £10,000, rising to an average of 59 per cent of estates worth between £25,000 and £40,000 and 54 per cent of estates valued at £40–50,000. It then falls steadily to 7 per cent of estates worth over £2 million. These figures show the considerable importance of residential property in the range of estates between £10,000 and £100,000, averaging 51 per cent of the total value of estates. It is here that the impact of rapid house-price inflation has had its greatest impact, and it can be argued that owner occupation and house-price inflation have together created a new class of middle wealth-leavers. Above this level, residential property is progressively less important compared to other, traditional, sources of wealth, such as land and stocks and shares.

The role of house-price inflation in increasing the value of smaller estates is shown in Figure 3.4, which compares data for 1968–9 and 1982–3. In 1968–9, prior to the onset of rapid price inflation, residential property comprised 15 per cent of estates worth under £1,000, 37 per cent of estates valued at £1–3,000 and 52 per cent of estates valued at £3–4,000. The proportion then fell to 40 per cent of estates between £4,000 and £10,000, and 29 per cent from £10,000 to £15,000. House property was thus of greatest importance in estates between £3–4,000. In 1982–3 house property was most important in estates of £10–80,000 where it accounted for over 50 per cent by value. House-price inflation has thus played a major role in increasing the value of estates containing house property.

The asset composition of estates passing at death in 1982–3

Residential property is now the single largest component of estates by value, accounting for no less than 40 per cent of total assets. But the relative importance of different assets differs according to the size of estate. Table 3.10 shows the relative importance by value of the major asset types for different-sized estates. These asset types are grouped into those that are proportionately most important in big estates (land, household goods, securities and trade and partnerships), and

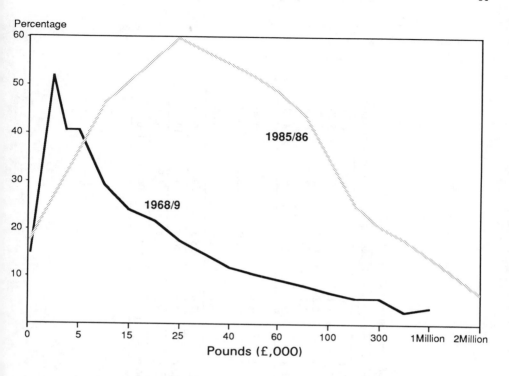

Figure 3.4   Residential property as a proportion of estate value by size

those that are proportionately more important in small estates (government and municipal securities, cash and interest bearing-deposits and insurance policies).

The proportionate importance of these assets types in the large and small estates is inversely related. In estates under £10,000 municipal and government securities and cash and insurance policies accounted for 76 per cent of assets compared to just 25 per cent in estates worth £200–300,000 and 15 per cent in estates worth over £1 million. In these large estates, land, household goods and stocks and shares accounted for about 70 per cent of asset value compared to 5 per cent in estates under £40,000. House property is most important in the middle range of estates.

While the importance of residential property is far greater in smaller than it is in larger estates, it forms a very important part of middle wealth-bands from £10,000 to £100,000. It is in these bands that the impact of house-price inflation on inheritance has been greatest, and there is a strong case for arguing that owner-occupation and house-price inflation have created a large group of middle wealth-owners that scarcely existed thirty years ago. The size of the group will grow rapidly over the next thirty to forty years.

Geographical variations in the importance of residential buildings

All the figures discussed above are national figures that say nothing about

Table 3.10   The relative importance of different types of asset by size band of estates, 1982–3

	>£2 m.	£1–2 m	2–300,000	80–100,000	60–80,000	25–40,000	<10,000
Land	24.2	13.4	8.1	2.9	1.9	0.4	0.06
Household goods	20.2	5.6	2.5	2.4	2.3	2.1	3.20
All securities	17.9	48.4	34.8	15.2	10.8	2.6	1.20
Trade and partners	5.2	3.7	2.9	1.7	0.8	0.4	0.40
Sub-total ('wealthy')	67.5	71.1	48.3	22.2	15.8	5.5	4.80
Government and municipal securities	4.7	6.3	7.2	8.3	7.4	4.7	9.90
Cash and deposit	8.0	7.0	15.5	25.5	29.0	26.0	56.90
Superannuation and insurance	0.8	2.6	2.4	3.2	2.9	3.5	9.40
Sub-total ('poor')	13.5	15.9	25.1	37.0	38.3	34.2	76.20
UK residential	9.3	8.9	20.4	35.8	40.2	54.4	14.60
Miscellaneous	9.7	4.1	6.2	5.0	5.7	5.9	4.40
Total	100.0	100.0	100.0	100.0	100.0	100.0	100.00

(*Source*: Inland Revenue, 1987.)

sub-national variations. The Inland Revenue therefore kindly prepared a series of special tables for us using hitherto unpublished statistics showing the breakdown of estates passing at death in 1980–1 by asset type and size of estate for each of the four countries of the UK. The figures for residential property are shown in Table 3.11, which shows that the bulk (87 per cent) of estates in the UK containing residential property are in England. Scotland has 6.4 per cent. More importantly, the proportion of estates containing residential property varies considerably from 55 percent in Wales and 50 per cent in England to 38 percent in Scotland and 36 per cent in Northern Ireland. The Scottish figure reflects the historically low level of owner-occupation in that country. The value of residential property as a proportion of the total net capital value of estates also varies markedly from 46 per cent in England and 44 per cent in Wales to 33 per cent in Scotland and 28 per cent in Northern Ireland. This reflects the differential value and structure of assets in each country. House prices in Northern Ireland are considerably below the average for the rest of the UK.

Table 3.11 National variations in the importance of UK residential property, 1980–1

	% of Estates including UK buildings	UK residential as % of capital value of estate	% of UK Total residential	% of UK value	Average value of residential
Wales	55.0	44.2	4.9	3.9	16,694
England	50.0	45.6	87.1	86.6	21,854
Scotland	38.0	33.0	6.4	7.3	18,040
Northern Ireland	36.0	28.1	1.6	2.2	18,680
UK average	48.6	44.4	100.0	100.0	21,328

(*Source*: Special tabulations prepared by Inland Revenue.)

It is clear from these figures that, whether measured in terms of the proportion of estates or as a proportion of their total value, residential buildings are far more important in estates in England and Wales than they are in either Scotland or Northern Ireland where other assets, particularly land, are more important. These geographical differences in the importance of residential property in estates are taken up again in Chapter 6.

Summary and conclusions

We have shown that housing inheritance in the early to mid-1980s accounted for approximately 40 per cent of 'equity extraction' or capital leakage from the owner-occupied housing market when the sales of council houses and private rented property to home owners is left out. The volume of equity extraction increased sharply in the early 1980s. But while the number and proportion of estates containing house property rose only slightly between the late 1960s and the mid 1980s, the value of house property in estates increased dramatically as a result of price inflation 2.5 times the inflation rate of other asset values. House property now makes up 40 per cent of the total value of estates and is by far and away the most valuable, single element in inheritance. The importance of house property is particularly marked in the middle range of estates from £10,000 to £100,000, and it can be suggested that house-price inflation has created a group of middle wealth-owners far larger than thirty years ago.

While the number of estates with house property should continue to increase for the rest of this century, the growth in the value of residential property in estates will remain largely dependent on house-price inflation. The number of estates containing house property will not grow substantially until the early decades of the next century as the rapid growth in home ownership over the last thirty years works its way through into housing inheritance. The characterization of Britain as a 'nation of inheritors' is rather premature, although it may be more appropriate by the early years of the next century. The social inequalities in the distribution of housing inheritance by class, tenure and region are taken up in Chapter 6. Chapter 4 examines likely future growth of housing inheritance.

4

DEMOGRAPHIC TRENDS AND FUTURE HOUSING INHERITANCE

Introduction

As was argued earlier, the current nature and scale of housing inheritance is a product of a number of factors including the growth of home ownership, rising house prices and demographic trends within the UK. In Chapters 2 and 3 we discussed the rise in home ownership and house prices, noting in particular the impact of house-price inflation on the value of property in estates. While the number of estates containing property only increased by 19 per cent over the period 1968–9 to 1984–5, the value of the property rose by over 690 per cent. Over the period 1985–9, house prices roughly doubled and we can therefore expect to see further large increases in the value of property in estates. This, combined with continuing growth in the level of home ownership, would suggest we can expect further increases in property-related inheritance.

In this chapter we consider how demographic trends are currently influencing the pattern of property inheritance. As Holmans (1983) has noted, the demographic forces at work influencing both the demand and supply of housing have been much neglected within housing analysis. While basic population trends have been considered, little attention has been given to the ways these interact with and produce changes in the housing market and, by extension, with the property-inheritance process. Notwithstanding this neglect, Britain is, in reality, witnessing major changes in its demographic structure. A slow aggregate increase in the population, a low birth rate and increased longevity are producing important shifts in the age structure of British society. The working population will decline while the number of the elderly will rise. While certain factors may slow the rate of inheritance, it is likely that the numbers of estates will grow significantly in the decades beyond the turn of the century, as the number of deaths rises reflecting the ageing of the population. Popular perception would have it that there should be a substantial increase in property-related inheritance now reflecting the growth of home ownership in the inter-war period and in the early 1950s. However, the impact of this rise in home ownership (as already charted in Chapter 3) has been muted by the general expansion of the population throughout the century (37 per cent growth from 1900 to 1985) and the increase in longevity. This suggests that the major impacts are still to come. Our aim here is to review current trends and then, looking ahead, consider how, using much simplified assumptions, these will develop over the next forty years.

Demographic trends

Demographic or population trends have an effect upon housing inheritance in a number of interrelated ways. First, the overall size of the population and, in particular, the number of households sets a broad limit on the number of dwelling units produced, occupied and that can ultimately be inherited. Obviously, the rise in second- and third-home ownership or the presence of portfolios of rental property can affect individual estates and these will influence the ultimate outcome, but in most cases an estate will contain one residential property or none at all. Second, and perhaps the most critical factor with respect to inheritance, are the rates of household formation and dissolution. The generation of new households enhances the demand for housing and ultimately influences the supply of dwellings to be inherited. As we shall show, household-formation rates have fluctuated over the decades, as have the rates of household dissolution, and it is changes in the latter rate that appear to be restraining the growth in housing inheritance.

Household-formation rates are influenced by a third important factor – trends in marriage, divorce and remarriage. While there is an important and growing never-married group of households (see Holmans and Nandy, 1987) marriage, divorce and remarriage are a potent force within the dynamics of the housing market and it is these patterns of behaviour that ensure that inheritance by a spouse remains the most common outcome of the death of a property owner. Subsequently, a fourth factor – the number of children – clearly influences the impact of any single inheritance (see Chapter 5). Here the decline in family size has had a 'concentration' effect, although there are important class and cultural differences. There are thus a number of ways in which demographic trends can influence the property-inheritance process. Clearly they are only 'activated' once households pass into and through home ownership and, as we have already noted, it is the increase in the number of households in this tenure in conjunction with massive price rises and specific demographic trends that has made the inheritance issue so important.

Population

The rise in housing inheritance has to be seen within the context of the continuing growth and reshaping of the population of the UK. In 1960, the UK's population stood at 52.4 million. By 1985 it had reached 56.6 million. It is now projected to rise to 60.0 million in 2025 – an increase of 6 per cent on the 1985 figure (OPCS, 1987). Significantly, from 2025 the UK's population is then projected to decline, falling over the next 25 years to 58.2 million in 2051. The number of deaths has stayed constant at around 650,000 persons per annum but, by 2041, it will rise to 790,000 persons per annum (a 21 per cent increase). Within the UK there are, then, quite divergent trends between the different countries (these are only projected up to 2025). The projections suggest that, while England and Northern Ireland can expect to have growing populations up to 2025, Scotland's population will decline through the period and Wales will record a rise up to 2001 and then fall (Table 4.1).

Table 4.1   Projected population, persons 1985–2025, UK and constituent countries (m.)

	UK	England	Wales	Scotland	Northern Ireland
1985 (actual)	56.6	47.1	2.81	5.14	1.56
1991	57.5	47.9	2.83	5.12	1.61
2001	59.0	49.3	2.87	5.10	1.68
2011	59.4	49.9	2.84	4.97	1.73
2021	59.9	50.5	2.81	4.82	1.75
2025	60.0	50.7	2.79	4.74	1.76

(*Source*: OPCS, 1987, Table 16.)

These population changes have significance in terms of both the overall demand for property and the number of estates that will come forward, and for the regional variations that will emerge.

Households

The number of households in the UK are also expected to rise, from 21.1 million in 1989 to 23.9 million in 2001 – a growth of 2.3 million or roughly 11 per cent. Unlike the population as a whole, OPCS only project households to 2001. Even so, a number of trends emerge. England's households grow at a faster rate than those of Wales (11 per cent growth, 1985–2001, compared to 8 per cent for Wales). This aggregate growth is made up of both growth and decline with respect to specific categories of households, as Table 4.2 shows. Married-couple households decline over the period 1986–2001 by 3.5 per cent in England, and 5 per cent in Wales. At the same time, one-parent households increase and, most significantly since they are likely to include a large number of elderly people, one-person households rise by 39 per cent in England and 40 per cent in Wales (though the number of one-person households, 60–5 + , is projected to increase to 3.9 million in 2001 it will only make up 55 per cent of all one-person households, down from 62 per cent in 1987).

In Table 4.3 the number of households in England over the period 1986–2001 is broken down by the age of the head of household (the table includes both female- and male-headed households). As can be seen, households headed by persons aged 15–29 (the key first-time buyer age-group) will decline from 1991 – falling by 22 per cent in the period to 2001. By contrast, households headed by persons aged 30–44, 45–59/64 and 60/65 and over, rise by 20 per cent, 19 per cent and 9 per cent respectively over the period 1986–2001. The number of households headed by persons of retirement age (60/65 +), i.e. the core, potential, benefactor group, rises by nearly 500,000 over the 15-year period though, because of the general rise in the total number of households, these households remain roughly constant at 30 per cent of the total.

Table 4.2   Households by type, England and Wales, 1986–2001

	(000s)				% increase/decrease			
	1986	1991	1996	2001	1986–91	1991–6	1996–2001	1986–2001
England								
Married couple	10,724	10,559	10,449	10,350	−1	−1	−1	−3.5
Lone parent	1,661	1,868	2,013	2,074	12	8	3	24.0
One person	4,452	5,099	5,691	6,184	14	12	9	39.0
Other	1,206	1,378	1,465	1,475	14	6	7	22.0
All households	18,044	18,903	19,617	20,083	5	4	2	11.0
Wales								
Married couple	643	630	621	609	−2	−1	−2	−5.0
Lone parent	99	109	114	115	1	5	1	16.0
One person	249	287	322	349	15	12	8	40.0
Other	58	61	61	59	5	—	−3	−2.0
All households	1,049	1,086	1,118	1,131	3	3	2	8.0

(*Source:* DOE, 1987, Table 2, p.1.)

Table 4.3   Households by age of head of household, England, 1986–2001

Age	Year (000s)				% change			
	1986	1991	1996	2001	1986–91	1991–6	1996–2001	1986–2001
15–29	2,317	2,425	2,190	1,877	5	−10	−14	−19
30–44	4,972	5,318	5,616	5,952	7	6	6	20
45–59/64	5,416	5,563	6,075	6,428	3	9	6	19
60+/65+	5,339	5,596	5,736	5,826	5	2	2	9
All	18,044	18,903	19,617	20,083	5	4	2	11
Annual household formation rate (average over 5-year periods)		172	143	93				

(*Source:* DOE, 1987, Table 3, p.2.)

This overall rise in the number of households disguises a steady fall in the net annual increase in households in each of the 5-year periods to 2001. In the 5 years to 1991, there is a net increase in England of 172,000 households annually. This falls to 143,000 in each of the next 5 years and plummets to 93,000 in the last 5 years to 2001. Within these totals the proportion of the net annual increase made up by the increase in elderly households falls from 30 per cent in 1986–91 to 19 per cent in each of the subsequent years. The demographic data would suggest that post-2001 there will be a substantial rise in the proportion of the net annual increase made up by elderly households as the early post-war baby-boom households move into retirement.

Clearly, the flow of households into retirement has great significance for the inheritance of property. Many may become or already be the beneficiaries of property inheritance and they themselves are likely to generate properties that will be inherited. However, in demographic terms, there are a number of key factors that complicate this picture. The first of these is increased longevity. Currently, males live to an average age of 72 years and females to 78. By 2024 it is expected males will live an average of 75 years and females 80 years. This is an extrapolation of past trends. Current thinking is that this may be optimistic. The population of the very elderly (75 years and over) in the UK is projected to rise from 3.67 million in 1986 to 4.41 million by 2001, 4.78 million by 2021 and reaching a peak of 6.3 million in 2041 (an increase of 74 per cent on the 1986 figure). Although property inheritance may ultimately take place, the impact of this increase in longevity may be to slow any increase in the rate of inheritance concomitant upon the steady growth of elderly households discussed above.

A further factor to consider is the impact of marriage, divorce and remarriage rates upon the inheritance process, e.g. by slowing the release of property to beneficiaries other than the surviving spouse. Marriage rates have increased slightly from a low in the mid-1980s. In 1987 total marriages (first time and remarriages) stood at 398,000. Remarriages now constitute 35 per cent of all marriages, though it should be noted that the proportion (and number) involving a widow or widower has fallen. Roughly 75 per cent of men 65 and over are married and this, combined with the increased longevity (particularly of the female partner), has the effect of dampening the rate of inheritance of property by beneficiaries other than the spouse.

Divorce can also significantly disrupt the inheritance process by changing the housing careers of the individuals involved. Holmans and Nandy (1987), in their research on household formation and dissolution and tenure, noted that owner-occupiers were less likely to divorce (one can speculate as to why and whether this will have changed since 1981, the end of the period they were considering). Moreover, as they go on to show divorce 'amongst owner occupier households leads to a net increase in the number of owner occupied households' as households split into two. Although the number increases, the actual proportion of owner-occupier households among those married in 1971 and divorced in 1981 falls sharply. These changes can alter the inheritance potential in number and value significantly. On divorce and break-up of a home-owning household, an initial trading down is likely by at least one partner or even a temporary move out of owner-occupation. If one or both of the divorcees do not remarry, then the potential inheritance may be diminished. If they do remarry then it is possible they will remarry an existing owner and restore their housing career. Indeed, some may do better than that because, having divorced but remained an owner, they will then be property rich. Under a variety of such circumstances the children of the original marriage may thus benefit from two estates.

In conclusion, it is evident that Britain is witnessing major changes in its demographic structure. A slow aggregate increase in the population, a low birth rate and increased longevity are producing important shifts in the age structure of British society. The working population will decline while the number of the elderly will rise. While certain factors may slow the rate of inheritance, it is likely that the numbers of estates will grow significantly in the decades beyond the turn of the century as the number of deaths rises reflecting the ageing of the population. Popular perception would have it that there should be a substantial increase in property-related inheritance now reflecting the growth of home ownership in the inter-war period and in the early 1950s. However, the impact of this rise in home ownership (as charted in Chapter 3) has been muted by the expansion of the population throughout the century and the increase in longevity. This suggests that the major impacts are still to come.

Having reviewed some of the ways in which the population is changing and their likely impacts upon inheritance, we now turn to developing a forecast of property inheritance over the next fifty years. As we have sought to show, the current pattern of inheritance is lower than might have been predicted. We suggest this is because of the slow build up of the level of home ownership and the impact of growing longevity. Over the next two decades, home-ownership rates will probably stabilize at a maximum of between 75 and 85 per cent. Moreover, it is likely that ownership levels will be more even across the older age-groups, reflecting rapid growth in recent years. All of this suggests we are therefore moving into a period when the flow of inherited properties could increase substantially and, in the section that follows, we examine this contention through a demographically based projection of property inheritance.

Future trends

Levels of home ownership have continued to rise in each successive age cohort of the population. Thus, taking the 15-year period 1972–87, which is covered in the published volumes of the *General Household Survey*, the home-ownership rate among 70–79-year-olds has gone up from 23.5 per cent to 28 per cent, while that for 80-year-olds and over has risen from 8 per cent to 11 per cent. Such increases over a relatively short period are not dramatic but they do point up the way the rate has edged upwards. In consequence, each cohort passing into retirement (and ultimately dying), has more owners within it. Expressed in generational terms, more children are likely to have home-owning parents who will bequeath property to them – a factor expressed in probability terms in Chapter 6. The likelihood of such beneficiaries already being an owner is also increasing. The coming together of these two trends offers a future prospect of greater levels of property inheritance that, if current behaviour is any indication, will lead to high rates of property sales as the beneficiaries liquidate their newly acquired asset.

The model

In order to examine these issues further, a simple forecasting model was developed using official projections of population by marital condition in 5-year periods up to 2031. Using age-specific mortality rates and attaching 1986 tenure by marital-condition data, it was possible to project the numbers of owners dying, the numbers of properties transferred to surviving spouses in each 5-year period and, reflecting the marital condition of the owners dying, the number that would be released to the succeeding generation. This distinction was important because, as is evident earlier, a large number of properties are transferred to a surviving spouse. Under such circumstances, no vacancy occurs and the property is not released until the surviving spouse dies. However, where the owner was an individual (e.g. a single, widowed or divorced person), a property is released.

Base data

The inadequacies of data have posed limits to the model that could be constructed. Broadly, mortality data relate to individuals while tenure data relate to households. In an examination of inheritance of property from deceased owners, the most useful data would be individual mortality rates by tenure. Sadly, such data do not exist and it is necessary to use data that allow an approximation of this. As indicated above, we constructed the model using the 1985 projections of population by marital condition in selected age-groups as the base-data set. The data distinguish between single, widowed, divorced and married individuals and they are projected in 5-year age-groups to 2026.

For the purposes of the model, the age-groups from 50 to 54 were utilized (i.e. nine groupings up to and including 90 +). The age-groups below 50 were ignored because it was felt that very few property releases would be generated by individuals in these age-groups (in 1987 deaths in the 0–44 age-groups accounted for less than 5 per cent of total deaths – OPCS, 1989, Table 19). In the event of death, property would probably be transferred to a spouse who him or herself would move forward into the 50 + category. Because of the absence of household-by-age-group projections beyond 2001, we are forced to equate marital condition with households. Single, widowed and divorced persons (aged 50 +) are assumed to form separate households. While there is evidence of cohabitation, especially among pre-50-year-olds, the incidence declines sharply with the older age-groups. Certainly this will change over time as the generations for which cohabitation was a more normal existence come into their later years, though this may be tempered by their subsequent experience of marriage! For married individuals it is assumed they form shared households and then, with the death or otherwise of their partner, they move forward into the single, widowed or divorced categories. In reality the assumptions in this approach are at least as robust with respect to households as the formal household projection. This relies on the projection of 'headship' rates and these have proven quite hard to predict accurately over the last few decades.

Having established the base data on which the model is developed, we then applied the 1985–6 age-specific mortality rates as derived by OPCS (1987) for the UK. These rates are given for males and females and are given as the mid-points of the standard 5-year-age-groups. Thus, for the 50–4 age-group, the mortality rate is calculated for 52-year-old females and males. As is shown later, the model then utilizes these rates in conjunction with a home-ownership rate to project the inheritance and then the release of property. The home-ownership rate is derived from the Department of the Environment analysis, the *Labour Force Survey* (*LFS*). This gives tenure by type of household and age of head of household for England for 1986. The proportion of married-couple owner-occupier households by age of head of household is given in Table 4.4.

Table 4.4 Proportion of married-couple owner-occupiers in England, 1986, by age of head of household

40–4	45–9	50–4	55–9	60–4	65–9	70–4	75–9	80–4	85 +
81.6	80.8	77.4	74.4	67.7	64.9	61.5	62.0	59.0	58.7

(*Source*: DOE from *LFS*, Table B–111.)

The data set from which this is extracted provides ownership rates by other types of households, namely, lone parent, multi-person and one person. There was no way of linking these categories directly to single, widowed and divorced, and we therefore decided to apply the married rate to all categories. That means the model will over-estimate the number of inheritances and releases because the married ownership rate is higher than for the other categories. For example, in the 60–4 age-group, the rate varies from 67.7 per cent of married couples to 42.7 per cent of male single-parent heads. Equally, the data is for England and therefore the English ownership rates are applied to UK data. Again, this raises problems, but it is worth recalling that Scotland's low ownership rate is balanced to a limited degree by higher rates in Wales.

The actual form of the model is as follows. These data were embedded in a model framework comprising essentially a cohort survival model with additional parameters to ensure that, for example, it was the death of a surviving spouse that resulted in the release of a dwelling for an owner-occupying couple. This forecasting framework, in the form of a micro-computer program, allowed the researchers flexibility to vary time periods for the estimates, and to make varying assumptions as to the proportion of owner-occupation currently pertaining to the different age cohorts – in fact, remaining constant over the forecast periods.

In general, the model has the form:

$$I^t = \sum_{i=1}^{s} \sum_{j=1}^{a} \sum_{k=1}^{q} (P^t_{ijk} M^t_{ij}) O^t_j,$$

where I represents inheritance over interval, t, s is sex, a is age-groups and q is status (i.e. single, widowed and divorced persons). P represents a cohort of the population in these categories alive at the beginning of time interval, t, and m is the mortality rate for the interval. O represents the proportion who are owner-occupiers at the beginning of the interval. In practice, a 5-year interval was used in the model giving a convenient square matrix form (i.e. 5-year groups aging over successive 5-year intervals).

The results are given in tabular form in Table 4.5 and are graphed in Figure 4.1. The number of property transfers increases steadily over the forecast period as do the number of releases. Averaged out over each year, the numbers grow from

Table 4.5 Property transfer and release, 1986–2031 (000s)

Years	No. of properties 'Transferred'*	No. of properties released	Average transfers* per annum	Average release per annum
1986–91	1,723	841	344	168
1991–6	1,892	938	379	188
1996–2001	2,062	1,036	412	207
2001–6	2,244	1,134	449	227
2006–11	2,420	1,230	485	246
2011–16	2,616	1,343	523	269
2016–21	2,816	1,455	563	291
2021–26	3,032	1,588	606	318
2026–31	3,217	1,715	643	343

Note
* Transfers comprise traditional inheritance, i.e. passing of property to a non-spouse relative (typically a succeeding generation) plus spouse-to-spouse transfers.

(*Source*: Forecasting model.)

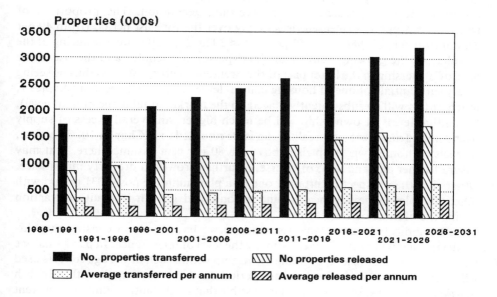

Figure 4.1 *Property transfer and release, 1986–2031 (Source: Forcasting model)*

344,000 transfers and 168,000 releases in 1986 to 643,000 transfers and 343,000 releases in 2031 (an 87 per cent increase in transfers and a 103 per cent increase in releases). In proportionate terms the rate of increase in transfers slows over the forecast period from an average 10 per cent per-annum increase in 1986–91 to a 6 per cent increase 2026–31. Indeed, by the end of the period, the annual average number of transfers has fallen back to the rate evident around the turn of the century. The rate of releases also falls from an average of 11.6 per cent in 1986–91 to 8.1 per cent in 2026–31.

The forecast suggests that property transfers and releases will continue rising throughout the period under consideration (i.e. 45 years). We would expect this because the levels of ownership are higher in each younger group and, as they age, so that pushes up the ownership level in the next higher-age category. Moreover, the population is still increasing and that has a major impact on the rising number of transfers and releases. The forecast indicates a doubling of the total number of transfers and releases over the period 1986–91 to 2026–31. Our forecast of 207,000 for the year 2000 compares well with the Morgan Grenfell forecast of 202,000 for the same year. However, because our forecast is over a longer period we are able to develop a clearer view of the impact of the growth of home ownership over the last forty years. It indicates that we can expect to see the number of properties actually inherited through property release to double in the next forty years.

The forecast period is not sufficiently long to tell whether transfers and releases will then stabilize as a consequence of home ownership having reached a roughly constant level across all age-groups. There is a suggestion from published statistics that the current 20–9 year age-group might not achieve the ownership levels of the present 30–9 age-group because of the disruption caused by recession 1981–6. In our view it is likely that, as a group, they will recover from this and achieve ownership levels equivalent to the preceding generation. The proportion of transferred properties released rises slowly over the forecast period (from 49 per cent of transfers in 1986–91 to 53 per cent in 2026–31), reflecting the ageing of the population, the growing number of single-person households and the rise in the level of ownership in the latter part of the twentieth century. We will thus be seeing a very substantial volume of housing being released and, as we show in Chapter 7, much of this will be subsequently placed on the market (double the present level). Given that levels of ownership will be much higher, an overall excess of supply over demand may become a reality – an issue returned to in Chapter 10. Of course, if levels of home ownership rise above the 80 per cent assumed here, that may ensure further demand and, of course, a further growth in property inheritance. Otherwise, the prospect is certainly one of a plateau in the post-2031 period with inheritance levels having peaked and a continued growth in equity extraction during the lifetime of benefactors.

As we indicated earlier, the assumptions we have made in constructing this model mean it will possibly over-estimate the level of inheritance. In particular, we have assumed that the level of home ownership within each of the age cohorts used will remain stable over the forecast period (and we have applied the English married-persons rate). However, it is possible that a substantial number of current public-sector tenants will buy their dwelling over the next few years as a consequence of rent increases, reduced housing benefit eligibility, enhanced discounts on the right to buy and, possibly, an extended rents-into-mortgages scheme. If this does happen we will then find that the levels of ownership will rise. The BMRB survey (1989) indicated that the level of home ownership amongst 55–64-year-olds could rise from 71 per cent to 75 per cent in ten years' time if people were able to make their preferences a reality. At the same time, the survey showed that among those aged 65 or over the level could fall from 61 per cent to 59 per cent. Overall, the survey indicated a massive preference for home ownership allowing Coles (1989a, p. 8) to conclude that 'there remains significant scope for growth in owner occupation'. It is therefore possible that our over-estimate will turn out to be an under-estimate and that inheritance will be greater than predicted here. In reality, the number and value of property-related wealth inheritances are dependent on a complex array of factors, many of which are unstable and are therefore difficult to predict (e.g. interest rates, house prices). In Chapter 10 we examine the prospects in further detail.

5

PATTERNS OF BEQUEATHING

Introduction

The existing literature on inheritance and wealth holding generally is sparse. Atkinson's (1972, p. 59) assertion that 'inheritance in Britain is an extraordinarily neglected subject' remains true today, although commentators through the years have all agreed on the importance of inheritance in sustaining and entrenching material inequalities in society.

The way in which inheritance impacts upon the distribution of wealth depends heavily upon the conscious bequeathing decisions of wealth leavers as well as formal laws governing the transmission of wealth at death. It is recognized that inheritance is a crucial mechanism governing the shape of society but surprisingly little is known about how it works in practice. Who exactly are the inheritors? What factors influence the ways in which estates are divided up? In this chapter we seek to answer these and related questions by looking at the small number of existing studies of inheritance and wealth and by presenting the findings of our own analysis of a large sample of recent wills.

The role of inheritance in wealth distribution

The first major study of inheritance in Britain was carried out by Josiah Wedgwood in the 1920s. As part of a wider investigation into the economics of inheritance, he gave a comparative account of the laws and customs of inheritance in England and Wales and in France. He concluded that the three major determinants of wealth distribution in society were unequal inheritances and gifts, unequal economic abilities and unequal luck. Wedgwood believed that inheritance perpetuated and could accentuate inequalities in wealth holding. He listed six main ways in which inheritance can foster inequality. These were

1. the laws and customs governing inheritance and bequest;
2. systems of taxation;
3. the extent of charitable bequests;
4. marriage customs;
5. the size of families; and
6. the degree of stability of economic and political conditions.

Inheritance laws and customs

Under English law, individuals can dispose of their property in any way they choose, but most European countries restrict the rights of the wealth leaver in order to protect the interests of the surviving family. Wedgwood compared the two systems by outlining the strict provisions of the 'Code Napoleon' operating in France, Holland and Belgium. Under the code, the children of a dying man were entitled to a fixed proportion of the estate, and only the remainder could be disposed of freely. If a man left one child then it was entitled to half of the estate. If he left two children then each was granted a third, and so on. The same provisions applied if grandchildren only survived. The entire estate could be freely disposed of only if no relatives in the direct line survived. Until they finally petered out, similar provisions survived in many parts of England and Wales until the early eighteenth century.

The implications of severe legal restrictions on the freedom of bequest are enormous. In extreme circumstances, such as those that followed the Russian Revolution of 1917, wealth inheritance may be abolished altogether and, in general, complete freedom of bequest is more likely to concentrate wealth than a system that guarantees a fixed proportion of the wealth left in estates to surviving relatives. In fact, as we shall see, in England and Wales it has been a long-established custom to bequeath in a way broadly consistent with the laws of succession laid down in the Code Napoleon. Very little inherited wealth leaves the immediate family circle. In Britain, the rule of custom rather than statutory laws of succession ensures that surviving family members receive the bulk of any wealth left at death.

Tax systems

The potential effects of a severe tax regime and steeply progressive rates of death duties can be considerable. In practice, as is shown in Chapter 9, the British experience, beginning with Lloyd George's Budget of 1909 and ending with the virtual abandonment of the policy in 1983 and 1988, has been to try to use inheritance taxation to bring about greater equality in wealth holding.

Charitable bequests

Wedgwood's third way in which inheritance can affect inequality is the extent to which charitable bequests are made by the dying population. These bequests, like the death duties taken by government, affect the amount of wealth eventually reaching individual beneficiaries. From his own study of high-value estates, he concluded that in England and Wales about 5 per cent of wealth is given to charity – a figure that has been confirmed by more recent studies. Giving wealth to charities can clearly reduce inequalities but, in Britain at least, large sums are likely to be given away only under exceptional circumstances, such as on the death of a spinster or widow with no surviving relatives.

Marriage customs and family size

If it was the case that people of different social classes and levels of income and wealth intermarried freely, there would be a tendency for inequalities perpetuated by inheritance to even out gradually over time. In fact, men and women in Britain and in most societies tend to marry partners from a similar class and wealth position as themselves. Even today, although there is undoubtedly more social mobility than there was, class strongly influences the choice of marriage partner. 'Assortative' rather than 'random' mating is the norm. It is still the case that, in general, the rich marry the rich and the poor marry the poor. Because of this the overall distribution of wealth in society is maintained.

The size of families

The size of the families raised by rich and poor parents also has a bearing on the value of the inheritances falling to the children of each. In Britain, Wedgwood concluded that, on the whole, poorer parents have larger families than richer parents. His findings, based on census material from the early part of this century, were that 'the average upper-middle class family is only two-thirds of the size of the average working-class family' (Wedgwood, 1929, pp. 94–5). Although the proportion may have changed, it is undoubtedly still true that the poor have bigger families than the rich. This fact tends to increase the inequalities in wealth holding resulting from inheritance in Britain.

Economic and social conditions

Wedgwood identified the degree of stability in economic and political conditions prevailing in a State as his final important factor. As a general rule, the longer established the country, the more important inheritance is likely to be in entrenching wealth inequality. In newly colonized countries, such as the USA or Australia, opportunities exist for individuals to build up substantial wealth on their own behalf. Under these circumstances 'native ability, industry and luck play a more important – though by no means sole part – in determining the distribution of wealth' (Wedgwood, 1929, pp. 97–8).

Social and economic stability generally strengthen the influence of inheritance on wealth holding. In particular, stability in price levels favour those who wish to live off invested money, deposited at an adequate rate of interest and assured buying power. The unwary investor could soon find the value of his or her assets falling if money were to lose its value but, as Wedgwood rightly pointed out, much inherited wealth has traditionally been in the form of land – an asset that, historically, has not depreciated as money depreciates. Generally speaking, 'rapid changes in the value of money make both chance and intelligent risk-bearing more important factors in [the] distribution [of wealth], so that both inheritance and savings proper become relatively less important' (*ibid*. p. 101).

Drawing in part upon Wedgwood's study, Atkinson (1972) concluded that the relationship between the inherited wealth received by one generation and that received by the next is dependent upon three factors:

1. The degree to which the elder generation built upon or squandered its inherited wealth, thereby affecting the total sum transferable to the next generation.
2. The ways in which the estates of the first generation are allocated to beneficiaries from the second. This reflects the laws and customs of inheritance, the degree to which charitable bequests are made and the effects of estate taxation.
3. Demographic factors, including family size and marriage patterns.

Modelling the effects of inheritance

Several economists have modelled the way in which inherited wealth can affect wealth holding and income distribution in society at large. Blinder (1973) expressed the distribution of inherited wealth of one generation as a function of the distribution of the terminal wealth of the preceding generation. He built in a number of assumptions on the customs governing inheritance and the economic status of marriage partners. His general conclusion (*ibid.* p. 626) was that 'with existing institutions the passing of generations can be expected to break down the inequality of wealth only very slowly. A heroic guess might be that inequality would be reduced 50% in a century'.

Using a similar approach, Pryor (1973) showed the marked effects that differences in fertility between the economic classes can have on the distribution of wealth. Atkinson (1971) had earlier used estate-duty returns to establish the distribution of wealth by age. He compared this actual distribution of wealth amongst the dying population with a hypothetical distribution arising in a society where all individuals of equal age have equal earnings and where no individuals inherit wealth or leave bequests. Building in a number of assumptions about patterns of saving and consumption, population growth and age-related growth rates in earnings, Atkinson calculated the total wealth that would be enjoyed by the richest groups in society. His 'observed' distribution derived from the estate-duty records proved to be weighted much more heavily towards the richest groups. He judged this to be due to inherited wealth. Oulton (1976) later refined Atkinson's assumptions, repeated the exercise and concurred that inheritance is the single most important influence on wealth inequality in Britain.

Empirical studies on inheritance

Most empirical studies on inheritance in Britain have used the probate records as their main data source. Wedgwood (1929) used them to compare the estates of wealthy children with the estates of their parents. He looked at two samples of estates above £10,000 left in the mid-1920s and found that only a small minority of the wealthy offspring had not been the beneficiaries of substantial inheritances. Harbury (1962) repeated Wedgwood's investigation using records from the mid-1950s and concluded that there had been very little change in the relative importance of inheritance in the making of the personal fortunes of Britain's top wealth leavers over the decades. Harbury and McMahon (1973) repeated the exercise using a sample from 1965 and found little change. Both in 1956–7 and in 1965, 58 per cent of sons leaving more than £100,000 had fathers who had left more than £58,000. Overall, there had been remarkable stability in the relationship between the level of wealth left by offspring and the wealth left by their fathers. Harbury and McMahon, in common with other writers, were quick to point out the limitations of using estate-duty figures as a measure of inherited wealth. Such figures take no account of gifts between the living and fail to take account of the role played by 'informally inherited' advantages acquired through education, attitudes, social and business contacts, and so on.

Harbury and Hitchins (1976) carried out a further study on the estates of the wealthy and those of their fathers using probate records from 1973. They found that the proportion of high wealth leavers preceded by wealthy fathers had declined by a statistically significant level compared to the earlier studies. The authors suggested that this may have been due to increasingly severe tax rates on large estates, increasing avoidance of estate duty through undeclared gifts and other devices and to increasing opportunities for men of humble origin to make their own fortunes. Extending the study to wealthy women, Harbury and Hitchins (1977) concluded that only about 5 per cent of a sample of women leaving more than £200,000 in 1973 had built their fortunes by entreprenurial means. Inheritance and marriage emerged as the most important sources of wealth for rich women testators: 'some 60% of rich sons (daughters) of rich fathers marry daughters (sons) from wealthy families' (*ibid.* p. 131).

Also using data from 1973 (the final year for which full details of the estate duty paid on each estate were made public) Horsman (1978) studied the pattern of dispersal of personal wealth at death in a sample of 285 high-value estates (all above £50,000). The records also allowed Horsman to discover the extent to which trusts were resorted to by high wealth leavers and the estate duty paid on estates of various size. He showed that high wealth leavers almost invariably leave the vast majority of their wealth to surviving members of their family. Of a total of 327 main beneficiaries, where the main beneficiary was defined as the recipient of the biggest single share of the estate (sometimes two or more individuals shared this distinction), all but 45 were clearly identifiable as family members (Table 5.1).

Table 5.1   Relationship of main beneficiaries to testator

	No.	%
Spouse	115	35.2
Child	99	30.3
Grandchild	4	1.2
Other relative: same generation	28	8.6
Other relative: next generation	36	11.0
Other	23	7.0
Not clear	22	6.7
Total	327	100

(*Source*: Adapted from Horsman, 1978, Table II.)

More than three quarters of the wills had set up trust funds as a means of avoiding estate duty. The estate duty exemption limit in 1973 was £15,000 and, despite the fact that the rate rose steeply beyond this threshold, Horsman found no direct correspondence between estate size and duty paid. In fact, the proportion of duty paid rose on estates between £50,000 and £300,000, stayed fairly constant up to £1,000,000 and then fell sharply on estates above £1,000,000. It would seem that the very wealthy are in a better position than their poorer counterparts to take advantage of tax-avoidance devices.

The Royal Commission on the Distribution of Income and Wealth, set up in 1974 and chaired by Lord Diamond, conducted its own survey of wills. It wanted to give authoritative answers on how inherited wealth is distributed among beneficiaries and what the impact of estate duty is upon inheritance. This was part of a much more comprehensive investigation of the distribution of income and wealth in Britain initiated by a Labour government keen to diminish wealth inequalities in society. The commission's standing reference was to 'help secure a fairer distribution of income and wealth in the community... [through]... conducting an analysis of the current distribution of personal income and wealth and of available information on past trends in that distribution' (Diamond, 1975, p. v).

The commission took a sample of 238 estates of £15,000 or more receiving probate in England and Wales in 1973. Their findings, in brief, were as follows:

1. The great majority of the wealth in most estates passed to relatives of the deceased. An average 60 per cent after-payment of duty went to close relatives (spouse and children) and almost 90 per cent went to all relatives.
2. In the estates of married people, a greater proportion of smaller estates was left to the surviving spouse than in larger estates (77 per cent in estates of £15–£50,000 to only 31 per cent in estates of £500,000 or more). In the estates of widowed people, a greater proportion of smaller estates was left to children than in larger estates (57 per cent overall but as low as 26 per cent in estates of £500,000 or more).
3. Large estates tend to be more widely and more equally distributed than smaller estates. The average number of bequests in estates of £15–£50,000 was 5. This figure rose to 24 in estates of £500,000 or more. Over half of the estates in the range £15–£50,000, but only a fifth of those of £500,000 or more, included a bequest representing more than 75 per cent of the disposable estate.
4. Bequests to charity were relatively insignificant, accounting for an average 5 per cent of the estate. However, this figure rose to about 15 per cent in estates of £500,000 or more.
5. In the average estate of £15,000 or more almost all property bequeathed to relatives went to individuals in the same generation (50 per cent) or in the next generation (46 per cent). As the average age at death of testators in the sample was 74 for men and 79 for women, most inheritances were therefore received by people already in middle or old age (see Diamond, 1977, Chapter 8).

Analysing bequests by the relationship of the beneficiary to the wealth leaver produced findings that were broadly comparable to Horsman's, although the

Safe As Houses

commission was able to go one better than Horsman by measuring the actual volume of wealth bequeathed (Table 5.2) rather than just the number of bequests.

Table 5.2   Analysis of bequests by type of beneficiary

| Range of estates | Total no. of estates | % disposable estates bequeathed to relatives | | | | |
		Spouses	Children and Issue	Other relatives	Friends	Charities
>£500,000	62	13.7	23.2	38.6	10.0	14.5
£100,000–£500,000	69	21.4	34.4	31.4	8.1	4.7
£50,000–£100,000	53	28.1	35.7	21.1	10.5	4.6
£15,000–£50,000	54	38.0	28.0	24.6	4.4	5.0
Weighted average totals		32.4	30.4	25.6	6.4	5.2

(*Source*: Adapted from Diamond, 1988, Table 83.)

The Diamond study agreed with previous empirical studies on inheritance that the bulk of inherited wealth is passed on to family members regardless of estate size, but that immediate family numbers (spouses and children) were less favoured in very large estates than in those of more moderate size. The Diamond sample was taken from wills receiving probate in 1973 – an era when estate duty was still severe on large estates – and the study confirmed that estate duty was significantly diminishing the net size of large estates. The average rates of estate duty paid on the four size-classes of estates sampled were, in ascending order, 8.8, 23.6, 43.3, rising to 53.4 per cent on estates of £500,000 and over. Clearly, therefore, the tax was playing a major part in limiting the sums that could be legally inherited by beneficiaries, although the figures could take no account of two important forms of wealth transmission: gifts made by the wealth leaver more than seven years before death and surviving spouse settlements that, together with deliberate tax evasion, could substantially decrease the size of the taxable estate at death (see Whalley, 1974).

Bequests and the characteristics of wealth leavers

Although most wealth left at death is bequeathed to family members, the identity of these family members varies according to the sex and marital status of the wealth leaver. Looking at marital status first, the Diamond Commission found that wealth leavers gave most of their wealth to their 'nearest available' relatives – in the case of married people, the surviving spouse, among widowed people any surviving children, and so on – but, as Table 5.3 shows, there were significant variations between estate sizes.

The proportion of the estate left by married people to their spouses was found to be inversely related to estate size. The same was true of bequests made by widowed people to their children. Among married wealth leavers, proportionately more wealth was left to children, grandchildren, other relatives, friends and charities from high-value estates than lower-value estates. It would seem that wealth from higher-value estates tends to be dispersed more widely and more evenly than

Table 5.3   Analysis of bequests by marital status of testator

| Estate size | % disposable estates bequeathed to relatives | | | | |
	Spouses	Children and Issue	Other relatives	Friends	Charities
Married persons					
£500,000 and over	31.1	30.1	24.3	3.5	11.1
£100,000–£500,000	44.9	41.4	8.7	2.2	2.8
£50,000–£100,000	58.8	29.3	10.4	0.7	0.8
£15,000–£50,000	76.9	14.2	5.6	0.1	3.2
Weighted average totals	66.3	22.4	7.7	0.7	2.9
Widowed persons					
£500,000 and over	0.1	25.6	41.8	13.9	18.6
£100,000–£500,000	—	45.4	36.2	14.0	4.4
£50,000–£100,000	—	61.6	16.2	22.1	0.1
£15,000–£50,000	4.2	61.3	24.7	5.7	4.2
Weighted average totals	2.5	57.4	25.6	10.6	3.9
Single persons					
£500,000 and over	—	—	68.8	17.2	13.9
£100,000–£500,000	—	—	77.2	12.7	10.1
£50,000–£100,000	—	—	61.9	13.7	24.4
£15,000–£50,000	—	—	74.8	13.3	11.9
Weighted average totals	—	—	72.5	13.4	14.1

(*Source*: Diamond, 1977, Table 85.)

wealth from lower-value estates and suggests an increasing fragmentation of larger estates over time *vis-à-vis* estates of more modest size.

While marital status was found to bear a strong relationship to the way in which the estates were disposed of, striking differences were also apparent between the sexes. As Table 5.4 shows, although both sexes strongly favoured their 'nearest available' relatives it would seem that married men and single women are inclined to give more of their wealth to remaining relatives and charities than are single men.

Table 5.4   Analysis of bequests by sex and marital status of testator

| Type of testator (all estates combined) | % disposable estate bequeathed to relatives | | | | |
	Spouses	Children and Issue	Other relatives	Friends	Charities
Married males	70.3	20.1	5.3	0.7	3.6
Married females	54.0	29.9	14.0	1.0	1.0
Widowed males	8.7	65.4	18.7	6.3	0.9
Widowed females	—	54.5	28.2	12.3	4.8
Single males	—	—	51.4	47.4	1.2
Single females	—	—	75.9	7.6	16.5

(*Source*: Diamond, 1977, Table 86.)

Taking a sample of 370 estates in England and Wales exceeding £50,000, where death occurred in 1981, the Inland Revenue conducted its own investigation into the connections between the sex and marital status of wealth leavers and their beneficiaries (Inland Revenue, 1984, Table 4.7). Their findings were in broad agreement with those of the Diamond Commission and, on the basis of both studies, it is possible to pick out six major relationships between wealth leaver (of higher-value estates) and beneficiary:

1. The surviving spouse received the bulk of the wealth of her dying husband (Diamond – 70 per cent, IR – 83 per cent).
2. The surviving spouse received the bulk of the wealth of his dying wife (Diamond – 54 per cent, IR – 73 per cent).
3. Surviving children and grandchildren received the bulk of the wealth of dying widowers (Diamond – 65 per cent, IR – 70%).
4. Surviving children and grandchildren received the bulk of the wealth of dying widows (Diamond – 54 per cent, IR – 54 per cent).
5. Other relatives received the bulk of the wealth of dying single or divorced men (Diamond – 51 per cent, IR – 60 per cent).
6. Other relatives received the bulk of the wealth of dying single or divorced women (Diamond – 75.9 per cent, IR – 59.9 per cent).

Limitations of the existing empirical studies

The empirical studies of inheritance go a long way towards telling us how different types of wealth leavers usually dispose of their wealth, but all of the studies looked at restricted their interest to high-value estates only. Horsman's sample of wills, for example, all had a minimum gross probate value of £50,000. Only 3 per cent of reported estates in England and Wales were worth as much as this in 1973, his year of study. Similarly, only 16 per cent of estates were worth more than the £15,000 lower limit set by the Diamond Commission for their sample. More recently, the Inland Revenue sample, which took a lower limit of £50,000 for estates where death occurred in 1980–1, excluded 91 per cent of all estates reported.

The Diamond Commission's reason for only sampling estates above the (then) estate-duty threshold of £15,000 were that the impact of inheritance on the overall distribution of wealth, which was the commission's prime concern, was felt to be greatest in the case of sizeable estates. Estates worth more than £15,000, though relatively few in number, accounted for 61 per cent of the total net capital left at death in 1973–4, the year chosen for study by the commission.

In the past there has been some justification for looking only at the higher-value estates since wealth holding, and wealth leaving, on any significant scale in Britain has traditionally been confined to just a small élite. Their bequeathing behaviour together with the fact that, even today, around half of the dying population leave no marketable wealth, has had the greatest impact on the overall distribution of wealth amongst the living. Recently, however, as is shown in Chapter 3, the proportion of wealth held and left by the top 10 per cent of the British population has been declining rapidly. Although the share held by the bottom half has altered little, there has been a marked redistribution within the top half in recent years. Inland Revenue estimates demonstrate that inequalities in wealth holding and leaving were considerably reduced, therefore, within the wealthier half of the population, and moderate wealth holding became more important as Britain entered the 1980s.

As we have shown, the most significant factor behind the rising importance in moderate wealth holding, and leaving, lies in the rapid inter-war and post-war growth in home ownership and substantial house-price inflation over the past two decades. The traditional élite, the top 10 per cent of wealth leavers, has been much less affected by the growing importance of housing wealth. For them, land and stocks and shares have continued to represent more significant elements of their wealth, but the growth of housing wealth and accompanying evening out of wealth holding and wealth leaving within the wealthier half of the population mean that the bequeathing behaviour of moderate wealth leavers are starting to become much more important that they used to be for patterns of wealth distribution amongst the living. It is essential to establish, therefore, how or if this expanding class of moderate wealth leavers differs from their wealthier counterparts in their bequeathing behaviour if we are to understand who the eventual beneficiaries of the 'new' housing wealth (much of it bought post-war by first-time buyers) are going to be. It cannot simply be assumed that wealth leavers bequeathing estates in which the owner-occupied house is the primary asset will act in identical ways to their much richer, and longer-established, contemporaries. In the next part of this chapter we present the findings of a study of a large sample of recent wills covering all sizes of estate, designed to shed some light on these, and related, issues.

A study of 1,000 London wills

To assess whether there are differences between estates of differing size and type, a random sample of 1,000 wills granted probate in London in 1981 was taken from the Probate Registry. The year 1981 was chosen because this was the last year for which exact gross probate valuations were provided for all estates. From late August it became no longer necessary to give exact figures for estates worth less than £25,000. Of the 1,000 wills, 71 fell into this category and have accordingly been excluded from Table 5.10 (p. 94). Following a review of the methodology used, we look at patterns of bequeathing for all sizes of estate and compare our findings with those of earlier studies. The study highlights major differences in bequeathing behaviour between the sexes, between wealth leavers of different marital status and shows that the volume of wealth left also varies significantly according to the sex and marital status of the wealth leaver.

Methodology

The Probate Registry contains 228 collated books of wills probated in London in 1981. Books are arranged chronologically and within each book wills are arranged alphabetically by surname of the deceased. The sample was chosen by taking five wills at random from each of the first 200 books for 1981. Almost all wills give an address for the wealth leaver. This address was checked against the final known address shown in the registry Calendar Books. Provided the addresses tallied and/or were both London addresses, the will was included in the sample. The Calendar Books provide for each wealth leaver their name, final address, place of probate, gross value of estate, date of death and date of probate. In 125 cases the final address differed from that provided on the will but was still within Greater London, so was kept in the sample. A further 82 final addresses were outside London, so they were discarded and replaced.

There is no necessity for wills to give the number of beneficiaries nor their relationship to the wealth leaver. Some wills are written in such a way that it is hard to determine these matters. A common clause takes the form 'I leave everything to any surviving children, to be shared equally'. Another gives the name and address of a beneficiary without giving their relationship. It proved possible to make a reasonable assessment in some of these cases and assign them accordingly. It was often clear, for example, that the spouse was the major beneficiary even though the relationship may not have been explicitly stated. Overall, the relationship proved impossible to assess in 8.8 per cent of cases. These have been categorized as 'no major beneficiary clearly stated'. This is comparable to other studies. Horsman, whose work (1978) we referred to earlier, assigned 6.7 per cent of main beneficiaries in his sample to a 'not-clear' category.

In certain cases it proved difficult to decide which had been the major beneficiaries of the estate. Wills often state that particular assets are to go to one beneficiary, the remainder to another. It was usually possible to decide on the basis of the estate's total value and the nature of the specified assets who had been the major beneficiary and to classify the case accordingly. Recipients of minor legacies and beneficiaries of small portions of an estate where the bulk had been left to others were left out of the analysis. In cases where an estate was divided jointly between a number of beneficiaries, each was treated as a major beneficiary.

Further difficulties arose in identifying beneficiaries because of the workings of trust-fund arrangements. Many higher-value wills contain clauses that restrict the ways inheritors can use their inherited assets. A common example gives the surviving spouse occupancy of the marital home for the rest of his or her life but directs that the house is then to pass to any surviving children. In the analyses that follow, the spouse was regarded as the major beneficiary if, judging from the total estate value, the house was clearly the major part of the estate.

Any study using wills to investigate bequeathing behaviour runs up against the problem that the named beneficiaries on the will are not necessarily the eventual recipients. Wills are often made many years before death and, whereas changes in family circumstances or the death of named beneficiaries may lead to the will being changed, there is no guarantee. Some wills contain reversionary clauses to be put into effect should the first-named beneficiary or beneficiaries die or be disinherited but there is no way of knowing by looking at the will whether or not such clauses were in fact invoked. In the following analysis it has been assumed that the first-named beneficiaries on the will did in fact receive their inheritances.

Devolution of the estates

Table 5.5 shows that, regardless of estate size, most wealth was bequeathed to close family members. Almost half of the estates in the sample (453 of 929) were left entirely to surviving spouses, and a further fifth (202 estates) were received by a child or children only.

Table 5.5 Relationship of major beneficiaries % and (number) to testator by total estate value (£000)

| | Estate size (upper limit) | | | | | | |
	£10	£25	£40	£60	£100	>£100	Average
Spouse only	43.4	49.5	49.3	58.8	50.0	56.7	48.8
	(139)	(93)	(101)	(57)	(34)	(29)	(453)
Child/ren only	23.1	22.3	24.4	18.6	16.2	13.7	21.8
	(74)	(42)	(50)	(18)	(11)	(7)	(202)
Grandchild/ren only	0.3	0	1.0	1.0	0	0	0.4
	(1)	(0)	(2)	(1)	(0)	(0)	(4)
Other relative(s) only: same generation	6.3	8.0	5.9	5.1	0	9.8	6.1
	(20)	(15)	(12)	(5)	(0)	(5)	(57)
Other relative(s) only: next generation	5.9	1.1	2.4	3.1	7.3	2.0	3.8
	(19)	(2)	(5)	(3)	(5)	(1)	(35)
Others (including combinations of other categories)	6.6	5.3	9.8	6.2	8.9	7.8	7.2
	(21)	(10)	(20)	(6)	(6)	(4)	(67)
No major beneficiary stated	10.9	9.6	5.3	6.2	11.8	7.8	8.8
	(35)	(18)	(11)	(6)	(8)	(4)	(82)
Charity only	3.4	4.2	1.9	1.0	5.8	1.9	3.1
	(11)	(8)	(4)	(1)	(4)	(1)	(29)
Totals	320	188	205	97	68	51	929
Total (%)	99.9	100	100	100	100	99.9	100

Overall, the proportion of estates left solely to a surviving spouse (48.8 per cent) is slightly higher than other studies have found. Horsman (1978) found that 40 per cent of his high-value sample of wills gave a surviving spouse as main immediate beneficiary. Similarly, in an early pioneering study of wills, Fijalkowski-Bereday (1950) found that 42 per cent of the main bequests in a high-value sample (281 estates worth more than £10,000 in 1944–5) were left to spouses. In our study, 53 per cent of the higher-value estates (above £60,000) were left entirely to spouses. Although there is considerable fluctuation between the size categories there is a general rise in the proportion of estates left intact to a surviving spouse with rising estate value, reaching a peak of 57 per cent in the highest category (above £100,000). This differs from the findings of other studies. The Diamond Commission (1977, Table 83) found that the percentage of disposable estate bequeathed to spouses declined rapidly with rising estate value, from 38 per cent in the £15–50,000 class to just 13.7 per cent in the over £500,000 category. Generally, though, our study supports the conclusion of previous studies that inherited wealth tends to be left to spouses before children and to children before other beneficiaries. For those estates not left entirely to immediate family members, there is limited evidence that wealth from the highest-value estates reached a slightly wider range of beneficiaries than that from low value estates. In the 'above £100,000' range, 9.8 per cent of estates were left to 'other relative(s) only: same generation' compared to 6.3 per cent in the 'below £10,000' range. This suggests that the close intra-familial character of bequeathing behaviour may be even more entrenched in small and medium estates than it is in high-value estates.

Gender differences in bequeathing behaviour

The study uncovered major differences between men and women in their bequeathing decisions. Table 5.6 shows that over three times the proportion of men than women named a surviving spouse as sole beneficiary. Just over half (56 per cent) of the women in the sample left their entire estate either to their husband or to a child or children. The figure for male wealth leavers was much higher as 82 per cent. Much more women's wealth, therefore, was left to beneficiaries outside the close family circle. Similarly, more than five times the proportion of female estates than male estates were left intact to more distant relatives in the succeeding generation or to charity.

There may be a number of reasons for the wider dispersion of women's wealth.

Table 5.6 Major beneficiaries % and (number) by sex of wealth leaver

	Males	Females	Overall
Spouse only	69.9 (376)	22.9 (107)	48.3 (483)
Child/ren only	12.2 (66)	32.9 (151)	21.7 (217)
Grandchild/ren only	0.4 (2)	0.4 (2)	0.4 (4)
Other relative(s) only: same generation	4.1 (22)	9.5 (44)	6.6 (66)
Other relative(s) only: next generation	1.1 (6)	6.3 (29)	3.5 (35)
Others (including combinations of other categories)	5.2 (28)	10.0 (46)	7.4 (74)
No major beneficiary clearly stated	5.9 (32)	12.1 (56)	8.8 (88)
Charity only	1.1 (6)	5.8 (27)	3.3 (33)
Total (%)	99.9	99.9	100
Total (No.)	538	462	1000

One probable explanation is simply that women usually outlive men, meaning that fewer women than men have spouses to leave their estates to. It also seems possible that women spread their wealth slightly more widely than men. The Inland Revenue study, summarised in Table 5.7, would suggest this to be the case.

In the Inland Revenue sample, married males were found to have left 83 per cent of the net capital value of their estates to their spouses and 15 per cent to children. The corresponding figures for married females were lower (73 per cent) and higher (22 per cent) respectively. Similarly, widowers left more of their wealth (65.8 per cent) to their children than did widows (52.9 per cent), and nearly twice the proportion of female wealth (52.9 per cent) was left to other relatives, strangers in blood and charities than male wealth (30.6 per cent). Overall, as a consequence both of differences in the marital status of male and female wealth leavers and differences in bequeathing choices, much more female wealth (54.4 per cent) than male wealth (30.5 per cent) left the close family circle of spouse and children.

Although, in our study of 1,000 wills, it was not always possible to distinquish the marital status of wealth leavers in the way that the Inland Revenue was able to, our findings generally suggest that, across all sizes of estate, the major beneficiaries were the wealth leaver's closest living relatives. It was overwhelmingly the case that where a spouse was named as major beneficiary he or she was the sole beneficiary. In only 11 and 5 cases respectively were there other major beneficiaries alongside a wife or husband and in these cases the other recipients were almost always children of the wealth leaver.

Marital and gender differences in wealth leaving

Some of the most interesting findings of the study concern the differing amounts of wealth left by males and females. The average size of estate for all 927 giving an exact estate value (excluding 2 very large estates of £1.5 million and £8.5 million) came to £32,354, but the average female estate was only £26,859 – just 70 per cent of the average male estate of £38,441. This major difference in the average value of male and female estates is given another dimension when it is considered that the aggregate amount of wealth left by women is even lower. In 1927, women left 44 per cent of the wealth left by men. By 1954 this proportion had grown to 64 per cent (Revell, cited in the Diamond Commission, 1975, Table 44). In the present study, women (who made up 46 per cent of the total sample) left only 60 per cent of the wealth left by men. This continuing difference between the sexes might be expected given women's traditionally subordinate position in the economy but it goes against expectations since women usually live longer than men and, if married, receive the bulk of their husband's wealth. Some insight into these differences can be gained by looking at particular groups of wealth leavers in the sample. Men who left their entire estates to their widows left an average £36,222. Women who left their entire estates to their widowers left an average £32,707, surprisingly close to the male figure. Comparison with Revell's work would suggest a slight closing of the gap in wealth leaving between married men and married women. In 1927, married women's estates were worth, in aggregate, only 13 per cent of married men's estates. By 1954 the proportion had risen to 17 per

Table 5.7 Devolution of estates by sex and marital status of deceased, and relationship of beneficiary, England and Wales, deaths, 1981

Relationship of beneficiary	Males				Females			
	Married	Widowed	Single or divorced	All	Married	Widowed	Single or divorced	All
Spouse	83.0	—	2.1	39.8	73.4	—	—	5.9
Children	15.0	65.8	3.5	29.7	22.3	52.9	9.0	39.7
Grandchildren	0.5	3.9	1.9	1.9	2.3	1.6	0.5	1.4
Other relative(s)	0.4	14.3	58.9	16.3	0.3	23.1	59.9	30.2
Strangers in blood	0.8	14.4	24.2	9.8	0.2	18.4	26.0	18.7
Charities, etc	0.3	1.6	9.4	2.5	1.5	4.0	4.6	4.0
All beneficiaries	100.0	100.0	100.0	100.0	100.0	100.0	100.0	100.0

(*Source:* Inland Revenue, 1984, Table 4.7.)

cent (*ibid*. Table 4.4). Our findings would indicate that the figure was around 26 per cent in 1981. It may be that more married women are dying testate than before. Another reason for the relatively high average value of these married women's estates may be that valuable assets, notably the marital home, are more often being held jointly by the marriage partners than was once the case. A study by Todd and Jones (1972) showed that in 1971 just over half (52 per cent) of owner-occupying couples owned their home in joint names, and 3 per cent were in the wife's name. It may be that a higher proportion of jointly owned houses are now working through into estates.

The picture that emerged for women who described themselves as widows or spinsters on their wills was very different. The widow's average estate was £29,379 and spinsters' estates averaged just £22,975. It is likely that many widows eat into any inherited or accumulated wealth in the years following the death of their husbands to support limited incomes or to give away as gifts before their own deaths. The low figure for spinsters' estates can be accounted for on two grounds. First, spinsters suffer from women's generally disadvantaged economic position. Like all women they are less likely than men to accumulate wealth. Second, unlike married women, they have no husband to leave wealth to them or to own property in common with.

Our 1,000-wills study confirms that, regardless of estate size, there is a very strong tendency for wealth leavers to keep wealth within the immediate family. Overall nearly half of all estates were left intact to a surviving spouse with a further fifth going to a child or children as the only major beneficiaries. Women who described themselves as widows on their wills left their wealth more often to children or relatives of the same generation than to any other groups – inheritors who represented the closest available relatives for these women. Whilst women dispersed their wealth slightly more widely than men, the average sums involved were 30 per cent lower, and the study provides no evidence that the current and future growth in moderate wealth leaving will be accompanied by any wider dispersion of inherited wealth beyond the immediate family than has already been well established for high-value estates. It seems very likely that the beneficiaries of the 'new' housing wealth will be a single, or several, close family members. Inherited housing wealth, disproportionately held in estates of moderate value, will be kept in the family. However, there is a distinction to be drawn between the initial recipients of inherited wealth and those who benefit over the longer term. The greater longevity of women implies that widows receive the bulk of male wealth but intergenerational wealth transfers are much more common from female estates. At least 74 per cent of male estates in our sample were left to relatives in the same generation as the wealth leaver. The equivalent figure for female estates was only 32 per cent. When we consider this together with a possible closing of the gap in aggregate wealth leaving between men and women and the evidence from Inland Revenue study that women choose to disperse their wealth rather more widely than men, it is clear that this has major implications for our understanding of the dynamics of inheritance. Although male wealth is, on average, 30 per cent larger than female wealth, it is the volume of female wealth and female bequeathing behaviour that are increasingly going to dictate the wider effects of inherited wealth on the living, since the bulk of intergenerational wealth transfers are from female estates.

In this chapter we have shown that the customs of bequeathing mean that inheritance operates overwhelmingly within the family and we have demonstrated that the growth in moderate wealth leaving, much of it based on rising home ownership and house-price inflation, is not likely to bring about any wider dispersion of inherited wealth beyond the close family circle. We have not, though, dealt with the inheritance of housing wealth directly. Unfortunately, the probate records in England and Wales do not allow us to differentiate with any certainty those estates containing housing from those without. In Scotland, however, the situation is rather different. There, the Sasine Records enable the researcher to identify clearly estates with a housing component. In the final part of this chapter we review the only study to date to look at the bequeathing of estates with a definite housing element, before going on (in Chapter 6) to present some of the findings of a national survey of housing inheritance, revealing the class, tenurial and locational characteristics of households that have inherited housing wealth.

The bequeathing of housing wealth

In the only study of its kind, Munro (1988) was granted access to the commissary records held at the Glasgow Sheriff Court. These record the transfer of any property to heirs or executors from individuals who die in Glasgow or in a number of areas to the north of the city. From a sample of 1,500 records relating to deaths in 1984, Munro found 453 estates (30.2 per cent of the total) to contain housing wealth. To allow comparisons between estates with housing wealth and those without, details were taken for all of the records of the age and sex of the wealth leaver and the total value of the estate. For those estates containing housing wealth some further information was gathered: the relative importance of housing and non-housing wealth within the estate, the value of housing (net of mortgages and debts) and details of who the beneficiaries were.

A number of marked differences were found between estates with housing wealth and those without. First, the presence or absence of housing wealth was found to have a significant bearing on the overall size of estates. Our own study of 1,000 London wills highlighted a major difference between the average size of male and female estates – female estates being only around 70 per cent as valuable as male estates. The gap was closer in Munro's sample, where the average female estate was worth 83 per cent of the average male estate. As Table 5.8 shows, the differential value of the housing wealth owned by each sex played a pivotal role in generating this disparity.

A higher proportion of men than women in the sample left housing wealth (33.5 per cent compared to 27.4 per cent), and the value of men's estates, both those containing housing wealth and those without, exceeded the value of women's estates. It would seem, then, that male wealth leavers not only left housing wealth more often than women, but also that the value of their housing wealth was also greater than women's. Some further insight into these gender differences is

Table 5.8   Value of estate by gender £ and (number)

	Without housing wealth	With housing wealth	Overall average
Male	13,459 (461)	47,201 (232)	24,755 (693)
Female	13,062 (586)	40,555 (221)	20,591 (807)
Overall	13,237 (1,047)	43,959 (453)	22,515 (1,500)

(*Source*: Munro, 1988, Table 4.)

possible by splitting the sub-sample of estates containing housing wealth down by marital status, as well as by gender (Table 5.9).

One explanation (not considered by Munro) for the gulf in values between married men's and married women's estates may have to do with the comparative frequency with which the marital home is held outright by the male spouse and the corresponding rarity for married women to own the home by themselves. As we stated earlier, in 1971 (in England and Wales), just 3 per cent of homes were held in the wife's name, compared to 45 per cent in the husband's name. The married-male estate value may therefore more frequently reflect the entire home than is the case with married female estates, where it may be more usual for the housing-wealth element to represent half of the home.

Table 5.9   Average value of estate (£) by marital status and gender

	Male	Female	Overall
Single, widowed or divorced	52,007	41,992	44,545
Married	45,331	31,742	43,203
Overall	47,201	40,555	43,959

(*Source*: Munro, 1988, Table 5(B).)

The inheritors of estates with housing wealth

We showed in the earlier part of this chapter that the inheritors of estates of all sizes tend to be drawn from a close circle of immediate family members. Munro's analysis of estates containing a housing element took this finding one stage further by demonstrating the volume of wealth in these estates going to different inheritors (Table 5.10).

From this evidence it appears that married 'housing-wealth' leavers leave almost everything to their spouses. This initial transfer between spouses can be viewed as a transitional arrangement, rarely involving, at least to begin with, any housing sale or move. The more significant housing-wealth transfers occur on the death of single, widowed and divorced people, at which stage slightly more than a third of their wealth pass down to a child or children, with a surprisingly high 18 per cent being bequeathed to nieces and nephews. Some 57 per cent of their wealth therefore passed to the following generation but, while we know their family

Table 5.10   The total wealth (%) bequeathed passing to different inheritors

Inheritor	Total estates	Estates left by married	Estates left by single, widowed or divorced
Spouse	43.2	96.0	—
Son/daughter	22.5	3.6	37.9
Brother/sister	8.3	—	15.0
Parent	0.2	—	0.4
Grandchild	1.1	—	1.9
Nephew/niece	10.3	0.2	18.3
Other relative	5.3	0.2	9.3
Non-relative/unknown	6.7	—	12.1
Church/charity	2.7	—	4.9
Total	100.0	100.0	100.0

Note
45% of the wealth was left by the married group and 55% by the single, widowed or divorced.

(*Source*: Munro, 1988, Table 8.)

relationship to the wealth leavers, we know very little else about them. In Chapter 6 we shall examine the characteristics of those individuals and households who have benefited from housing inheritance to date by drawing on the findings of a large specially commissioned survey of housing inheritance in Britain.

6

A NATION OF INHERITORS?

Introduction

We showed in Chapters 3 and 4 that the post-war growth of home ownership is beginning to percolate down into housing inheritance on a large scale and that this is likely to grow significantly by the early decades of the next century, if present trends continue. This has implications for the intergenerational transmission of wealth and its distribution over different social classes, regions and tenures. In the past, when home ownership was far more limited than today, and private housing accounted for a smaller proportion of total wealth, housing inheritance was confined to the children and other relatives of private landlords and a small minority of middle-class home owners. Today, as we showed in Chapters 2 and 3, housing constitutes a larger proportion of both total wealth and the total value of estates passing at death. The growth of home ownership and rising house prices have created a large new group of middle wealth-owners and have widened the distribution of wealth. The key question to be addressed in this chapter is the related one of whether the growing importance of housing inheritance will widen the distribution of inheritance within society. Inheritance has traditionally played a key part in the maintenance of wealth inequalities, as Chapter 5 shows. Will housing inheritance serve to break down these inequalities? Some commentators suggest that it will. Peter Saunders's (1986, p. 158, emphasis added) has argued that:

> with 60% of households in the owner occupied sector in Britain (and an even higher proportion in some other countries such as Australia and the United States of America), not only is a majority of the population now in a position to accumulate such capital gains as may accrue through the housing market, but *for the first time in human history, we are approaching the point where millions of working people stand at some point in their lives to inherit capital sums far in excess of anything which they could hope to save through earnings from employment* . ... Taken together with other potential advantages enjoyed by owner occupiers ... the inheritance factor strongly suggests that consumption location may be every bit as important as class location in determining life chances.

What Saunders is suggesting is that housing inheritance is not only independent of social class but also that housing-related wealth may be as important as class location. This is a radical argument that will be assessed below. The importance of inheritance has also been noted by Conservative politicians. Mrs Thatcher stated in 1979 (15 May) that the Conservative policy of giving council tenants a right to buy their homes

> will be a giant stride towards making a reality of Anthony Eden's dream of a property owning democracy. It will do something else – it will give to more of our people that freedom and mobility and that prospect of handing something on to their children and grand-children which owner-occupation provides

Ten years on, Eden's dream of a property-owning democracy appears to have made the giant stride that Mrs Thatcher envisaged, and in 1987 the Chancellor of the Exchequer, Nigel Lawson, suggested that

> Britain is about to become *a nation of inheritors* (emphasis added). Inheritance, which used to be the preserve of the few, will become a fact of life for the many. People will be inheriting houses, and possibly also stocks and shares. All this is highly desirable for it leads not only to the further diffusion of property in society, but to a more stable and responsible society.

A nation of inheritors is a splendid phrase, and Nigel Lawson was clear that house inheritance will become far more widespread than hitherto. The financial press have also taken up the debate over the possible distributional implications of housing inheritance. In an editorial, 'Growing rich again', *The Economist* (1988a, p. 13) stated in its characteristically forceful fashion that

> The bequest, that staple of Victorian melodrama, is about to make a dramatic comeback. But those who inherit will be no Forsytes or Pallisers. Most bequests will be large relative to the incomes of those who receive them. ... Most of the legatees will be in their 40s or 50s. They will already have bought homes of their own.

It is now quite widely accepted that housing inheritance is an important and widespread phenomenon that will bring benefits to large numbers of people. It has also been argued that it will act to reduce inequalities of personal wealth. Morgan Grenfell (1987, p. 2) argued that it will 'tend to broaden the distribution of wealth in the personal sector'. This is indisputable, but the question is, by how much and who stands to gain? The Morgan Grenfell report suggested that house inheritance will boost personal wealth 'for a majority of the population', and will lead to 'a redistribution of total assets towards second generation owner-occupiers' (*ibid.* p. 11).

Is it true, as both Morgan Grenfell and *The Economist* suggest, that housing inheritance will lead to a redistribution of assets towards second-generation owner-occupiers, and is it correct that housing inheritance will benefit a majority of the population as Morgan Grenfell suggest? This is more questionable, particularly if the beneficiaries are middle-class home owners. As Sarah Hogg (1987) has suggested, the case for a wider distribution of wealth is only true up to a point: 'while more people will receive a substantial inheritance, the gap between second-generation owner-occupiers and council-tenant families will be widened'. Forrest and Murie (1989, p. 37) have also suggested that 'Wealth accumulation and inheritance through housing will be highly differentiated and may ... accelerate rather than smooth out social divisions'. They have also argued that marked regional differences in housing tenure, house prices and rates of house-price inflation will be reflected in an uneven pattern of housing-wealth accumulation, which will tend to concentrate house wealth disproportionately in the more buoyant and affluent parts of Britain and that patterns of housing inheritance may accentuate this geographical variation. If Hogg and Forrest and Murie are right, the argument that housing inheritance will benefit a majority of the population is undermined, along with Saunders's argument, that the rise of widespread housing inheritance will further weaken class divisions and introduce new dimensions of social stratification. It is this question of the incidence of housing inheritance by social class, housing tenure and region, and its implications for the distribution of wealth, that we want to examine in this chapter. Put simply, will housing inheritance serve to break down existing inequalities in wealth ownership or will it reinforce them?

To answer this question we need to know who inherits houses, what the incidence and probability is of housing inheritance for different groups of the population living in different areas, what the socioeconomic characteristics of beneficiaries are and how they differ from non-beneficiaries. It is particularly important to assess the extent to which housing inheritance is class or tenure related, and the extent to which it reflects or cuts across existing class inequalities.

We know from the Inland Revenue figures in Chapter 3 that there are currently about 145,000 estates passing at death each year that include house property. But, as the Mintel (1987) analysis of Inland Revenue data showed, only 70 per cent of estates were those of single individuals. The other 30 per cent were of married people and, in these cases, the family house is very likely to pass to the surviving spouse. If this is correct, there are only about 100,000 'finally dissolving' owner-occupied households each year instead of the 150,000 estimated by Morgan Grenfell (1987). If the average number of principal beneficiaries is 3, as our NOP survey data suggests (see below), then some 300,000 people could inherit a share of house property each year. This is 0.7 per cent of the population aged 18 or over and almost 1.4 per cent of households. Over 10 years some 3 million people could inherit house property. And, as Chapter 4 showed, this figure could double by the year 2030 – other things being equal. These are large figures and appear to support Saunders's view (1986, p. 158) that 'millions of working people stand at some point in their lives to inherit'. Certainly, millions of people will inherit, but the term 'working people' is a very ambiguous one. It implies that house inheritance will be widely distributed over all social classes. To determine who inherits house property, their social class, tenure and geographical distribution we need a survey of beneficiaries as there is no existing published data.

Who inherits: the problem of finding and interviewing beneficiaries

The principal problem with survey research on beneficiaries is that of locating them. Because under 1 per cent of adults inherit per year, beneficiaries are relatively few and far between. There are two ways of locating them. The first involves sampling probated wills held at Somerset House and interviewing the beneficiaries, and the second involves some kind of random national survey to identify beneficiaries. We initially opted for the first course, and drew a sample of 1,000 wills probated in London in 1981, where both the deceased and one or more beneficiaries had a London address with a view to tracing and interviewing the beneficiaries (see Chapter 5). This provided a very valuable source of in-depth interviews with beneficiaries in London, and some of the findings are discussed in Chapter 9. But, as a source of systematic information on the beneficiaries and the incidence of housing inheritance, it was a total failure! First, half the wills sampled left the estate to a spouse. This knocked out half the sample. Second, a large number of wills were written in the 1950s and 1960s and, even where an address was given for the beneficiaries, there was a strong probability that they had since moved or died. As a result, we only contacted a very small number of beneficiaries, and most of them had lived in their current home for many years. The sample was therefore very small and biased towards elderly non-movers.

We therefore had to locate an alternative way of identifying and surveying the beneficiaries, preferably on a national basis. Because the number of beneficiaries is annually relatively small, a national survey has to have a large sample in order to locate reasonable numbers of beneficiaries. Fortunately, NOP (a large survey research firm) conducts regular national, random, omnibus surveys on which they include different sets of questions. They have a team of interviewers permanently in the field and the costs of the surveys are spread across all the users. By using a filter question asking all interviewees if they had ever inherited over £1,000, and following up with detailed questions to those who replied 'yes', a national random-sample survey was affordable. We therefore commissioned NOP to include a number of questions on housing inheritance in two successive, stratified, random-probability omnibus surveys between 22 April and 2 May 1988. The standard NOP sample design was used. A stratified random-cluster sample of electors drawn from the electoral registers in 540 parliamentary constituencies was used in addition to a random sample of non-electors drawn from households of the selected electors. A total of 3,250 adults aged over 18 were contacted by NOP – a success rate of 58 per cent. Of these, some 3,100 answered the inheritance questions – a response rate of 95 per cent of those contacted and an overall response rate of 55 per cent. Because the response rate is higher among women than men, higher in the north than in London, higher among the elderly than the young, the sample of 3,100 was weighted to 3,300 to make it representative of the population by age, sex, social class and region. The random-sample design enables the survey findings to be generalized to the national population with a reasonable degree of confidence. On the assumption that the non-responses were not significantly biased, we estimate that the results of the survey are representative of the total population aged over 18 to within + or − 2 per cent, where major frequency counts are concerned. Respondents appeared to have a high level of knowledge and recall of housing inheritance as there were very few 'don't knows'. If the responses were biased, this may undermine some of our findings about the scale and incidence of inheritance – but this is almost impossible to determine.

For most questions in the survey, respondents were asked whether they or other members of their immediate household had inherited. This was done for two reasons. First, because inheritance is often used to benefit households rather than individual recipients, and the household is often the effective housing decision-making unit. Second, and more importantly, as the number of cases of property inheritance each year are relatively small, we wanted to obtain data on as large a number of cases of inheritance as possible. As a result, the appropriate population for the results to be measured against is the total number of *households* in Great Britain rather than the total population. OPCS estimated that there were 21.260 million households in Great Britain in 1985. This means that the sampling fraction for the survey was 1/6,858 on an unweighted basis and 1/6442 on a weighted basis.

Inheritance and inequality: the results of the NOP survey

Of the weighted total of 3,300 respondents, 506 or 15 per cent lived in households where one or more members had received an inheritance of over £1,000 at some stage of their lives. Of these cases, some 302 (60 per cent) and 9.1 per cent of the total sample included house property or money derived from the sale of house property. Unfortunately, the questionnaire did not clearly distinguish housing transfers between spouses on the death of one partner and other types of inheritance. But, as the family house generally passes to a surviving spouse under the law of succession, it is thought that most of the cases of housing inheritance identified were *not* between spouses. The data show that 22 per cent of beneficiaries lived in the property by the beneficiary following death. On this basis, a maximum of 22 per cent of cases may have involved spouse transfers. But as this figure includes brothers and sisters living with the deceased, children living with a parent and cases where the beneficiary moved into the house after inheritance, as well as resident spouses, it is believed that the number of spouse beneficiaries is unlikely to exceed 10 per cent of cases. Preliminary data from a larger recent survey by the authors suggest that the true figure is near 6 per cent.

On the assumption that the figure of 302 cases of inheritance is a reasonably accurate reflection of the distribution of housing inheritance in British households, multiplying this figure by the sampling fraction of 1/6442 suggests that there are approximately 1.945 million households in Britain currently containing members who have inherited house property at some stage in their lives. Of the 302 cases of household property inheritance, 245 households (81 per cent) had inherited once, 49 (16 per cent) had inherited twice and 8 (3 per cent) had inherited 3 or more times. This suggests a total number of cases of housing inheritance of about 2.4 million.

Of the 302 cases, 188 involved respondents who had inherited themselves. In this case, the relevant population is the number of adults aged over 18 in Britain (41.98 million) and the sampling fraction is 1/12722. Multiplying the number of respondents by the sampling fraction suggests that there are currently 2.392 million persons in Britain who have inherited house property. This is 0.4 million more than the number of households containing members who have inherited. But this seeming discrepancy is explained by the number of multiple inheritances in households, and the estimates of 2.364 and 2.392 million from the two methods are very close.

A check on the accuracy of these estimates is provided by the Inland Revenue figures of the number of estates containing house property inherited each year. They suggest an average of 140,000 a year from 1968–9 to 1984–5. On the basis of the Mintel figures, this suggests 100,000 estates per year left by single individuals. An average of three main beneficiaries per estate would give 300,000 beneficiaries per year or 3 million over a 10-year period. This figure is very close to the survey estimates.

Who inherits house property?

What light does the survey throw on inheritance and inequality? Housing inheritance is not a random event that impinges on all members of the population with equal probability. On the contrary, it is highly unequal in its incidence, and an individual's chance of inheriting is strongly influenced by their age, social class, tenure, region and, not least, by their parental tenure. Because the great majority of beneficiaries are children of the deceased (see Chapter 5), the probability of housing inheritance is greatly influenced by whether one's parents or one's spouse's or partner's parents owned their own homes.

We discuss the social dimensions of inheritance shortly. First, it is necessary to look at the natural inequality of age. Because most inheritances are received from parents or from grandparents, aunts and uncles (Chapter 5), there is an inevitable generational bias to house inheritance. It is widely accepted that the majority of beneficiaries are middle aged when they inherit but, to date, this has been a matter of informed speculation rather than fact. Looking at the age of 188 respondents who inherited themselves, the survey confirmed that most beneficiaries are middle aged when they inherit property. Only 4 per cent of beneficiaries were aged under 20, 15 per cent were in their 20s and 14 per cent were in their 30s, compared to 25 per cent in their 40s, 24 per cent in their 50s and 13 per cent in their 60s. Just 3 per cent were 70. Overall, 67 per cent of beneficiaries were aged 40 or over.

Though very important, the age distribution of beneficiaries is almost entirely a consequence of the structure of family life and reproductive cycles. Given that most housing inheritances are received from parents, age is the principle influence on *when* an inheritance is received. But the probability of *whether* an inheritance is received at all is primarily socially and economically determined, and it is to the social attributes of beneficiaries and the determinants of inheritance that we now turn.

Looking first at the number of beneficiaries by current tenure, of the 302 cases, 266 (88 per cent) of households were owner-occupiers, only 20 (7 per cent) were council tenants and 16 (5 per cent) were rented tenants. It could be argued that this is largely a result of beneficiaries becoming owners after inheritance but, when inheritance was cross-tabulated against tenure at time of inheritance, the overwhelming majority of beneficiaries were found to be owners at inheritance. This is an important finding that confirms that house property is predominantly inherited by existing owners, and the incidence of inheritance between tenures was also very unequal. Table 6.1 shows that 12.7 per cent of owner-occupied households had inherited compared to 2.1 per cent of council households. Owners were therefore six times more likely to inherit than council tenants. The distinctions are even sharper where outright owners (21.7 per cent) are concerned,

Table 6.1 The incidence of property inheritance by tenure

	Mortgaged owners	Outright owners	Council tenants	Private renting	Other	Total
Inheritance	99	167	20	7	8	302
Total sample	1,319	770	940	179	80	3,298
Percent	7.5	21.7	2.1	3.9	10	9.1

but these differences are primarily age related as mortgagees are generally much younger than outright owners. The best comparison is between owners and council tenants as a whole. As we argue shortly, housing tenure is not itself a cause of differences in the incidence of inheritance but a reflection of more fundamental differences in parental tenure and social class.

A similar, if slightly less marked, picture was found regarding social-class differences in the incidence of housing inheritance. Using the occupationally based class categories for household heads defined by NOP and other market-research firms, Table 6.2 shows that 17 per cent of households with class A and B heads (professional and managerial) had inherited compared to 11 per cent of C1s, (junior non-manual), 10 per cent of C2s (skilled manual), 5 per cent of Ds (semi-skilled and unskilled) and 4 per cent of Es (economically inactive). Class A and B households were therefore *four* times as likely to contain a beneficiary as class D and E headed households. The differences were even sharper where cases of multiple inheritances were concerned. Overall, 1.7 per cent of households inherited more than once but, as Table 6.2 shows, the incidence of multiple inheritance varies from 7.5 per cent of class A and 5.1 per cent of class B households to 2.8 per cent of C1s, 0.6 per cent of C2s, 0.5 per cent of D and 0.4 per cent of E households. The incidence of multiple inheritance is some 15 times as great among A households as among Ds and Es. It is clear from these figures that the incidence of housing inheritance is very strongly class specific. The higher a head of household's social class, the greater the probability of a member inheriting house property and the greater the probability of multiple inheritance.

Table 6.2 Social-class differences in property inheritance

	A	B	C1	C2	D	E	Total
Inheritance	11	70	79	91	29	23	302
Total sample	67	415	722	935	600	560	3,298
Percent	16.4	16.9	10.9	9.7	4.8	4.1	9.15
Multiple inheritances	5	21	20	6	3	2	57
Percent	7.5	5.1	2.8	0.6	0.5	0.4	1.7

There were also marked geographical differences in the incidence of housing inheritance. Some 22 per cent of beneficiaries lived in the South East (outside Greater London) compared to 13 per cent of the total sample. Conversely, Scotland had only 5 per cent of beneficiaries compared to 11 per cent of the total sample. As a proportion of the sample living in each region, 16 per cent of households in the South East had inherited compared to 6 per cent in Yorkshire & Humberside and a low of 4 per cent in Scotland. Put differently, people in the South East have four times the chance of inheriting as people living in Scotland, three times of those in Yorkshire & Humberside, double those in London and almost twice the chance of people in some other regions (Table 6.3).

Table 6.3   The regional incidence of housing inheritance

	Number of households	Total in sample	Percentage incidence
South East	67	415	16.1
South West	29	281	10.3
West Midlands	25	243	10.3
East Anglia	12	117	10.3
North	25	247	10.1
North West	43	473	9.1
East Midlands	20	235	8.5
Wales	25	306	8.2
Greater London	25	323	7.7
Yorkshire & Humberside	17	299	5.7
Scotland	15	361	4.1
Great Britain	302	3,298	9.1

This reflects several factors, first being the differences in tenure structure between the regions. The level of home ownership is far higher in the South East (outside Greater London) than in Scotland or some other northern regions. Currently, 75 per cent of households own their own home in the South East compared to under 50 per cent in Scotland. The low figure for London reflects the high levels of private and council renting in inner London and the low level of home ownership, under 30 per cent in 1981. Outer London has been largely owner-occupied since the 1930s but this is offset by the level of renting in inner London. Second, and more importantly, current tenure differences reflect long-term differences. Home ownership levels in the South East have been relatively high from the 1930s onwards when the region experienced rapid growth of home ownership. Between 1919 and 1939, 45 per cent of houses built in England and Wales were built in the South East, and most were built for owner occupation. Conversely, the scale of home ownership has only recently begun to increase in Scotland. These differences play a key role in the incidence of parental home ownership, and thus the likelihood of properties being available for inheritance.

The figures above referred to the geographical distribution of *beneficiaries* by region. They said nothing about the distribution of the inherited property itself or the extent to which the two coincide. This is of considerably interest, however, for, as Forrest and Murie (1989) suggested, there may be a tendency for regional flows of housing inheritance to gravitate towards the South East. The number of housing beneficiaries in our survey is small, so the analysis of inter- and intraregional flows must be treated with caution. Also, the small number of surviving spouses in the survey, most of whom will continue to live in the marital home, will overstate the number of intraregional inheritances. These caveats aside, it is striking that the majority of beneficiaries inherited property located in the region in which they lived. The lowest figure (69 per cent) was for the South East, but in most regions the figure exceeded 80 per cent, and in Scotland all the property inheritances derived from within the region. The figures show a high level of intraregional inheritance flows, but interregional flows into the South East are far larger than those into other regions. This lends some support to the idea that inherited housing wealth is likely to gravitate towards the South East.

We also asked inheriting households about the value of the property or the property share they inherited. There were a total of 340 cases of property inheritances and we obtained values for 234 of these. This information was collected by size band and the values were calculated for the mid-point of the relevant band. Also, the data related to inheritances over a considerable period of time, although half of inheritances were received since 1981. The results must be seen as indicative rather than definitive given the relatively small number of cases within each region and the allocation procedure employed, but they do suggest that there were wide regional variations in the average value of property shares going to inheriting households. Only three regions exceeded the national average of £16,757, and values of inheritances going to households in the East Midlands and East Anglia were only just over £18,000, compared to an average of £26,584 for households in the South East – almost 60 per cent above the national average. In the North and North West, on the other hand, the average value of property shares was £10,970 and £9,390 respectively – 65 and 56 per cent of the national average. Just as households in the South East are more likely to have inherited housing than households in other regions so, too, its value is likely to be much greater than that received by households in other regions (Figures 6.1 and 6.2).

It is clear from these figures that housing inheritance is very unequally distributed and that middle-class home owners and those living in the South East have a much higher chance of inheritance than working-class council tenants or those living in Scotland. This is an important finding that contradicts the views of those such as Saunders who argue that housing inheritance is independent of social class. On the contrary, housing inheritance seems to be strongly class related and we will take this point up again later in the chapter when we look at its probable future distribution. These findings also raise interesting questions about the causes of these differences. In particular, they raise the question of whether the tenure, class and region of beneficiaries are causes or correlates of differences in incidence of housing inheritance.

Little consideration is required to realize that these variations are correlates and not causes of the differences in the incidence of housing inheritance. To put the question rhetorically, would it make any difference to an individual's chance of inheriting for them to become a manager or professional, to become a home owner, or to move from Scotland to the South East? The answer is clearly 'no', and the reason is to do with the nature of the inheritance process, which involves transmission of property from one set of individuals to another. Seen in this light, it is clear that *the key to the differential incidence of housing inheritance lies not with the social and economic characteristics of beneficiaries but with the characteristics of the testators*. The social class or tenure of beneficiaries is a good

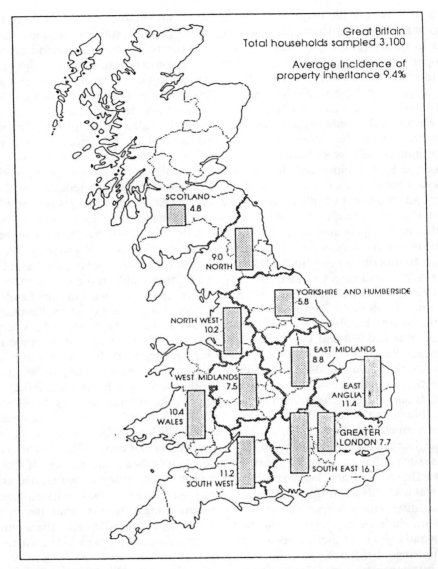

Great Britain
Total households sampled 3,100

Average incidence of
property inheritance 9.4%

SCOTLAND
4.8

9.0
NORTH

YORKSHIRE AND HUMBERSIDE
5.8

NORTH WEST
10.2

EAST MIDLANDS
8.8

WEST MIDLANDS
7.5

EAST
ANGLIA
11.4

10.4
WALES

GREATER
LONDON 7.7

11.2
SOUTH WEST

SOUTH EAST 16.1

*Figure 6.1   The regional incidence of property inheritance 1988; % households inheriting
property or proceeds from the sale of property (Source: Harmer and Hamnett
1990)*

measure of the inequalities of housing inheritance as they affect beneficiaries, but
they are extremely unlikely to play a part in determining the incidence of property
available for inheritance. This is a result of parental tenure, and its class and
regional variations. The generational nature of inheritance demands that we look
backwards for the root causes of contemporary inequalities in incidence of
inheritance.

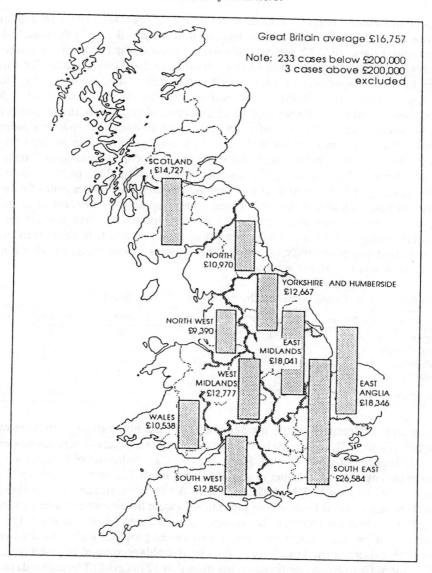

Great Britain average £16,757

Note: 233 cases below £200,000
3 cases above £200,000
excluded

SCOTLAND
£14,727

NORTH
£10,970

YORKSHIRE AND HUMBERSIDE
£12,667

NORTH WEST
£9,390

EAST MIDLANDS
£18,041

WEST MIDLANDS
£12,777

EAST ANGLIA
£18,346

WALES
£10,538

SOUTH WEST
£12,850

SOUTH EAST
£26,584

Figure 6.2   Average value of property shares received by inheriting households in each region, 1988 (Source: Harmer and Hamnett 1990)

Excluding transfers between spouses, Chapter 5 showed that most property passes from parents to the children or grandchildren and from uncles and aunts to the next generation (Royal Commission on the Distribution of Income and Wealth, 1977; Inland Revenue, 1984). It is therefore suggested that it is parental tenure that is the key cause of differences in the incidence of inheritance and that this is related to the characteristics of beneficiaries through the links between parental class and tenure, and the class and tenure of their children. Research shows that parental tenure is related to children's tenure (DoE, 1977; Jenkins and Maynard, 1983; McDowell, 1982). Jenkins and Maynard (1983) showed, using longitudinal data, that 72 per cent of owners' children in 1950 were themselves owners in 1975. They also showed that children of 1950 owners were 2.4 times more likely to be owners in 1975 than the children of non-owners. The NOP findings confirm this. Looking at parental tenure of the sample of 3,300 respondents, Table 6.4 shows that in 25 per cent of cases only the respondents parents owned. In 11 per cent of cases, only their partner's or spouse's parents owned, in 18 per cent of cases both sets of parents owned and in 44 per cent of cases neither set of parents owned. But when owner-occupiers and council tenants are compared, 69 per cent of the parents of owners or their partners owned, compared to just 27 per cent of council-tenant parents. And 24 per cent of owner-occupiers had both sets of parents owning compared to just 4 per cent of council-tenant parents. Conversely, whereas 31 per cent of owners had neither set of parents owning, this rose to 74 per cent of council tenants. It is clear from these findings that the probability of ownership increases according to whether none, one or both sets of parents were owners.

Table 6.4 Parental home-ownership by current tenure of Recipient (%)

Home ownership by	Mortgagor	Outright	All owners	Council	All
Respondent's parents	29	29	30	13	25
Spouse's parents	13	12	13	9	11
Both parents	30	21	26	4	18
Neither parents	28	38	31	74	44
n = 3,298	100	100	100	100	100

The class differences in the incidence of parental home-ownership were even sharper (Table 6.5). Whereas 53 per cent of parents of class-A households both owned, this fell steadily to just 5 per cent of class-E households. Conversely, neither parents owned in 12 per cent of class-A households rising steadily to 70 per cent of those in class E. Respondents in class A were six times as likely as those in class E to have one or both sets of parents who were home owners. The incidence of parental home-ownership is strongly class related. Not surprisingly, the incidence of parental home-ownership also varies geographically. In the South East both parents owned in 23 per cent of households compared to just 9 per cent in Scotland. Conversely, neither parents owned in 32 per cent of households in the South East and 60 per cent of households in Scotland.

Table 6.5 Parental home-ownership by class of head of household (%)

Home ownership by	A	B	C1	C2	D	E	Total
Respondent's parents	24	24	32	28	23	17	25
Spouse's parents	11	14	12	12	11	8	11
Both parents	53	43	22	16	10	5	18
Neither parents	12	19	34	44	56	70	46
n = 3,298	100	100	100	100	100	100	100

The tables show the uneven incidence of parental tenure, but they do not directly link parental tenure to inheritance. The figures in Table 6.6 show that beneficiaries are much more likely to have one or both sets of parents owing their own homes than non-beneficiaries. Of 99 head of household beneficiaries, 50 per cent had one set of parents owing and 33 per cent had both sets of parents owning, while just 17 per cent had no parents owning. The equivalent figures for non-inheriting household heads were 30 per cent, 15 per cent and 55 per cent respectively. In aggregate, 83 per cent of beneficiaries of housing inheritance had one or both sets of parents as owners, compared to 45 per cent of non-inheriting household heads. We can conclude that inheritance is strongly related to parental tenure.

Table 6.6   The incidence of inheritance by parental home-ownership

Parental ownership	Beneficiaries		Non-beneficiaries	
	(Heads of household only)			
Respondent's parents	41	(41%)	260	(20%)
Spouse's parents	9	(9%)	128	(10%)
Both sets of parents	32	(33%)	200	(15%)
Neither parents	17	(17%)	708	(55%)
Totals	99	(100%)	1,296	(100%)

The future of housing inheritance and wealth inequality

Taken collectively, these figures indicate that the incidence of housing inheritance is extremely unequal among different social classes, tenures and regions. It is also very strongly related to parental tenure. Put crudely, households stand a far higher chance of inheriting house property if they are middle-class home owners living in the South East and whose parents also owned than they do if they are working-class council tenants living in the north whose parents did not own. While the spread of home ownership has greatly widened wealth ownership in Britain, housing inheritance has not weakened the existing inequalities of class and tenure. Rather, it appears to reflect them closely. The biblical comment that 'unto those who have shall be given' can be modified to read 'unto those whose parents are home owners shall be given'. Far from constituting a new dimension of inequality as Saunders has suggested, housing inheritance currently seems to reflect existing patterns of inequality.

But is the current structure of inheritance inequality likely to be maintained in the future? The answer to this would seem to be no, for the simple reason that the existing pattern of housing inheritance reflects the social differentials in home ownership of a generation ago. At that time, home owning was still largely confined to the middle classes, and the inheritances of today are a product of the pattern of home ownership thirty or more years ago. Not only was the incidence of home ownership much less than it is today but it was also still predominantly middle class. Today, however, home ownership is far more extensive and, despite the marked class differences in its incidence, it has slowly percolated down into the skilled working class and below. In 1961, 67 per cent of managers and professional-headed households owned their own home, against 53 per cent of junior non-manual workers, 40 per cent of skilled manual, 29 per cent of semi-skilled and 22 per cent of the unskilled. By 1981, 83 per cent of managers and professionals owned compared to 70 per cent of junior non-manual, 58 per cent of skilled, 42 per cent of semi-skilled workers and 31 per cent of unskilled workers (Hamnett, 1984). This widening of ownership will have an effect on the distribution of housing inheritance in the future. As Rubinstein (1986) has noted,

> the growth of property ownership will have its effects on future generations, as more and more people inherit substantial amounts of money. Even now, only half of the deceased population leaves any property counted for probate purposes, but this proportion is bound to rise continuously as the newly propertied age and die off.

A simple model of the future distribution of housing inheritances

This more extensive and more widely based structure of ownership has considerable implications for housing inheritance in the future, for it is the contemporary structure of home ownership that will largely determine the structure of housing inheritance in the future. This can be demonstrated using a simple model of changing tenure structure over time. If we assume that

1. there are two tenures – owner-occupation and renting;
2. house inheritance occurs via owner-occupation alone;
3. the probability of house inheritance by any individual reflects prevailing parental tenure structures;
4. the probability of house inheritance by couples is a product of the incidence of parental home-ownership;
5. that the pairing of couples is random rather than class (and tenure) selective;
6. that all parental homes are available for inheritance by their children; and
7. all children can expect a share of the parental home,

we can deduce a simple probability model of the likelihood of housing inheritance amongst couples. The pairing of couples, of course, is assortive rather than random, but we will discuss the implications of this when we have outlined our simple model.

In the situation that prevailed up to about 1919, some 90 per cent of households rented and only 10 per cent owned their homes. In these circumstances, the probability of a couple inheriting a parental home is very slim. The probability of neither parent owning their homes is $90\% \times 90\% = 81\%$. The probability of both parents owning is $10\% \times 10\% = 1\%$, and the probability of one set of parents owning is $10\% \times 90\% \times 2 = 18\%$ (9-per-cent probability for husband's parents and 9 per cent for the wife's). It is readily apparent that with this tenure structure, 4 out of 5 couples stand no chance of property inheritance from parents as neither parents will own their homes. Other sets of probabilities can be produced for different tenure structures and this is done in Table 6.7.

It is apparent from Table 6.7 that, given the very restrictive assumptions outlined about, there is a regular relationship between the structure of tenure at

Table 6.7   Probabilities of owner-occupied housing inheritance from neither, one or both sets of parents in specific tenure structures

% of households		Neither set of parents owning	One set of parents owning	Both sets of parents owning
Owning	Renting			
10	90	81	18	1
20	80	64	32	4
30	70	49	42	9
40	60	36	48	16
50	50	25	50	25
60	40	16	48	36
70	30	9	42	49
80	20	4	32	64

any given time and the probabilities of couples having neither, one or both parents owning and, hence, of inheriting parental property. The situation prevailing in 1919 was extreme and it is apparent that very few couples had a chance of inheriting owner-occupied property. However, by 1945 the structure of tenure was close to the 30/70 split. Under these circumstances just over half of all couples have a chance of inheriting a house – broadly the situation prevailing today, given the generational lag. It is also apparent from Table 6.7 that the probability of housing inheritance in the future will be much greater than it is today. The home-ownership rate is currently about 66 per cent, and it is likely to approach 70 per cent by the early 1990s. Under this tenure structure, 90 per cent of couples can expect, other things being equal, to inherit a share of the parental home(s) in thirty to forty years' time. But, of course, things are not equal. Pairing is class- and tenure-selective rather than random and we can therefore expect that the children of home owners are more likely to be partners of children of other owners rather than partners of council tenants. In the extreme situation where children of council tenants only partner one another, and children of owners only partner one another, the structure of housing inheritance in future would reflect precisely present tenure structures. In this situation, the 70 per cent of owners' children could expect to inherit a share in two homes, while the 30 per cent of tenants' children would get nothing.

The reality will be somewhere between the two extremes of totally selective class and tenure pairing and random pairing, whereby only 10 per cent of couples would get nothing. We can safely predict (other things being equal) that over the next thirty years between 10 per cent and 30 per cent of couples will not inherit any house property from their parents. The growth of home ownership will open up the possibility of house inheritance to a far larger proportion of the population than at present and will serve to reduce the inequalities of wealth inheritance. But, at the same time, the division between those who inherit and those who do not will become much sharper. In the past, only a minority of the population inherited owner-occupied houses. In the future, if current trends continue, only a small minority will not inherit. Instead of having a privileged minority we will have a privileged majority. The minority may be a permanent under-class of rent payers living in run-down council estates with no capital assets of their own and little hope of inheriting any. The future for them is bleak. The current housing-tenure division is likely to remain a division in terms of intergenerational wealth transfers.

The above discussion is concerned solely with the incidence of housing inheritance. It has said nothing about differential values of housing inheritances. These are very substantial and reflect differences in house types, regional differences in house prices and differences in family size. Taken in combination, the effects are considerable. Whereas the only child of middle-class parents in a prosperous London suburb may inherit a house worth £200,000, the children of working-class parents living in a terraced house in the north of England may only inherit £30,000 between them. If the inheritance is shared between five children they would only get £6,000 each. At the outside, there are some children who will inherit houses in central London worth over £1 million. For them, housing inheritance will have a very different meaning. These are stereotypes, of course, and the permutations are virtually endless, but they rest on a very strong factual basis. Single beneficiaries of high-priced housing will do far better from housing inheritance than multiple beneficiaries of cheap housing. So the incidence of housing inheritance only accounts for part of the inequality – the rest results from what is inherited, how much is it worth and how many people share it.

Conclusions

Anthony Eden's dream of a property-owning democracy has become a reality for two thirds of the population and, as home ownership percolates down into housing inheritance, Nigel Lawson's idea of a nation of inheritors will also become a reality for a growing number of people. But, just as the property-owning democracy is unlikely to exceed much over three quarters of the population, so the nation of inheritors will also be limited to a similar-sized group, probably consisting of the same people. As the benefits of owner-occupation spread to a larger proportion of the population, so the divisions between the haves and have-nots of housing and wealth ownership are likely to become steadily sharper. Saunders (1986) is correct in that, for the first time in human history, millions of working people stand (within the next thirty years) to inherit house property, but millions will also be excluded. And those who are excluded are likely to be less-skilled individuals whose parents do not own. Although the class divisions of housing wealth are changing, they have by no means disappeared, and class position will continue to influence inheritance for many decades to come.

This analysis assumes that house property will continue to be available for housing inheritance in the future. But, as we argue in the final chapter, this may not prove to be the case. Until relatively recently, housing options for the elderly were very limited and most old people had little choice but to leave their house to their children or other relatives. However, with the growth of retirement homes, sheltered housing for the elderly and the variety of equity-release schemes for elderly home-owners now on offer, it looks likely that a steadily larger proportion of home owners' equity will be released prior to death to help finance old age. In many ways this is a desirable development if it helps the capital-rich, income-poor elderly to improve their quality of life in old age. But equally, the financial institutions have come to see the locked-up housing capital as a market to be developed and they could attempt to extract as much housing capital as possible prior to death. Government health-and-welfare policy may also go in this direction in an attempt to relieve government of the burden of care for a growing elderly population. This argument is taken up again in the final chapter.

7

HOUSING INHERITANCE: USES AND IMPACTS

Introduction

In the previous Chapter we discussed some of the findings from our national survey of inheritance. Approximately 9 per cent of households had inherited house property suggesting that, if applied to the population as a whole, around two million existing households will have inherited in this way. As we indicated, the distribution of property-inheriting households was not evenly spread across social classes, age-groups, regions or housing tenures. We concluded that there was strong evidence to suggest that property inheritance is currently reinforcing to patterns of equality.

In this chapter our purpose is to look in detail at how individuals and households have used their property inheritance. Having considered the use to which households put their inherited property, the analysis then focuses upon the impacts these decisions have on the housing and finance markets and it is here that we are able to place the inheritance process in context. In many respects it is these 'macro' effects that have been the centre of attention, and this chapter examines them in some detail.

Property inheritance: uses and implications

The popular image of inheritance is that it is simply a case of receiving an unearned increment that can be disposed of at whim. At the level of an individual this is correct, and as our case studies in Chapter 9 show, households do make a wide range of choices. For example, if most beneficiaries use their inheritance to trade up and buy bigger houses, then a significant proportion of the upward filtering within the housing market could be 'driven' by the inheritance process. Clearly it is important to establish the facts. However, depending upon the relative incidence of those choices, the aggregate impact upon specific markets can be considerable.

There are a number of competing and contrasting views as to how households are likely to make use of inherited property or property wealth (i.e. shares in the proceeds of sale) and what impacts these have upon the British economy and British society. Within the serious press there have been a number of analytic commentaries on housing inheritance. As noted earlier, *The Economist*, in an editorial of 9 April 1988, entitled 'Growing rich again', commented (p. 13).

> So the bequest, that staple of Victorian melodrama is about to make a dramatic comeback. ... Most of the lucky legatees will be in their 40s and 50s. They will already have bought homes of their own so they will sell their parents' homes to a new generation of young housebuyers. Most of those who inherit their parents' homes will have begun to plan their own retirement. They may spend a little more than they would otherwise have done in the final decades of their working lives, but they will regard the proceeds of their parents' thrift mainly as an insurance against poverty in their own old age. So for the time being, they will save, converting their parents' physical assets into financial assets of their own. Many will have quite as much money in occupational pensions as they are prepared to save in this illiquid form. They will choose instead the greater flexibility of stock exchange securities or various sorts of bank deposits.

The editorial goes on to talk about the 'wealthfare state', where the new rich can buy better services at a price. *The Economist* acknowledges it will be a less egalitarian country as a consequence. In putting forward these arguments about the growing importance of property inheritance, *The Economist* drew upon the 1987 Morgan Grenfell report entitled 'Housing inheritance and wealth'. In a useful but largely speculative analysis, the bank asserts that the lump sums derived from property inheritance will not be reinvested in the property market but will find their way into a range of financial assets, such as unit trusts and building-society accounts that are easily traded and, to a lesser extent, into consumer demand for luxury goods. This redeployment of funds out of physical housing assets and into financial assets would, the bank claims, lead to a fall in net equity in housing and a rise in personal-sector assets. The report assumes that housing consumption will not rise with the 'new rich' buying bigger or more houses.

In addition to the Morgan Grenfell report and a number of other commentaries (such as that by Mintel, 1987) there is an emergent academic literature in the issue of inheritance, its use and implications. Munro (1988), like Morgan Grenfell, suggests that there could be negative price effects from mass inheritance, i.e. the release of property by beneficiaries will add to existing supply to create market gluts and thus prices will fall. She re-emphasizes the point that inheritance will occur when beneficiaries are in their middle- to-old age. This implies their housing career is unlikely to take them to a larger property – indeed, her prognosis on price suggests that she sees beneficiaries continuing to trade down despite the inheritance.

In contrast to the arguments in this literature, Lowe (1987) suggests that a considerable portion of the money released from property inheritance will find its way back into housing to sponsor up-market moves (thus implying a considerable elasticity of demand for housing). He also suggests there will be a tendency to increase the investment in and use of private health care, private education and other important services that can be bought outside of the Welfare State or State provision in general. Such an argument meshes with thinking within government about how to reduce the cost of State provision and to enhance choice (the former Junior Health Minister, Edwina Currie, has herself suggested that home equity be used to purchase health care). Equally, Lowe is joining a developing debate on consumption cleavages and the ways in which home ownership and, by extension, the inheritance of house property, is contributing to a divide in British society between the haves and the have-nots (see, for example, Lowe, 1988; Forrest and Murie, 1989; Saunders, 1988; Saunders and Harris, 1987, 1988).

Perhaps the earliest and most sustained commentary on housing wealth and inheritance has come from Murie and Forrest. In 1980 they outlined five possible effects of property inheritance: trading up, presumption of parental assistance, multiple ownership and a growing rented sector, investment in building societies and increased consumption. They subsequently developed their earlier position on wealth and inheritance (Forrest and Murie, 1989) by looking more closely at the sociology and social geography of housing in an examination of the way people move through the housing market over their life time (i.e. housing careers). They point to a number of factors that might affect the distribution of housing inheritance and limit its impact within individual families. Thus the size of the family (i.e. the total number of beneficiaries to any will) and the family's attitudes to wealth and inheritance will have an important effect, and both of these factors, will vary by class and ethnic background. For example, a working-class family may be larger and have a stronger propensity to spend on consumption than a typical middle-class family. The geography of home ownership is sufficiently varied that, in different regions, the propensity of social groups to inherit property will vary markedly (as we ourselves show in Chapter 6) and, for the reasons advanced by the authors, its subsequent impact will also vary.

Forrest and Murie also raise the question of home-equity plans that certainly have the potential to reduce significantly housing wealth during the lifetime of the benefactor and, thus, reduce the significance of housing inheritance. The current evidence suggests that for some elderly persons the conversion of the value of their property into an equity plan that ensures they retain ownership of the dwelling and receive a cash sum and an income, is attractive (*ibid*, 1989). On their death the proceeds of the sale of the property are divided between the company that provides the equity plan and the beneficiaries. So far, use of the schemes has been limited but the research shows that most of those participating have used the cash for consumption generally rather than for maintenance and repair. Thus not only is value of the property inherited divided up but the property itself may also end up in a substantially deteriorated condition. This is clearly a point of great importance when we think about the future.

It is apparent from this brief review of the relatively limited literature in the area that there are a number of competing and contrasting views as to how households are likely to make use of inherited property and the impacts that flow from these decisions. In summary these are a follows:

Uses
1. Beneficiaries will keep the inherited property to live in themselves.
2. Property will be retained by beneficiaries to create a growing rental sector. Alternatively if sold, the property might become part of the rental sector.
3. Property inheritance will lead to trading up as beneficiaries increase their housing consumption.
4. Property inheritance will lead to enhanced consumption by beneficiaries.

5. Property inheritance will result in parents giving increased aid to children to establish themselves in the housing market.
6. As property rises in value, so there will be a growing tendency for the existing owners to extract some of the equity value.

Impacts
7. Inherited property will be sold and the cash raised will be put into a range of financial assets. This could lead to a fall in net equity in housing and a rise in personal-sector assets.
8. The incidence and impact of property inheritance will have marked class and race dimensions with a range of implications for British society.
9. The release of property could trigger price falls as supply begins to exceed demand.

In part these views derive from the differing stand-points that underpin each analysis. The Morgan Grenfell report (1987), for example, reflects the concerns of a major bank, while the work of Lowe (1987, 1988 and 1989) links to his role as a social-policy analyst. Most of these studies rely exclusively on published aggregate data, which can only allow a limited analysis of the issue. In essence, beyond some basic comments on the total volume of property inheritance, analysts have been forced to speculate on the range of outcomes we have discussed here. In our study we are able to go an important stage further, i.e. to look at the ways households have *actually* made use of the properties they have inherited. From this evidence we are then able to discuss with some certainty the implications their actions have for the housing and finance markets and, more generally, for British society (assuming, of course, that patterns of behaviour do not change radically in the future).

The use of inherited property

What did beneficiaries do with their inherited property? Of the 302 households inheriting at least one dwelling, 198 or two thirds sold the property (or properties) more or less immediately. However, 67 of the beneficiaries decided to live in the house or flat inherited. If the 8 cases where the property was lived in by someone else is added to this, it gives a total of 75 cases or *nearly one quarter* where the dwelling was retained for living in. (As discussed in Chapter 6, a large number of these are likely to be spouses of the deceased.) Perhaps surprisingly, given this figure, only 11 of the beneficiary households took the alternative choice of renting the property out, and only 5 did this long term.

Table 7.1 summarizes what happened to the property inherited. It should be noted that our data do not allow us to determine whether the current occupiers of the properties that were retained had previously been resident in that property. As can be seen, the proportions discussed above vary sharply when broken down by sole or joint beneficiary. Sole beneficiaries were more likely to retain the property for living in, while joint beneficiaries normally sold the property immediately – no doubt as a way of arriving at a more easily divisible inheritance. What is evident from this is that the number of beneficiaries has a significant effect on the way in

Table 7.1   What happened to the property on inheritance

Action by beneficiary	All (no.)	All (%)	Sole Beneficiary (no.)	Sole Beneficiary (%)	Joint (no.)	Joint (%)
Sold more or less immediately	198	66	40	44	153	79
Lived in by beneficiary	67	22	36	40	27	13
Lived in by other	8	3	3	4	4	2
Rented then sold	6	2	4	5	2	1
Rented	5	2	4	5	—	—
Other	11	4	2	2	7	5
Total	295	99	89	100	193	100

Note
Excludes don't-knows.

(*Source*: NOP survey (Q5), weighted.)

which the property is used (44 per cent of sole beneficiaries sold more or less immediately compared to 79 per cent of joint beneficiaries). Moreover, as can be seen from Table 7.1, the volume of inherited property rented out is very small in comparison to other uses. Indeed, inspection of the detailed tabulations shows that of the 12 properties that were being rented at the time of death, 8 were sold; beneficiaries moved into 2; and only 2 remained as rented units. Only 3 properties owned and lived in by the benefactors became rental units, making the total of 5 rented out. Joint beneficiaries, in particular, appear to prefer to sell and to divide the cash rather than rent the property out and share the income.

Table 7.2 contrasts the previous tenure of beneficiaries with their current tenure. Whereas 163 recipients lived in dwellings that were owned outright at the time of inheritance, only 115 of them are currently outright owners, while 38 are current mortgaged owners. It can be suggested that most of the 38 were living in a parental home owned outright at the time of inheritance and have now bought. Ten, however, have moved into council renting and other tenancies. But, of the 84 recipients who were living in mortgaged households at the time of inheritance, 36 are now in mortgaged households and 46 in outright owned households. This suggests that many of this group have subsequently managed to buy after they had inherited. Similarly, of the 17 living in council tenancies at the time of inheritance, 10 are now living in owner-occupation. They may also have managed to buy after inheriting but the data do not permit a firm conclusion. What is clear is that some 247 recipients lived in owner-occupied households at the time of inheritance and now 266 are owners. There has clearly been a shift into ownership though whether this has come about as a result of inheritance is impossible to say with certainty.

The evidence suggests that most beneficiaries sell their inherited property. The question then is, how is the money released by the sale of inherited property used by the beneficiaries? Table 7.3 indicates how the households surveyed deployed the cash. It distinguishes between how *most* of the money was used and how any of the money was used. The uses have been grouped into 'property-related purchases and home improvement', 'financial investments' and 'consumption-related expenditure' as a means of summarizing the responses. Considering how *most*

Table 7.2 Beneficiaries of property inheritance: previous tenure by current tenure

Previous tenure	(No.)	(%)	Current Tenure											
			Outright owner		Mortgagor		LA/HA*		Private rented		Other		Total	
			(No.)	(%)	(No.)	(%)	(No.)	(%)	(No.)	(%)	(No.)	(%)	(No.)	(%)
Outright owner	163	54	115	70	38	23	8	5	1	1	1	1	163	100
Mortgagor	84	28	36	43	46	55	1	1	1	1	—	—	84	100
LA/HA*	17	6	3	18	3	18	10	58	1	6	—	—	17	100
Private rented	13	4	5	38	—	—	1	8	5	38	2	15	13	100
Other	17	6	6	33	7	38	—	—	—	—	4	22	17	100
Don't know	8	3	3	37	4	50	1	12	—	—	—	—	8	100
Total	302	100	168	56	98	32	21	7	8	3	7	2	302	100

Note
LA = local authority; HA = housing association.

(Source: NOP survey (Q7).)

Table 7.3　Use of money released from property inheritance

	Any money used (No.)	(%)	Most money used (No.)	(%)
Buying first home	24	9.0	21	12
Moving up market	8	3.0	8	4
Buying second home	4	1.5	4	2
Assist children/grandchildren to buy	4	1.5	4	2
All property purchase	40	15.0	37	21
Home improvement	30	11.0	11	6
All property (purchase and improvement)	70	26.0	48	27
Investing in building society	60	22.0	49	27
Bank	23	9.0	15	8
Shares/unit trust	10	4.0	8	4
Other investments	19	7.0	15	8
All finance	112	42.0	87	49
Holidays	17	6.0	8	4
Buying car	19	7.0	7	4
Education children/grandchildren	6	2.0	2	1
General assumption	42	16.0	27	15
All consumption	84	31.0	44	24
Total	266	100.0	179	100

Note
Excludes don't-knows and refusals. Note that clm 1 will include multiple responses.

(*Source*: NOP survey (Q11a and 11b), weighted.)

money was used, it is evident that property-related expenditure was *not* the major category. Only 21 per cent of households spent *most* money on property purchase and a further 6 per cent spent most of it on home improvements giving a total of 27 per cent for this category. Relatively few beneficiaries spent most of the money on up-market moves, second homes or assisting children/grandchildren to buy, and most of this group spent it on first-home purchase. Most beneficiaries directed the majority of their spending into financial investment with building-society investments leading the way. Of households, 27 per cent put most of the cash released into building societies, 15 per cent into banks and 8 per cent into shares and unit trusts. In total, 49 per cent of households put most of the cash released into financial assets.

Consumption-related expenditure was preferred in roughly the same proportion as housing, with 26 per cent of households putting most money into general consumption, holidays, cars and education. Education attracted very little interest – only 1 per cent of households spent most of their inherited money in this area and only 2 per cent had spent any money on it.

The overall balance of expenditure changes across a number of categories when we look at whether households used *any* money on specific items. In terms of the total proportion of spending decisions, consumption played a slightly larger role while both property and financial investment were slightly lower. This shift is understandable since many households, even though reserving the major expenditure for investments, would still choose to spend a certain amount of money on consumption.

The deployment of the money released from inherited property reveals a strong preference for financial assets at least in the short term. This finding is at odds with a number of the suggested uses referred to earlier but closely in line with the speculative suggestions put forward by Morgan Grenfell (1987). What we cannot predict from these results is how individuals will use these financial assets in the long term. The possibility remains that beneficiaries will move from financial assets back into property, though the probability is low, as we discuss later. In the next section we consider the implications of these patterns of use for the housing and finance markets.

As we suggested earlier, patterns of use are likely to be influenced by the background of the beneficiary, i.e. class, tenure and region. In Table 7.4 a summary cross-tabulation shows the relationship between these factors and the broad categories of expenditure. The small numbers prevent further disaggregation and even this table must be treated with caution. With regard to social class, it can be seen that households in the higher social-class categories used slightly more of their inheritance on financial investment and less on consumption.

A slightly higher proportion of households in the C1 and C2 category used inheritance to enhance their property position and for consumption, although financial investment still dominates. Renters spent nothing on property (including improvement and assistance to relatives), although the numbers are very small. Their spending was highest on financial assets as was that of the owners. Finally, by region, there is considerable variation with property expenditure being slightly more significant in London and the South East (ignoring Wales and Scotland where numbers are very small), while financial investment is a particular feature of the Northern region. In the Midlands and East Anglia consumption concerns dominate.

In Chapter 6 we discussed the background of beneficiaries and the relationships between property inheritance, social class and parental tenure. The dominance of home ownership among beneficiaries is readily apparent from Table 7.4. This high level of home ownership probably acts to encourage a focus on financial investment at least in the short term. But we cannot tell whether the households will utilize the inheritance in the property market at a later stage. However, given that our beneficiaries cover the age spectrum and presumably the housing-career cycle, we might have expected to see evidence of property-market moves within the sample. Buying a house for the first time was the major property-related expenditure (setting aside home improvement) and this was most commonly associated with social classes C1, C2 and D, where ownership rates have lagged behind social classes A and B.

Property inheritance can have a very wide range of effects and consequences. For example, at the level of an individual, the financial security it offer may bring greater stability to a household by allowing changes of job, the purchase of an essential good or service or simply peace of mind. This may be particularly true for

Table 7.4 Use of most money by background of beneficiary

	Property (No.)	(%)	Finance (No.)	(%)	Consumption (No.)	(%)	Total (No.)	(%)
Social class								
A + B	12	23	30	58	9	18	51	100
C1 + C2	29	29	44	44	28	28	107	100
D + E	7	24	15	52	7	24	29	100
Tenure								
Owners	47	30	72	46	36	23	155	100
Renters	—	—	11	58	8	42	19	100
Region of residence								
Northern (North, North West, Yorks. & Humber.)	8	19	24	56	11	26	43	100
Midlands and East Anglia	12	26	16	35	18	29	46	100
London and South East	20	33	30	49	11	18	61	100
South West	3	25	6	50	3	25	12	100
Wales	4	40	5	50	1	10	10	100
Scotland	3	38	5	62	—	—	8	100

Note
Excludes don't-knows.

(*Source*: NOP survey (Q11b), weighted.)

people who have retired or are about to retire and, as our data show, a great many beneficiaries are elderly. However, while effects at the level of an individual household are important, it is the aggregate impact of these upon British society in general, and the housing and finance markets in particular, that are of most importance and it is to these issues we now return.

Housing-market impacts

At the beginning of this chapter we discussed a number of views of the likely impacts of property inheritance upon the housing market. Briefly these were as follows:

1. It may give assistance to those seeking to enter the housing market either directly through the inheritance or through assistance from parents or relatives who have inherited.
2. It might allow existing owners to increase their consumption of housing by trading up, improving or extending their existing property or by buying a second home.
3. Through retention of the properties inherited, it might contribute to an expansion of the rental sector.
4. It could affect house prices either positively or negatively. Enhanced consumption power via inheritance could stimulate the demand for particular types of property and/or locations. Alternatively, the release of inherited property could exceed the demand for property and thus prices might stabilize or even fall.

To this list we would add further factors for consideration. Inheritance may result in *cross-regional flows* of funds with property being inherited in one area, its cash value realized and transferred and applied in another area, although, as we show in Chapter 6, most beneficiaries live in the region in which the benefactor resides. Second, by enhancing the housing-market position of beneficiaries it will further contribute to the housing market's role in the creation of social cleavages. Third, it will contribute potentially to a re-orientation in the housing finance market with, for example, the emergence of more stringent mortgage-allocation policies, on the assumption that households will have access to inherited wealth and the growth of home-equity plans. Beyond these relatively specific sets of issues there is a general question about the magnitude of property inheritance and its place within the housing market and this provides an appropriate starting-point for our discussion.

Inheritance and the housing market

In earlier Chapters we pointed to the growing numbers of estates containing residential property and to the increasing numbers of elderly people who are home owners. Assuming our survey figures accurately represent the population, it is possible to estimate the number of current households in Great Britain that contain members who have inherited house property during their lives. These are discussed in the previous chapter but bear repeating here.

OPCS (1987) estimated that there were 21,260,000 households in Great Britain in 1985. Our weighted sample of 3,298 represents a sampling fraction of 1 in 6,442 households. Applied to the data on house-property inheritance, we estimate that there are 1,945,000 or 9 per cent of households where members have inherited house property (there is a sampling error of + or − 1.8 per cent on this estimate). Of these, 1.58 million or 7 per cent of households had inherited once, 316,000 (1.5 per cent) had inherited twice and 50,000 or 0.2 per cent had inherited 3 or more times. Applying the sampling fraction to the data on the use of property would suggest that, of the 1.94 million households, some 1.275 million would have sold the property (or received part or all of the proceeds of sale), 483,000 would have retained it for living in (primarily the sole beneficiaries) and 71,000 would have rented the property out. This is over a considerable period of time (pre-1950–88). Averaging these figures across a 15-year period (the distribution of inheritances shows that nearly 80 per cent fall into this period), this suggests that on an annual basis at least 85,000 properties that had been inherited would be sold, 32,000 would be lived in by the beneficiaries and 5,000 rented out.

Holmans (1986a) estimated that, in 1984, there were some 1,324,000 property sales (excluding sales by local authorities and housing associations), of which 1,148,000 were second-hand sales (including sales by private landlords to sitting tenants[1]). The sales by beneficiaries would represent some 7.4 per cent of this market and would therefore probably be insufficient to have a significant impact upon prevailing prices. However, our data do show that the geography of household dissolution and inheritance is skewed towards specific regions and, therefore, it is possible but probably unlikely that it could have a local price effect. This obviously requires further exploration. The release of property into the private-rental sector is also quite small (5,000 per annum) and dwarfed by the flows of property out of that sector – Holmans (*ibid.*) estimated sales to sitting tenants and with vacant possession at 86,000 in 1984 – so again there is little evidence to suggest that property inheritance would make a significant contribution to the growth of the rental sector. Indeed, as we pointed out earlier in this chapter, most of the rental property inherited was sold into owner-occupation so, in effect, inheritance is acting to erode the sector not enhance it.

While it is apparent that property inheritance has assisted the growth of home ownership through the sales of rented property into individual ownership and by providing some people with the means to buy their own dwelling, the evidence is that its impact on the home-ownership market is not great. Some 14 per cent of households used most of the cash proceeds to buy a house for themselves or to assist their children or grandchildren to buy. Applying this percentage to the number of households inheriting property and then grossing it up in terms of current households suggests that over 270,000 have been assisted by these means into home ownership – around 18,000 households per annum. Over 536,000 property purchases were made by first-time buyers in 1984, suggesting that inheritance would make only a small annual contribution (around 3.4 per cent) to that process though, if the number of first-time buyers diminishes, reflecting demographic changes, then its significance may grow slightly.

Trading up represented 1 in 5 of every property-related purchase and the purchase of a second home, 1 in 10. With regard to current households this would indicate that some 77,000 have traded up consequent upon inheritance and over 38,000 may have bought a second home. In annual terms this would suggest that about 5,000 households traded up and 2,500 bought a second home. In the housing-policy review undertaken in 1977 (DoE, 1977), it was estimated roughly two fifths of present owner-occupier moves were for trading up. Applying this proportion to the 794,000 moving-owners transactions in 1984 (as given in Holmans, 1986a), we can estimate that at least 320,000 transactions would have involved trading up.

Inheritance-assisted trading up would represent approximately 1.5 per cent of that total annually. Assuming the proportions have not changed significantly, this would suggest that the cash derived from property inheritance and used in trading up does not contribute to a significant proportion of total up-market moves in any year. With respect to second homes, the housing-policy review indicated that 5,000 were purchased in 1971. This would suggest that in this sector inheritance could be more significant, although the number of purchases has probably risen considerably since that time. Finally, improvement expenditure was the major expenditure for 6 per cent of households that inherited, i.e. around 116,000 of all current households and, on an annual basis, around 8,000 households – a tiny proportion of owners engaging in improvement work (Building Societies Association, 1986). Again, it is possible that inheritance funded some very major improvements and has a large share of that sector of the improvement market.

Our survey results therefore allow us to refute a number of claims made for the impact of housing inheritance. There is no evidence that it has induced price falls in the housing market or that it is a major contributor to the private-rented sector.

Indeed, inheritance has contributed significantly to the erosion of this sector through sales on inheritance. Assistance to first-time buyers, trading up, second homes and home improvement, while all individually significant, are not substantial within each market as a whole. So far, therefore, we must conclude that the impact of property inheritance upon the housing market is not as great as has been suggested. Obviously this might change over time as the forecast growth in dissolving owner-occupier households becomes a reality, but this is in the future and its impact could be neutralized by other factors, such as home-equity plans, which could 'soak up' much of the inheritance potential now present. We will return to these issues in the conclusion.

The financial market

It is apparent from the national survey that investment in financial assets is the most common outcome from property inheritance. It is to the form of those investments and the implications they may have for both finance and property markets that we now turn. Within the small literature on inheritance there have been a number of speculative suggestions as to the likely use of property-inheritance derived cash in the financial sector and the implications that may arise:

1. Beneficiaries may place the lump sums derived into secure interest-bearing assets that will produce an income stream. This suggests building societies may be a prime destination for the money.
2. The windfall gain may encourage speculative investment in stocks and shares.
3. The financial sector itself may devise products designed to extract property wealth during the *benefactor's* lifetime, thus reducing the ultimate value of inheritance. Alternatively, the sector may devise products aimed at those with an inheritance, i.e. they will focus upon attracting the large lump sums that will flow from cashing in the inherited property.
4. The expansion of property inheritance may diminish the need for additional pension-plan arrangements.
5. Mortgage demand may be enhanced to buy the properties released via inheritance. Thus in the long term, much of the cash deposited into financial assets will be fed back into the property market.

The evidence from the survey certainly shows that investment played an important role in the strategies of most individual beneficiaries (see Table 7.3). Some 42 per cent of the choices made by property inheritors involved investment in financial assets and, in 49 per cent of cases, this was how most money was used. Indeed, over one quarter or 27 per cent of all respondents placed most of the money in a building society. Moreover, deposits with the societies far exceeded investment in other assets. Banks attracted only 8 per cent of the total, shares and unit trusts 4 per cent and other investments 8 per cent. Respondents were therefore at least three times more likely to place money released with the building societies than with any other financial agency or instrument.

Evidently, financial investment does arise from property inheritance and the volume of money is considerable. As inheritance grows in importance we can expect to see more funds flow into financial assets. Equally, as the financial sector expands, so we can see more funds flowing into the property market, mainly via mortgages. House prices then become a crucial regulator of this process since they both set the requirement for mortgage funds *and* control the volume of funds released through the sale of inherited property. In the long term they also influence the growth of home ownership.

In the Stow Report of 1979, the building societies estimated that some 15 per cent of their gross income and 20 per cent of their net income (gross minus mortgage redemptions replaced by a new loan) came from 'last-time' sellers. These included people leaving owner-occupation for other tenures, household dissolution through death and the sales of private-rented housing. Dissolutions were estimated to produce £3,354 million out of the total £4,503 million produced by last-time sellers. Such lump-sum investments were recognized to be very important to the societies as the small-savings market was approaching saturation. The importance of attracting large sums of money, as opposed to the small sums that come via households saving a proportion of each month's income, was re-affirmed in the Gibbs Report of 1984. No precise estimates of funds through inheritance were given in this report, although the Building Societies Association confirm that they remain a very important source of income (personal communication, August 1988). On the restrictive assumption that only receipts of over £100,000 are likely to be inheritances, the Building Societies Association estimates that in some months around 25 per cent of net income comes through inheritance (e.g. in June 1988, £313 million out of £1,239 million net receipts were via deposited sums in excess of £100,000).

Our survey confirms the relative attractiveness of the building societies as places to deposit inherited wealth and it is evident from the above that it now constitutes a major income source for the societies. This has encouraged the societies to devise new products attractive to the large investor, i.e. they offer premium rates of interest for sums above a certain amount (£10–20,000), although they normally attach a penalty clause against sudden withdrawal. These products can be structured to produce income and/or capital growth.

Given the typical age of beneficiaries (44 per cent of those inheriting property were aged over 60 and 73 per cent were aged over 50), capital is likely to be held to produce an income. Whether this will reduce the demand for additional pension plans cannot be deduced from these data. Equally with regard to the question of an enhanced demand for mortgages, it is apparent that a considerable volume of property is released onto the market to be sold (over 90,000 properties annually). Since many of these properties will be owned outright with no mortgage and the remainder will probably only have a small outstanding mortgage attached, their release will generate a substantial demand for new mortgages. In addition, a number of outright owners in our survey have now taken out mortgages. Taken together this suggests that property inheritance is contributing to the demand for mortgages and therefore to the increase in properties mortgaged. This trend may be counterbalanced by existing owners who used their inherited-property-based wealth to pay off their mortgage and the persistence of high interest rates may encourages this. The data suggest around 6 per cent of total property purchases in

1984 would have involved the mortgaging of inherited properties that were being disposed of.

Grossing up the various elements, we can predict from the 102,000 estates where the property was sold that in around 28,000 cases most of the funds will flow into the building societies, in 8,000 they will pass into the banks and in 4,000 into unit trusts or shares. If the properties were sold at the average price of properties bought in March 1988 with the Nationwide Building Society (£49,052), minus 10 per cent to allow for transaction costs and the fact that properties are, on average, cheaper because of a lower quality due to lack of investment and updating (Holmans, 1986b; Hamnett, 1988) and all of the money was realized, some £1.7 billion would then flow into the financial sector (£1.2 billion to the societies, £0.34 billion to the banks and £0.17 billion to unit trusts and shares). For the societies this inflow would represent around 11 per cent of their net mortgage lending in 1987.

If the capital released flows back into the housing market, we have a financial circuit that feeds upon itself. The societies' lending sustains the market, which allows equity to be released. This in turn is deposited with the societies. The record price increases of recent years mean ever greater sums of equity are released but, equally, that ever larger mortgages are required. Incomes provide the 'natural' check on this process in that, ultimately, house prices cannot exceed the capacity to pay. However, inheritance could provide a limited mechanism for by-passing this because it would provide households with extra resources to meet higher prices. There is little evidence that this is happening at present but, because of the large inflows of capital, societies have been able to lend more generously and at very competitive rates.

Concluding comments

The patterns of use of inherited property suggest that in many cases the property is sold and the proceeds placed with a building society. There is little in the evidence that suggests there are substantial *direct* impacts upon the housing market though, as noted above, the secondary effects via mortgage lending might be considerable. Looking ahead, there is little to suggest that the pattern of use will change as the level of inheritance rises. The age at which people inherit and their job and housing-career positions are such that many will surely follow the current pattern.

Perhaps the two most obvious factors to consider with respect to future prospects are the emergence of equity-extraction schemes and likely house-price trends. The home-equity plans come in two forms – home-income plans based around an annuity and home-reversion schemes in which the incumbent sells the property to a company in return for an income (see Wheeler, 1986; Leather, 1987). In 1988, these were being used by around 50,000 households (*The Sunday Times*, 1988). As the figure suggests, they are very much in their infancy and, as yet, do not benefit from a tax treatment that encourages their rapid expansion. If their tax status was changed it is likely we could see a substantial increase in their use. This would then cut into the inheritance proceeds and have a dampening effect on the trends discussed earlier.

The benefits to be derived from equity extraction and, indeed, the whole question of the impact of property inheritance, hangs critically on the issue of house-price trends (both absolutely and relatively). If house prices stabilize or fall not only could the share of property-inherited wealth decline within the total of inherited wealth but also the benefits accruing to individual households may also be reduced. Price stability or falls may mean a static market in which sales are more difficult to complete with the consequence that more equity may remain in the form of property rather than passing quickly into liquid assets.

Note

1. Private-landlord sales to sitting tenants are included because, clearly, some beneficiaries are in this situation. The data for these estimates are drawn from Table F9 in Holmans (1986a).

8

BENEFICIARIES OF INHERITED WEALTH: CASE STUDIES

Introduction

In Chapter 7 we discussed the findings of a specially commissioned national survey to show how inherited housing wealth had been used by beneficiaries in our sample. We showed that there is a strong likelihood for inherited property to be sold and for most of the proceeds to be converted into financial assets. We went on to speculate about the possible effects of property inheritance on the housing and financial markets. The survey findings suggest that there are social-class and regional dimensions to the ways in which inherited wealth is used and, in Chapter 6, we indicated that the value of inherited property wealth to beneficiary households has varied markedly between different parts of Britain. In this chapter we seek to move beyond describing the scale and impact of property inheritance to consider the various roles that inheritance can play in the lives of individual beneficiaries.

The value of case studies

Whilst the aggregate figures provided by our national survey and the Mintel (1987) and Morgan Grenfell (1987) studies are of considerable value in painting a broad picture of the incidence of inheritance and the pattern of uses, they can not be regarded as giving a complete account of the subject. In brief, the quantitative treatment represented by our questionnaire survey embodies one of two distinct methodological approaches in social research. As originally described by Harre (1979), there is a distinction to be drawn between 'extensive' and 'intensive' research methods, each with their own characteristics and functions. Much of the book so far has been based upon extensive research, centred around the analysis of large-scale questionnaire results and formal statistics. Intensive research, by contrast, looks in-depth at small numbers of cases, typically using semi-structured and interactive interviews to produce qualitative material that is less amenable to numerical analysis and more open to interpretation by the researcher. Different kinds of questions are addressed by each approach and different kinds of account are produced. Extensive research seeks to answer such questions as 'what are the regularities, common patterns, distinguishing features of a population?' 'How

widely are certain characteristics or processes distributed or represented?'
Intensive research asks such questions as 'how does a process work in a particular
case or small number of cases?' 'What produces a certain change?' 'What did the
agents actually do?' (Sayer and Morgan, 1985, Table 6.1).

In earlier chapters we focused our attention primarily on the first series of
questions. In this chapter we address the second series by presenting the findings of
a small number of semi-structured interviews with a selection of recent inheritors
living in the South East of England. Our intention is to gain insight into the varied
social situations within which the event of inheritance has occurred in order to
understand how inheritance can change the lives of beneficiaries and why, and
under what conditions, inheritors use their new-found wealth in one way rather
than another. We must remember that using inherited property and wealth
necessarily involves making choices, the outcome is never pre-determined and,
although at root individual biographical circumstances and choices are unique,
individual beneficiaries are also locked into structures that guide and shape their
lives and decisions in definable ways. We maintain that identifying the dimensions
of these wider forces is of great significance if we wish to make sense of the
disparate decisions inheritors have made and will make in the future. We hope that
what follows conveys the feeling that inheritance occurs within a lifelong,
continuous series of actions and happenings, structured and interpreted in
personal, as well as common, ways.

Methodology

The case-study material derives from 27 interviews with major beneficiaries of
wills probated in London in 1981 and 1985. Our method of contacting
beneficiaries was to examine wills lodged and publicly available at the Probate
Registry in London's Strand. The name and address of a major beneficiary (other
than surviving spouses) to each estate was identified from the will and pre-paid
cards were sent out in late 1987 and early 1988 with a letter requesting an interview.
Two batches of letters were sent out. One batch related to 186 estates probated in
1981. The second batch related to 147 estates probated in 1985. It is rarely possible
to establish from the will whether an estate contained housing – just over 10 per
cent of the wills in our sample explicitly referred to a house or houses – so to
maximize our chances of contacting beneficiaries of estates with a housing
component we set lower limits on the estates to be included in the sample. All of
the 1981 estates were valued at £25,000 or more and all of the 1985 estates were
valued at £35,000 or more. Table 8.1 shows what became of letters from each
batch.

Table 8.1   Beneficiary interviews – destination of the letters

	Sent	Refused	Returned by PO	Unknown	Interviews
1981	186	3	58	113	12
1985	147	3	33	96	15
Total	333	6	91	209	27

This represents a contact rate of only 8 per cent, understandably low in view of the date of many of the wills and the likelihood of beneficiaries changing address. It should be stressed that the purpose of talking to beneficiaries was not to interview a group who would be 'representative' of all recent inheritors. No self-selected sample of interviewees, no matter how large, willing to answer questions of matters of personal finance and bereavement is likely to be completely representative of an entire population. Rather, our intention was to build up a relatively small number of case studies incorporating a wide range of biographical information as well as a range of more easily defined facts to do with the inheritance itself and the inheritor's housing, family and employment history. Semi-structured interviews were carried out with each inheritor centring around four main areas of interest: the nature of the inheritance, the inheritor's life and circumstances, information about the wealth leaver and the way in which the inheritance was used. In this way the event of inheritance could be placed within a rounded life history, providing the background needed to understand the impact of inheritance on individual lives and inheritors' rationale for using inherited wealth as they did. The interviews lasted between 45 and 90 minutes and were taped to ensure a free-flowing discussion. The intention was to allow each person to speak for themselves in their own words, whilst retaining a degree of control over the general course of the interview.

The inheritors

A wide range of information was collected on the inheritors and their housing, work and family histories. Although, as we have shown in an earlier chapter, inheritance customs mean that most major beneficiaries are well into middle age by the time they inherit, the age of those we spoke to varied greatly. The youngest was only 24 when she inherited, the oldest was in her mid-80s. Most, however (16 of the 27), were over the age of 50, and many of them married and with children (Table 8.2).

Table 8.2 Age of inheritor in the household at time of inheriting

	Single (unmarried, widowed, divorced or living with parents)	Married	Total
30 or less	3	1	4
31–50	2	6	8
51–70	4	10	14
over 70	1	0	1
Total	10	17	27

Our national survey demonstrated that a high proportion of inheritors of housing wealth are home owners when they inherit. This was also true for the inheritors we interviewed. Only four did not own their own homes at the time of inheriting and these were principally the younger recipients. Three were aged 30 or less and two of these were still living in the parental home.

Again, in keeping with established patterns of bequeathing, most of the older inheritors (11 of the 15 aged over 50) had benefited on the death of a surviving parent. Despite their age and, for most, a long history in owner-occupation, these inheritors had moved house infrequently, if at all, and over short distances. Six had owned only one property and only four had owned three or more. Although the method used to contact inheritors predisposed the sample towards those who had remained in their home after inheriting (rather than using their newfound wealth to move), it was striking just how static these elderly inheritors had been. None of the elderly inheritors had moved since inheriting and all but four had lived in their current home for more than 10 years prior to getting their legacies. In total, as Table 8.3 shows, all but five inheritors had remained in the homes they occupied before inheriting and few had owned many homes.

Table 8.3   Length of residence in current home prior to inheriting (yrs.)

Homes owned	10 or less	11–20	More than 20	Total
1	4	—	5	9
2–4	4	2	5	11
5 or more	1	1	—	2
Total	9	3	10	22

Although most inheritors had a history of housing moves in the rented, tied or privately owned sectors, these were moves generally confined to their present locality in or close to London. Twenty inheritors were born and still live in Greater London, although one or two had experienced short stays outside the capital, during service in the armed forces, wartime evacuation or spells of employment abroad or in other parts of Britain. By the time they inherited, most had long been living in what they regarded as a satisfactory home, typically a three- or four-bedroomed suburban semi- or terrace (Table 8.4). Fourteen of the inheritors' homes had been bought for less than £10,000, so even where there was still a mortgage the repayments tended to be minimal. Again, this is what we would expect given the usual age at which inheritance occurs and the 'intra-tenurial' nature of inheritance.

For most inheritors, their children had either left home or were about to leave home, so few envisaged any future need to move to a larger house in order to accommodate a growing family. Indeed, several inheritors have found themselves in homes that were too big once the children had gone and were considering moving to something smaller. These middle and early old-aged inheritors had no urgent need to move house, although the inherited wealth was often enough to have facilitated a considerable trading up.

Contacting inheritors from the information given on wills gave us no guarantee that they would have benefited from housing inheritance rather than wealth held in some other form although, as we have stated, no estates worth less than £25,000 were chosen in order to maximize the chances that there would be a housing element. In the event, 25 of the 27 estates either included housing or contained money from a recent property sale and, where housing was involved, it was almost

Table 8.4   Inheritors' housing and assets inherited

Inheritor's housing at inheritance	Assets inherited	Housing as % of estate value
3-bed 1938 semi	3-bed semi, £3,000	90
3-bed Vict. terr.	shares in family business	n/a
4-bed 1958 det.	2-bed flat, investments	50
3-bed 1924 terr.	flat, £6,000	85
4-bed 1930s semi	flat, £50,000	35
3-bed 1930s det.	half 3-bed semi, savings	70
rented room	£12,000	90
3-bed 1930s terr.	half, 3-bed det., investments	90
3-bed 1950 semi	half 3-bed semi, car, £20,000	80
3-bed 1956 semi	£25,000	70
with parents	£60,000	n/a
with parent	3-bed terr., £6,000	65
with parents	2-bed maisonette, investments	50
2-bed 1850s terr.	house proceeds, trust proceeds	?
4-bed 1930s semi	£40–50,000 in equities	n/a
4-bed Edw. terr.	half house proceeds, £1,250	95
4-bed 1930s det.	half proceeds from two properties	50
2-bed Edw. flat	£24,000	?
2-bed Vict. det.	2-bed Vict. det., £4–5,000	80
3-bed 1911 semi.	3-bed Edw. semi, investments	75
4-bed Edw. flat	2-bed flat, shares, bonds	65
3-bed 1964 det.	half house proceeds, £3,000	75
2-bed flat	house, investments	50
5-bed 1930s det.	£124,000 in investments	n/a
4-bed Edw. terr.	2-bed flat, investments	40
4-bed 1979 terr.	2-bed flat, investments	85
3-bed 1931 terr.	£6,500	95

invariably the most valuable asset in the estate, in several cases rising to 90 per cent and more.

The inheritors came from a wide variety of family backgrounds and occupations, ranging from a West-Indian immigrant from a poor family who had spent her working life in badly paid and insecure jobs in the clothing industry, to a woman from an established monied background who had never known financial hardship. Many inheritors, though, could be described as middle class, working in the professions or education. Incomes varied accordingly between inheritor households. Two inheritors were living solely on State pensions of no more than £2,500 a year. These were 'asset-rich, income-poor' inheritors, each inheriting the house that had previously been their home but with very little income to live on or to maintain their properties. Another, working as a consultant to a number of property companies, earned in excess of £50,000. Many inheriting households, in keeping with their employment status, were comfortably off. Twelve earned above £15,000. A further nine were unable or declined to state their incomes.

Apart from parental help with a first-property purchase (12 inheritors had received such assistance), most had reached their position in the housing market purely on the basis of earned income. Although employment emerged as the prime factor behind the inheritors' housing histories, only one or two had followed careers requiring frequent and disruptive moves. Most had been remarkably sedentary, corroborating our survey finding that only a small minority of property inheritors use their wealth to move house. They expressed a great reluctance to move as they had built up important local friendships and social ties they would be unwilling to give up. In addition, after a lifetime in or around London, few would give serious thought to moving away from the capital. Many thought that life in the country would be too quiet for them, although all were aware that the sale of their homes, added to their inherited wealth, would bring in enough money to buy something a great deal more luxurious elsewhere. For the elderly in particular, the emotional ties invested in their home and neighbourhood seemed to be of great importance.

The form of the wealth received by each inheritor depended not just on the nature of the assets left but also on the way in which estates were dispersed. As Table 8.4 shows, inheritors were left a great variety of assets, though almost all estates included a property element. Thirteen sole beneficiaries inherited property intact and one joint beneficiary was left a maisonette as her share of the estate. While most of the remaining estates also contained property, it was necessary to sell it in order to divide up the estate. This limited the ways in which the inherited wealth could be used. Rather than a tangible asset in the form of property, the inheritor received a lump sum of money. This distinction between housing inheritance and the inheritance of money from the sale of property turned out to be an important one. Inheritors of intact property had open to them a range of options not available to money inheritors.

Using the inheritance

In earlier chapters we presented our survey findings to show how inherited property wealth has been used by inheritors to date. We related these decisions to a number of household indicators, for instance, the inheriting household's tenure and class position, but the questionnaire survey did not allow us to explore inheritors' motivations in any great depth. Our interviews were designed to uncover individual reasons for acting, complementing the primarily descriptive focus of the questionnaire survey.

It became apparent from the interviews that there were a number of significant influences over how inheritances were used. Those who were left property intact chose to use it in ways closely related to their existing housing and family circumstances. Three inherited the house jointly occupied with the wealth leaver. Each continued to live in the house, not just because it had come to be their home but also because in these cases little easily realizable wealth had changed hands. Inherited wealth for these beneficiaries was not really surplus to their housing needs and, hence, opened up few opportunities to realize the capital left to them.

A wider range of options was available to those left a house or flat who were independent home owners. Six sold their inherited property soon after receiving it. One of these, a middle-aged married woman with two adult children, kept the house her mother left her for several months so that a niece would have somewhere to live while she was working in London. In general, though, the properties were put up for sale almost immediately. Already satisfactorily housed and, for most, with no obligations to children, those who sold had little reason to do otherwise. The sums they received were mainly put into equities, unit trusts and building-society accounts, with a view to supplementing their incomes in future years after retirement or drawing on these investments should the need arise. For these inheritors, future housing moves were far from their minds. The possibility of moving at some stage was mentioned but only if infirmity or a need to be closer to children demanded it.

Three inheritors who kept their inherited properties were motivated in different ways. One, a married woman home owner in her 40s, decided to keep her inherited flat to provide a home for one of her college-aged daughters. Another, a middle-aged woman who had recently married and left the South East, kept her mother's flat as a second home to use on visits back to London. The third, an affluent well-housed professional man with a young family, rented out his father's flat in Earl's Court in order to derive a rental income and benefit from its rapidly increasing capital value. At the time of interview, the problems of letting had induced him to put the flat on the market with the intention of using its sale value to bolster an existing portfolio of investments.

In cases where estates were divided up between two or more major beneficiaries, property was almost invariably sold off so that the proceeds could be shared out. Where large sums were involved the inheritor's existing housing, financial and family circumstances were again the predominant influences over how the wealth was used. One middle-aged married man, living in a comfortable inter-war semi, used the relatively small amount he received from his mother's estate to buy a better car and take a Far-Eastern holiday. The money was simply surplus to requirements and could be used on luxuries. Another inheritor, an elderly childless widow living alone in an inter-war three-bedroomed terrace, received £50,000 from her sister's estate. She owned a range of investments and her income more than covered her needs so she gave about 70 per cent of the inheritance to churches and charity. As she explained,

> I'd decided I'd like to use it for things that interested me – selfishly I spent some of it on myself and I bought three weeks of time-share at a hotel on the south coast, which meant that I had somewhere definite to go for holidays. After that I started spending some of it on the various churches that interested me. I gave some to leukaemia research, mainly because my sister died of leukaemia, and then anything to do with children or wildlife always needs money, and I've covenants with a number of different charities.

Neither of these inheritors was in any immediate or foreseeable housing need or had children in housing difficulties. Most of the inheritors who received only money were in a similar position and, for them, investing their inherited wealth in stocks, shares or unit trusts was the most common course of action. Since the inheritors felt no pressing need to use the money for any special purpose, most simply added it to existing savings. They were primarily middle or old aged, well housed, with adequate incomes and without family responsibilities.

Some inheritors were rather younger and a different set of issues concerned them. One married inheritor in his 30s used most of his inherited wealth to reduce the size of the mortgage on the family house and to pay for house repairs. Another moved into the maisonette she had inherited as her share of her aunt's estate. She had previously been living with her parents so the inheritance was her route into home ownership, a move that would otherwise have been problematic on her legal secretary's income. A third young inheritor, a chartered accountant in her 20s, was left £60,000 by her great-aunt. She was still living at home at the time so she used most of the money to help buy her first property, a luxury two-bedroomed flat in a fashionable part of north London. For her and the other unmarried inheritors interviewed, satisfying their personal housing needs emerged as the top priority in their thinking on using their inheritances.

More commonly, married inheritors with children tended to express a selfless attitude of putting their children's needs first where this was necessary. Sixteen inheritors were married with children. In seven cases the children had long since grown up and left home and had become established home owners in their own right by the time the inheritance came along. Usually the wealth came from the estate of a surviving parent and, by this stage, both the inheritor and his or her children were fairly well set up in owner-occupied housing so the wealth was simply added to existing savings. The children of another four relatively young inheritors were still of school or college age and, therefore, were in no immediate housing need. Again, most of the wealth was simply invested and each foresaw using the wealth if and when necessary to help their children into home ownership. The remaining five inheritors came into their legacies just before the expected departure of a child or children from the parental home and each helped financially with their offspring's first property purchase.

For married inheritors with children, the timing of the inheritance in the lives of the children critically influenced how the wealth was used. The inheritors we interviewed were all adequately housed home owners who could afford to put their children first if they needed help. This may not always be the case, although our questionnaire survey suggests that they are likely to represent a common type of inheriting household. As we show in an earlier chapter, most major wealth transfers, other than those between spouses, take place between a parent and children who are likely to be in middle or old age themselves with grown-up children of their own by the time they inherit. Given the probability that dying home owners will be the parents of home-owning children, unless family pressures intervene, the inheritors have little reason to do anything but channel their inherited wealth, in the first instance, into various kinds of investment rather than straight back into housing.

Case histories

The housing, family and employment experience of each individual inheritor is ultimately unique to that person. At a detailed level, their reasons for using inherited wealth in one way rather than another are also particular to the individual. However, although the biographies and decisions of the inheritors differed from each other, a number of common features did emerge from the interviews and some of these themes have been outlined above. In this final part of the chapter we illustrate these uniting strands by drawing on selected interview transcripts and summaries to convey in greater depth the processes shaping the inheritance decisions of the inheritors and the impact of inherited wealth in their lives.

As we have indicated, most of the inheritors interviewed were married, middle aged and with children and can, perhaps, be thought of as typical of today's housing-wealth beneficiaries. They were long-established and contented home owners and had experienced relatively stable housing histories in which any moves that had occurred were principally guided by the need to accommodate a growing family. The employment histories of this group were similarly fairly static – often the principal wage earner had been with the same employer for long periods, although reaching their current or final status in work often followed an initial period of frequent moves in or out of London prior to buying a first home.

Many of these inheriting households were second-generation home owners who had struggled to buy initially and, in later life, found themselves benefiting from their parents' housing decisions of many years before. The case of Mrs P incorporates many of the features associated with these middle-aged inheriting households:

Mrs P's parents came originally from neighbouring Suffolk villages. Her father, who had been in domestic service, came to London after the First World War and married in 1921. Her mother started work as a teacher, kept a few hens and sold their eggs and did some seamstressing. After a succession of jobs, Mrs P's father eventually became a chauffeur earning £3 a week. Initially they rented a flat in Clapham where Mrs P was born in 1927 but, in 1937, they were able to buy a house in Mitcham. It was a 1934, terraced, three-bedroomed property costing about £400. Mrs P's parents had saved assiduously to buy and therefore needed only a small mortgage.

On leaving school Mrs P trained as a nurse and, in 1955, after two years abroad, she came back to live in the family home and did two years further training. In 1961 she bought a new two-bedroomed maisonette near to her parents for £3,300 with the help of a mortgage. Her parents helped with the deposit. In 1970 Mrs P married and she and her husband bought the house in Epsom, which is still their home. It is a three-bedroomed detached property built in 1930, which cost them £10,000. Around the same time her ageing parents moved out of their house and bought Mrs P's smaller and more manageable maisonette. After Mrs P's father's death in 1975, her mother wanted to be closer to her daughter so, since the opportunity arose, she bought the house next door jointly with her daughter and son-in-law. Although it is a sizeable three-bedroomed detached house, this was a solution that saved the inconvenience and delay involved in building an extension to Mr and Mrs P's house.

In 1971, at the age of 44, Mrs P gave birth to a daughter and gave up her career in nursing. Her husband, an examiner in the patent office, now retired, was drawing a good salary so there was no financial need to keep working. When Mrs P's mother died in 1981 she became the sole beneficiary of the estate. This consisted mainly of the value of the house and some National Savings certificates. The house was kept empty for 18 months to two years after the death because there was a possibility that Mr P's father, beginning to suffer from Alzheimer's disease, might have needed to be cared for. In the event this didn't happen and the house was sold for a figure close to the probate value. The money was invested and made no appreciable difference to Mr and Mrs P's way of life.

Since that date, Mrs P's daughter has grown up and recently married. Mr and Mrs P have helped with the purchase of a 1960s two-bedroomed maisonette in Epsom, paying about two thirds of the cost. The newly married couple have a mortgage on the remainder. In one sense the inheritance money has been passed down to Mr and Mrs P's daughter, although they insist that they would still have been able to help to the same degree even if no inheritance had been received.

When Mr and Mrs P bought their home in 1970 they gave little or no thought to the investment possibility the property might represent. After all this was before the period of major house-price inflation. The house was bought purely as a place to live. They have long been in a position to move to a more expensive house if they wanted to but they have no desire to do so. They think that they will stay in Epsom for the rest of their lives unless infirmity makes it difficult to manage the house and garden, in which case they might move to something smaller nearby. Friends, shops and services are all close at hand so they feel it would be foolish to move out to somewhere where these facilities, which they are likely to need more and more as they age, are not readily accessible.

We have suggested earlier that many, perhaps most, property-inheriting households can be expected to have something in common with the case described above: in particular, the central importance of family relationships to the decisions made on using inherited wealth. Mrs P's case also illustrates just how recent has been the transition from relative poverty to relative affluence and significant wealth transfers within today's inheriting families. The spread of wider home ownership from the inter-war years onwards has subsequently led to the passing on of valuable assets between generations within families that had previously never known inheritance.

A second group of inheritors inherited rather earlier in life, in their 30s and 40s. Usually married, few were old enough to have adult children but, like their older counterparts, they, too, had attained a reasonable standard of owner-occupied housing by the time they inherited, mostly mortgage financed by the salary of the male spouse. Once again the inherited wealth was surplus to any immediate requirements. Its usual destination was to be put into various kinds of financial investments but all younger inheritors with children had the idea of using the wealth at some future date to help their children buy a first home or for other purposes. Mr W is typical of this younger type of inheritor, comfortably housed, with a high income and school-aged children:

Mr W's mother died in 1979, leaving his father with a house that was too big for him, so he sold it and moved into a two-bedroomed flat in Earls Court. His income was limited so selling the larger house released some money to be invested in equities, unit trusts and an annuity scheme to provide a steady income. The house was sold for £40,000 and the flat cost £17,000.

At the age of 20, in 1958, Mr W went into publishing and stayed in it for 17 years. After being made redundant for the third time, he entered investment management and has worked in that field ever since. His first home was a one-bedroomed flat in central London, bought as he got married in 1960 for £4,500. He and his wife were given wedding presents of £1,000 each and this money was used to buy the flat. They moved in 1964 to Amersham, a job-related move, and bought a three-bedroomed inter-war semi there for £6,000. Their first son was born while they were in Amersham and, in 1970, they moved back to London, buying a four-bedroomed Edwardian terraced house in Barnes for £9,750, which is still their home.

When Mr and Mrs W moved back to London they gave no thought to any possible increase in the house's value. As Mr W says, 'I've lived in this house for 17 years and certainly 17 years ago I didn't think of it as an investment. I thought of it simply as somewhere to live. I couldn't stand living out in Amersham having been born and bred in London. I just had to live in London and this was basically a house that we came across and thought we could do something with to make it a nice place to live in and that was the only reason we bought it, certainly not as an investment. Obviously, one sort of rubs one's hands these days when we look in an estate agent's and see what similar houses are going for.'

Mr W was the sole beneficiary of his father's estate. The flat was valued at £38,000 and he also received about £6,000 in investments. He has used the money to build up his own pension plans but rented out the flat for a number of years to generate a rental income of £125 per week, with the intention of cashing in eventually on an increased capital value. (At the time of interview the flat was about to be put on the market.) Mr and Mrs W have no aspirations to live anywhere else even though they are now in a position to move if they chose to. Their accumulated savings, of which the inheritance money is part, will be there if the children need it to start off their own housing careers at some future date.

Another inheritor with a young family has made more formal arrangements to ensure the welfare of her children:

with the money [from the sale of an inherited flat] ... my husband set up a Deed of Family Arrangement and the money is just used for the children's expenses. It's just used to support them on everyday things, I mean they are 10, 12 and 14, and it seems to be a very expensive age, especially the 14-year-old. If she's got to go skiing with the school or go on a French exchange we draw it out of that, and also their clothes and anything school-like.

The dynamics of inheritance mean that it is unlikely that people below the age of 30 will receive substantial legacies. Few direct wealth transfers of any size pass down to young adults but, when they do occur, the impact can be pronounced in the lives of the recipients. Three of the inheritors we interviewed were under the age of 30 when they inherited. Their early stage in the life-cycle and their positions in the housing and job markets guided them to use their inheritances in radically different ways from their older counterparts. For Ms S's inheritance was, quite literally, her way into home ownership:

Ms S inherited at the age of just 24, from her aunt who died in 1981. She received her aunt's maisonette, a car and assorted chattels. Ms S was living with her parents at the time, following periods in rented flats in London. She was working, and still works, as a legal secretary. She moved into the inherited property shortly after her aunt's death and stayed there for three years, selling it for £36,000 and buying her present home, a larger three-bedroomed neo-Georgian terraced house also in Petts Wood, for £46,000. Ms S moved because she wanted a bit more room and because the garden of her maisonette was too big to manage comfortably. She has no wish to move again in the foreseeable future. She pays a small mortgage, which allows her plenty of spending money for holidays and leisure activities. Some of the other inherited wealth was used to buy a new car, the rest was invested.

On inheriting, Ms S's immediate housing needs shaped her decision to move into the inherited property and subsequently served as a basis for buying a large and expensive house – a standard of property that bears little relation to her position in the labour market or indeed to her status as a single home owner.

A final illustration of the dramatic effects that inheritance (this time across two generations) can bring about in the lives of those at an early stage in the life-cycle is provided by the case of Ms D:

Ms D inherited around £60,000 from her great-aunt's estate of £112,000. The wealth was held in building-society accounts and in the form of a shop with a small flat above it. Ms

D was living with her parents when she inherited in 1985 at the age of 29. Although her salary as a chartered accountant would have allowed her to move into some form of owner-occupation, for some time she had delayed, but on inheriting used £45,000 of the money to buy an £84,000 one-bedroomed flat in a fashionable part of north London. As she explained, 'at the time I'd already decided I was going to look for a flat, and [the inheritance] ... just meant I had more money to spend on the flat. When I started looking I didn't actually know how much I would have available, but I certainly upped my sights afterwards while I was looking.'

Her decision to buy the flat was not motivated by the investment potential. She knew where she wanted to live and was able to buy there with the help of the inheritance. As she says, 'the fact that it has been a very good investment decision has been an added benefit but I don't think that would put me off buying it if I was told it was not a good investment.'

Conclusion

This chapter has looked at the ways in which a small number of recent (primarily) housing-wealth inheritors used their inheritances, their rationale for acting as they did and the impact of inherited wealth in their lives. In the main these were people who, comfortably housed and in middle or early old-age, found themselves receiving substantial sums or valuable properties bought during the major phases of expansion in owner-occupation between the wars or after 1950. The interviews, though relatively few in number, highlight a number of themes that may be more generally applicable to the mass of today's property inheritors. Our questionnaire survey indicated that few inheriting households use their inheritance to trade up (or down) market. Those inheritors we spoke to were also remarkably static. The age at which parental wealth is received by children – such transfers as we have seen account for the bulk of intergenerational bequests – and the 'intra-tenurial' character of housing inheritance mean that few beneficiaries have any pressing financial or housing needs. One strong finding that came out of the interviews was the priority older inheritors gave to the needs of their children when they considered how to use their inheritances. Their statements, together with our survey results, put a dent in any notion that housing inheritors act in economically optimal ways. The impression that came across repeatedly was that the wealth was simply surplus to requirements, making no appreciable difference to inheritors' ways of living. In the absence of anything else, most was simply invested and forgotten about.

For younger inheritors who were not in owner-occupied housing or were still financing sizeable mortgages, the inheritance of housing or a large inheritance made an enormous difference to their lives as a different range of priorities came into play. Although unusual, where it does happen, inheritance to young adults can facilitate an initial entry into home owning at a level bearing no relationship to income levels. In some cases inheritance may be the only way for some ever to own their own home.

A combination of factors to date has ensured that donors' wealth holdings have maintained or grown in value in the final years of life. House-price inflation, major reductions in inheritance tax and the cushion of State welfare benefits and 'free' social and health services have all had the effect of enabling donors to leave substantial assets to their beneficiaries. There are now doubts whether this will always be the case. The growing privatization of health care, increasingly severe capital-asset thresholds for the receipt of various State benefits and the growth, and growing, take-up of equity-extraction schemes targeted at the elderly all cast doubt on whether housing inheritance and its value to individual recipients will continue to grow as it has in recent years. These are themes we return to in the final chapter but, in Chapter 9, we consider the often neglected but crucially important and rapidly changing influence government exerts on inheritance through the tax system.

9

INHERITANCE AND TAXATION

Introduction

In Chapter 4 we showed how the changing tenure profile and demographic structure of Britain have the potential to bring about a major increase in the incidence of housing inheritance in the years after the turn of the century. Our projections based on present trends suggest that around 345,000 properties each year will be passed on by 2030 – more than twice the current figure. These figures alone tell us little about the impact of property inheritance in the lives of succeeding generations. In Chapter 5 we examined the role of the bequeathing decisions of wealth leavers, demonstrating the strong 'intra-familial' character of most wealth transmission and, in Chapter 8, we presented case-study evidence to demonstrate that housing inheritance can radically improve the life chances of individual recipients and their families.

However, for inheritance to have any influence at all in the lives of recipients, bequeathed assets must first survive inheritance taxation. How big a share of wealth left at death gets 'siphoned off' by government through the tax system? How has the tax regime changed over time and how is it likely to change in the future? Has the tax regime influenced patterns of giving? Are there legal restrictions on the disposition of estates? Clearly, answers are needed to all of these questions if we are to assess the wider effects of inheritance on patterns of wealth holding amongst the living.

In this chapter we consider the role of government and inheritance taxation in regulating wealth transmission at death. Through taxing estates left at death the government effectively becomes a beneficiary of estates above a minimum value. We outline the development of inheritance taxation in Britain, showing that the range and levels of taxation levied on estates have varied considerably over the years, and draw connections between the changing tax regime and the climate of political opinion forming the background to tax changes. We show that, because inheritance taxes have 'first claim' on assets left at death, they can severely affect the amount of inherited wealth reaching beneficiaries. These taxes can also influence the way in which inherited wealth is passed on to beneficiaries, through encouraging the setting up of 'tax-efficient' trusts and the giving of gifts prior to death. Furthermore, by exempting or reducing the tax rates payable on transfers to some categories of beneficiary, the government can influence strongly those who receive inherited wealth.

Inheritance taxation and government

British inheritance taxes have a long and complicated history. Their precise origins are not fully understood, but it is thought that taxing wealth transfers at death may have been started in Roman times by the Emperor Augustus (Inland Revenue, 1857, p. xxvi). The main purpose of death duties (from their introduction and until recently) was to raise money for the Exchequer. Only during this century have inheritance taxes been changed in order to bring about greater social equality. These two motivating factors – the government's need to raise revenue and a desire for social justice – both have implications for the amount of inherited wealth received by beneficiaries after tax. An understanding of the changing effects of inherited wealth on people's lives must therefore start by considering the changing series of laws seeking to regulate wealth transfers at death. In this way we may gain a greater understanding of how and why inherited wealth plays such an important role in contemporary life.

The early development of British death duties

As we have indicated, inheritance taxes in Britain have obscure origins and, for many centuries after the Roman period, probably did not exist at all in any formal sense. But towards the end of the seventeenth century the English Parliament introduced the first of a continuing series of British taxes on wealth transfers at death. In 1694, under the new Dutch King, William of Orange, a probate duty was brought in, paid by the executors or administrators of an estate for a stamped receipt on their grants of probate or representation. Those who had not paid the duty had no authority to carry out the provisions of the will. Only high-value estates, containing personal property worth more than £20, were affected by the tax, which, itself, was not large, just a flat-rate charge of five shillings, increased to ten shillings in 1698.

The probate duty, like many of its successors, was designed to raise money to finance war, in this case against the French. It was directly copied from a Dutch tax and its importation perhaps illustrates that, as Bertrand Russell put it (1984, p. 583) King William had indeed 'brought with him the commercial and theological wisdom for which his country was noted'. Almost a century after its introduction, in 1779, the flat-rate probate duty was replaced by an ascending scale of charges rising to a maximum of £2 10s on estates containing personalty worth more than £300.

A year later, in 1790, a new tax was introduced, the legacy duty. Like probate duty it was designed to raise money to finance war, this time the American War of Independence. It was to be paid by inheritors for stamped receipts for the legacies. The duty was progressive, rising with the value of the legacy and, as with probate duty, it applied only to personal property. The highest rate was only £1 on property worth £100 or more but even this small sum was easily avoided since, remarkably, there was no legal obligation to provide or demand such a receipt (Inland Revenue, 1857, p. xxiii).

Because neither tax applied to real property and because there was no legal need to pay the legacy duty, inheritance taxes brought very small sums into the Exchequer. This low yield prompted a reform of legacy duty in 1796. The law was changed, making executors or administrators liable for payment of the tax and, more significantly, the rate of tax was graduated according to the relationship of the inheritor to the wealth leaver. These blood relationship or 'consanguinity' rules stayed part of inheritance taxation for a century and a half, until 1949. Transfers to parents, grandparents, children and grandchildren were exempt from the tax but transfers to more distant relatives and unrelated people or 'strangers in blood' were taxed at between 2 per cent and 6 per cent. After a series of increases and extensions over twenty years, only bequests to widows remained untaxed (Table 9.1). From 1815 the tax remained virtually unchanged until major reform in 1894.

Table 9.1   Increases and extensions in the legacy duty, 1796–1815

Where a legacy shall be £20 or more	% rate of duty			
	1796–1804	1804–5	1805–15	1815
1. To father, mother or any lineal ancestor	—	—	—	1
2. To children and descendants	—	—	1.0	1
3. To brother sister or descendants	2	2.5	2.5	3
4. To uncles and aunts or descendants	3	4.0	4.0	5
5. To great uncles and great aunts or descendants	4	5.0	5.0	6
6. To any other collateral relative or strangers in blood	6	8.0	10.0	10

(*Source*: Sandford, 1971, Table 2.1.)

The reformed legacy duty and higher rates of probate duty quickly began to bring in much more money. In 1828, both taxes together raised more than £2 million for the first time, even though successions to real property, primarily to land and freehold dwellings, were still untaxed.

To end the exemption of real property from inheritance tax, Gladstone introduced a succession duty in 1853. The duty taxed successions on nearly all kinds of property not covered by legacy duty. Measures were taken to ensure that this new tax was not too severe (the tax was levied on the value of the life interest in the realty rather than its capital value) but, even so, its yield fell well below the level predicted by the Inland Revenue. One of the reasons suggested by the revenue for the shortfall was that land (a major element in real property at this time) was, on the whole, inherited by closer relatives than legacies of personal property and hence incurred the lowest rates of duty.

The Inland Revenue's *First Annual Report* of 1857 gives a clear indication of the amount of wealth going to inheritors with various relationships to the wealth leaver. As Table 9.2 shows, nearly £400,000 was collected at the 1-per-cent rate of legacy and succession duties during 1856 in England and Wales. This implies that assets worth one hundred times that amount (or nearly 60 per cent of the total sum

Table 9.2 The amount of legacy and succession duty paid at each rate in 1856, England and Wales

	Duty paid	Value of assets transferred at rate	% total asset value
£1 %	£387,960	£38,795,900	59.10
£3 %	£581,300	£19,377,050	29.50
£5 %	£117,288	£2,345,760	3.60
£6 %	£21,506	£358,300	0.60
£8 %	£1,970	£24,625	0.04
£10 %	£472,054	£4,720,540	7.20

(*Source*: Adapted from Inland Revenue, 1857, p.xxvi.)

transferred) had been left to parents, 'lineal ancestors', children and their descendants. This was twice the amount left to brothers, sisters and their descendants and eight times the 7 per cent left to very distant relatives and non-relatives.

Over succeeding decades the three death duties (legacy, succession and probate) brought in more and more revenue, doubling from just over £3 million in 1856 to over £6 million by 1880. Death duties were also becoming proportionately more significant to the total tax yield, rising from 5 per cent of the total to around 9 per cent over the same period. There is little doubt that rising national wealth rather than changing customs in the disposal of property accounted for the increase. (Sandford, 1971, p. 37).

The death duties were now important contributors to the Exchequer and, throughout the 1880s, a series of further increases and modifications were put in place to simplify their administration and to enable them to bring in even more money. Rates of probate duty were raised in 1880 and again in 1881. At the same time, Gladstone simplified the death duties by exempting from legacy or succession duty all property that would have been taxed at the 1-per-cent rate, a measure that covered, as we have seen, three fifths of the total sum transferred. This enabled many executors to settle their estates through a single payment of the probate duty rather than two separate payments as before and, on small estates of less than £300 gross value all death duty (probate, legacy and succession), claims could be settled by a standard payment of 45s. Another improvement was to charge the duty on the 'net' estate after the deduction of an allowance for debts. Previously the gross value of the estate had been subject to tax and a rebate granted later in respect of debts after a claim had been submitted.

The same Act of 1881 introduced measures to discourage evasion of probate duty through gifting large sums immediately prior to death. A new 'account duty' was to be paid at the same rate as probate duty on gifts made within three months of death – the forerunner of present-day regulations concerning gifts between the living, or '*inter vivos*'. At the same time, the rates of succession duty were raised in an attempt to bring receipts from that tax up to the level coming in from probate duty.

By now the death duties were proliferating and were becoming increasingly difficult to administer yet, in 1889, as an *ad hoc* measure designed to raise yet more money for the Exchequer, another death duty was created. The new (later known as 'temporary') 'estate duty' was a flat-rate charge of 1 per cent on all estates above £10,000 in value. There were now five separate death duties, each with its own special field of application:

> The probate, account and temporary estate duties were levied on the property of the deceased regardless of its destination. The legacy and succession duties were both inheritance taxes, acquisition duties on the beneficiary, graduated according to consanguinity. The probate, account and legacy duties applied almost entirely to personalty: the succession duty to realty, settlements taking effect on the death of the settlor, and to leaseholds – technically personalty but ranged with and taxed as land. The temporary estate duty taxed both realty and personalty.
>
> (*ibid*. pp. 41–2)

Thus the death duties had grown over two centuries from a simple flat-rate stamp duty on grants of probate or administration into a complicated system of charges levied according to the size of the estate, the nature of the property bequeathed, the relationship of the inheritor to the deceased or on a flat-rate principle. There was now a clear need for simplification and, in response, a comprehensive series of reforms to the death duties came into effect in 1894, establishing the structure that persists to the present day.

British death duties in the twentieth century

In the 1894 Finance Bill the liberal Chancellor, Sir William Harcourt, reformed the three death duties applicable to property left by the wealth leaver, regardless of its destination. As we have seen, these were the probate, account and (temporary) estate duties. In their place he substituted a new estate duty levied on the aggregate net value of all property, real or personal, settled or unsettled, passing on death. The tax rate rose according to the size of the estate, ranging from 1 per cent on estates worth between £100 and £500 and up to 8 per cent on estates worth more than £1 million. He also brought in a small extra levy called the 'settlement estate duty', which was applied in certain circumstances on settled property. This tax raised insignificant amounts and was repealed in 1914.

Harcourt wanted to end the favourable treatment given to real property by taxing its net capital value rather than just the life interest, but to arrive at an aggregate estate value some fair way of valuing real property had to be reached. This occupied most of the discussion on the Finance Bill in the House of Commons. The main argument against charging real property at full net capital value was that its owners already suffered by comparison with owners of personalty because they were liable to pay local taxation – they therefore deserved some respite at death. But the reformers had their way and, from then on, real property was to be treated in a broadly similar way to personal property.

The detailed progression of the estate duty embodied the idea that the tax should be closely related to the ability of the estate to pay, but many opponents of the bill felt that the new rates and method of valuation of realty were iniquitous and would have dire consequences. There were even those who feared for the livelihood of landlords and predicted the collapse of English farming (Hansard, 1894).

The Inland Revenue's statistics showed that wealth leavers continued to favour strongly their closest relatives. The 1 per cent duty on bequests to spouses, parents, grandparents, children and grandchildren had been abolished by Gladstone, although small sums were still being collected from this tax. Some 70 per cent of personal property passed to these groups, so only about 30 per cent of £210 million total net capital value of personal property on which death duties were paid were now also subject to legacy duty. As Table 9.3 shows, brothers, sisters and their descendants were receiving more than half of this taxable sum.

Table 9.3   Legacy duty – capital paying legacy duty and duty paid at each rate in year ended 31 March 1905, UK

In respect of legacy to	Rate of duty	Capital upon which duty was paid	% of total duty paid
A child, or a descendant of a child, of the deceased, or father or mother, or any lineal ancestor of the deceased	1	£4,816,000	7.2
A brother or sister of the deceased, or any descendant of a brother or sister	3	£41,085,732	61.8
An uncle or aunt of the deceased, or any descendant of an uncle or aunt	5	£4,587,040	6.9
A great uncle or aunt of the deceased, or any descendant of a great uncle or aunt	6	£796,500	1.2
Any other person	10	£15,161,190	22.8
Total		£66,446,462	

(*Source*: Adapted Inland Revenue, 1905, p. 115.)

The purpose of the death duties was still to raise money for the Exchequer and the reforms of 1894 proved spectacularly successful in achieving this. By 1898 they were bringing in more than £15 million, four fifths of which came from the probate and estate duties, and the death duties combined were contributing a larger and larger share of total taxation revenue, reaching 20 per cent by the turn of the century (Table 9.4).

Death duties and social reform

The pre-war liberal chancellors were quick to exploit the reformed tax system further but, for the first time, an increase in death duties was linked to a specific programme of social reform. Asquith increased the rates in 1907 partly in order to finance Britain's first non-contributory old-age pension scheme and this signalled a general change in political attitudes towards personal wealth taxation. Redistribution for the common good came to justify rapidly increasing rates of death duty on higher value estates. 'Social justice for all' was the theme of Lloyd George's 'People's Budget' of 1909, in which he pledged himself to 'raising money to wage implacable war against poverty and squalidness' (Hansard, 1909). He

Table 9.4　Changing importance of death duties within total Inland Revenue receipts (£m.)

	Total IR receipts	Net receipt of death duties			Death duties as % total IR receipt
		Total	Legacy and succession duties	Probate and estate duties	
1848–9	29.7	2.2	1.2	0.9	7.4
1858–9	35.8	3.4	2.2	1.2	9.5
1868–9	41.8	4.4	2.8	1.6	10.5
1878–9	49.4	5.6	3.3	2.3	11.3
1888–9	53.2	6.6	3.7	4.3	12.4
1898–9	78.3	15.7	3.6	12.1	20.1
1908–9	96.2	18.3	4.1	14.2	19.0
1918–19	623.7	30.8	5.6	25.2	4.9
1928–9	407.5	81.0	8.8	72.2	19.9
1938–9	520.8	77.5	11.0	66.5	14.9
1948–9	2,055.0	178.4	23.1	155.3	8.7

(*Source*: Adapted from Inland Revenue, 1950, Tables 1 and 5.)

increased the estate-duty rates, re-introduced legacy and succession duties on bequests to children, their descendants, parents and other lineal ancestors, widened the scope and raised these duties and even, under exceptional circumstances, extended the tax to spouses. On the eve of the First World War, the rates were again increased on all estates above £100,000 and, for the very wealthy, the tax was becoming severe, a maximum of 20 per cent. The government was beginning to take a substantial share of higher-value estates and, in addition, a 10-per-cent rate of legacy and succession duty on all bequests outside the immediate family circle was starting to act as a significant disincentive to the wide dispersal of wealth left at death. By 1920, only 7 per cent of the personal property subject to estate duty was left to persons other than relatives in the direct line or siblings (Inland Revenue, 1920).

Throughout the First World War there had been great reluctance to use death duties as a war tax but, when hostilities ended and with the country in severe financial difficulties, Austen Chamberlain, the chancellor of a coalition government, felt free to raise the rates considerably on higher-value estates. Nominally at least, the government was now claiming 40 per cent of estates worth £2 million or more. For Chamberlain and subsequent inter-war chancellors, financial need, rather than social justice, motivated a series of increases in the rates of death duties. As Conservative Chancellor, Winston Churchill raised the rates on middle-value estates in 1925 to finance a reduction in supertax in the hope of stimulating incentive and, in 1930, the Labour Chancellor, Snowdon, brought the maximum rate up to 50 per cent on large- and medium-value estates to help deal with the national debt. Three further increases followed in 1939 and 1940, 'the first associated with pre-war armaments expenditure, the others with the arrival of war' (Sandford, 1967, p. 14) and, by 1940, the top rate had become 65 per cent. In principle at least, the government had become the major beneficiary of high-value estates.

Death duties and the post-war settlement

If the inter-war rises in rates of death duties had been initiated purely by financial difficulties, the changes that immediately followed the Second World War were closely allied to a thorough-going programme of social reconstruction and reform. In 1946 the incoming Labour Chancellor, Hugh Dalton, brought the maximum estate duty rate up to 75 per cent, reduced rates on lower-value estates and brought the exemption threshold up from £100 to £2,000. In the process he exempted three quarters of all estates that would have been taxed. The legacy and succession duty rates were also raised considerably and a number of exemption clauses were introduced to favour leavers of smaller estates and their bequests to close family members. Dalton made no secret of his wish to bring about greater equality in the distribution of wealth. He was determined to close 'the gap which separates the standard of living of the great mass of our fellow citizens from that of a small privileged minority' (Hansard, 1946). Two years later, the new Labour Chancellor, Sir Stafford Cripps, abolished legacy and succession duties but more than compensated by considerably raising the rates of estate duty, particularly on medium-value estates. Yet despite the major rises of the early and mid-1940s, the death duties became much less important compared with other forms of Inland Revenue duty (Table 9.4). The prime reason for this lies with the massive growth in the tax yield from other sources, primarily income tax, but it seems probable that increasing tax evasion and avoidance also played a part (see Sandford, 1971, pp. 78–90).

With the abolition of legacy and succession duties in 1949, estate duty became the sole tax on wealth left at death. The next twenty years saw several rises in the exemption threshold but general stability in the rates imposed. It is likely that over this period inflation in property values and other assets increased the burden of estate duty since inflation boosts the monetary value of estates and brings them into higher tax brackets than they would otherwise have occupied.

By 1960, the British government was taking a far higher proportion of the wealth left at death than were those of most other countries. According to one commentator, Britain had 'the most severe system of inheritance taxation in the world' (Tait, 1960, p. 346). Yet in spite of a steeply progressive tax that rose to a maximum of 80 per cent of total estate value, death duties continued to decline as revenue producers compared with other taxation sources. They contributed only 4.9 per cent of all central-government taxation revenue in 1969 even though, nominally at least, the State was taking more than half of the value of all estates above £40,000.

The decline of death duties for redistribution

Over the past two decades, primarily because of a shift in political attitudes that questions the moral and economic justification for taking such a large share of the wealth left at death, there has been a considerable relaxation in the rates of duty and a series of substantial increases in the exemption threshold. Transfers between husband and wife are now exempt from death duties (before 1974 there had been a limit of £15,000 on such bequests) and since the advent of the first Thatcher

Table 9.5   Rates of inheritance tax/capital transfer tax, 1977–89 (lower limit of slice of chargeable gain (£000) on transfers on death)

Rate of Tax %	Oct. 77–Mar. 80	Mar. 80–Mar. 82	Mar. 82–Mar. 83	Mar. 83–Mar. 84	Mar. 84–Apr. 85	Apr. 85–Mar. 86	Mar. 86–Mar. 87	Mar. 87–Mar. 88	Mar. 88–Mar. 89	Mar. 89–Mar. 90	Mar. 90
10	25	—	—	—	—	—	—	—	—	—	—
15	30	—	—	—	—	—	—	—	—	—	—
20	35	—	—	—	—	—	—	—	—	—	—
25	40	—	—	—	—	—	—	—	—	—	—
30	50	50	55	60	64	67	71	90	—	—	—
35	60	60	75	80	85	89	95	—	—	—	—
40	70	70	100	110	116	122	129	140	110	118	128
45	90	90	130	140	148	155	164	—	—	—	—
50	110	110	165	175	185	194	206	220	—	—	—
55	130	130	200	220	232	243	257	—	—	—	—
60	160	160	250	270	285	299	317	330	—	—	—
65	510	510	650	700	—	—	—	—	—	—	—
70	1,010	1,010	1,250	1,325	—	—	—	—	—	—	—
75	2,010	2,010	2,500	2,650	—	—	—	—	—	—	—

(*Source*: Inland Revenue, 1989, Appendix A6; Budget statements 1989, 1990.)

government in 1979 a series of marked changes have been made to capital transfer tax/inheritance tax. When the Conservatives took office the first £25,000 of estates were exempt from tax, and the remainder was taxed at progressively higher rates rising to 75 per cent of estates of over £2 million. In the first Conservative budget in 1980, the lower exemption limit from tax was raised from £25,000 to £50,000 and all tax rates of under 30% were scrapped. In 1984, the maximum rate of tax was reduced to 60 per cent, and in 1987 the tax structure was greatly simplified with just four bands – 30 per cent on estates of over £90,000 rising to 60 per cent on estates of over £330,000. The most dramatic change came in 1988 however when the whole system of progressive taxes was scrapped and replaced by a flat rate of 40 per cent inheritance tax on estates of over £110,000. This lower exemption limit has subsequently been increased with inflation and now stands at £128,000. The idea of inheritance tax as a progressive tax on wealth has been totally abandoned, and by 1980 inheritance tax produced only 1.4 per cent of the total tax yield, a figure which has remained virtually static ever since.

Death duties in Britain are rapidly returning to the marginal tax role they held during the middle of the nineteenth century. The tide has turned against the idea that the taxation of wealth left at death should be used as one means of bringing about greater equality in wealth holding in society at large. As we have shown, this was an idea first put forward by the liberal government of David Lloyd George and had its heyday in the great reforming programme of the post-war Labour government. Notwithstanding the many legal and illicit ways of avoiding and evading death duties (see Rubinstein, 1986, pp. 47–8), in the two decades after the Second World War the State took a major part of all estates of any substance. However over the last decade, as Table 9.5 shows, the government has withdrawn more and more from taxing the transfer of wealth held at death. The only estates now likely to pay the full flat rate of 40 per cent on the chargeable slice are those lacking in the usual provisions for reducing the tax liability (trusts, agricultural land holdings, gifts *inter vivos*) and are disposed of in unusual ways. In recent years, inheritance tax has rightly come to be described as a 'voluntary' tax, so easy is it to avoid (Whalley, 1974).

10

THE FUTURE OF HOUSING INHERITANCE

Cond. 1970's

Introduction

Until the first major house price boom of the early 1970s, which doubled average house prices in three years, little attention was paid to house prices and the role of housing in personal wealth. Houses have always been expensive in relation to income and house buyers have always had to struggle to buy for the first time. But until the 1970s, home ownership was primarily seen in terms of its role of providing a roof over people's heads. Its main attraction was the degree of control and self-determination it offered, the freedom from the dictates of landlords and the chance of owning a home outright rather than paying rent indefinitely. Although home ownership was generally viewed as a sound investment and a hedge against inflation or a 'store' of wealth, it was not generally seen as a source of substantial capital gains or as an important retirement nest-egg.

However, by the late 1980s, after the third house-price boom within two decades and after national average house prices had risen by 1,000 per cent, it had become clear to many home owners that home ownership could also provide a major source of capital gains and ultimately become a source of real income. Home ownership had become a major element in personal wealth, and moving up the housing 'ladder' was seen by some, particularly the young middle-class owners in the South East, not just as a way of improving the quality of accommodation but also as a way of maximizing potential capital gains and personal wealth. The larger, and more expensive the house, the greater the potential capital gains and accumulated equity and all of it was tax free.

There is little hard evidence to back up these assertions about the changes in the way in which home ownership has been viewed, and the changes will not have been the same across different age-groups, social classes and regions. Older home owners, and those in some of the lower-priced regions, will probably have retained a more traditional attitude to home ownership and the perception of home ownership as a financial commodity first and foremost is probably confined to a relatively small minority of recent buyers in London and the South East. These caveats aside, we believe that many individuals are more aware of ownership as a source of financial gains than they were twenty years ago. It may not have had an overwhelming impact on their reasoning to buy in the first place, but their view of its significance will have developed during their tenure of the property. The house-price slump of 1989 and 1990 and high mortgage interest rates will have given this view a knock, particularly in the south of England where prices are 10–20 per cent below March 1989 (Halifax Building Society, 10 April 1990) and some recent buyers have undoubtedly made real losses. But this also happened in 1974–7, although not to such a marked extent, and the mortgage rate rose equally rapidly in 1977 to about 15 per cent, immediately prior to the late 1970s house-price boom. There is a general belief that house prices will begin to rise again in London and the South east by 1991–2 as rising real incomes reduce the house price:income ratio to more manageable proportions and growing numbers of buyers are attracted back into the market, and we would concur with this view. Already the house price:income ratio has fallen back from a peak of more than 5 (Amex Bank Review, 1990) and, with continued rises in incomes and a stagnant housing market, it should continue to fall. We would note, however, that there is at least one good reasons why it might not return to the 'historic' 3.5-times income. This is because the growing number of working women and two–income households have increased household purchasing power and house prices. In this respect the mortgage:income ratio is a more sensitive measure of market conditions. The 1989–90 house-price slump is not the first, nor will it be the last, given the cyclical nature of house-price inflation in Britain (Holmans, 1990).

Following upon the growth of home ownership, the rise in house prices and the rapidly growing importance of home ownership in personal wealth has come a dawning realization that housing inheritance is also going to be of growing importance in Britain in the future. Inheritance in general has always been an issue of considerable importance for wealth economists in advanced Western capitalist countries, because of its key role in maintaining intergenerational wealth inequalities. Inheritance transmits advantage from one generation to another and, as such, it can contribute significantly to the different opportunities available to individuals and, collectively, to groups and classes. Until recently, little attention has been given to housing inheritance as an issue in its own right within inheritance. However, as we have argued throughout this book, the last few years have seen a sudden surge of interest in housing inheritance in Britain. Overall, it would not be too great an exaggeration to say that housing inheritance has been rediscovered as an important issue for the 1990s. We say 'rediscovered' because housing inheritance has long been important for a small minority of individual owners and private landlords and their beneficiaries. What is new is the prospect of widespread housing inheritance on a large scale. It is the potential scale and implications of mass inheritance that has attracted so much attention in Britain today.

In contrast, outside Britain (and probably the USA) little attention seems to have been paid to housing inheritance, and the sudden surge of interest in housing inheritance in Britain is unique. This raises important questions about why this level of interest has occurred in Britain, but not elsewhere. We would argue that the explanation lies in the unique conjunction of two interrated events in Britain. The first is the pace of the post-war expansion of home ownership. Home ownership has long been high in the USA, Canada, Australia and New Zealand. In North America about half of all households owned their own homes by 1945 (Harris and Hamnett, 1987) and this level was reached in Australia by the early 1950s (Kendig, 1984). Since then, the proportion in these countries has risen to about 70 per cent, only slightly higher than the current level in Britain (for a useful summary of home-ownership trends in a number of countries, see Building Societies Association, 1989). However, in these countries as in much of Europe, the rise in the level of home ownership has been slow and gradual. In Britain, however, the transformation into a nation of home owners has been much more rapid and occurred largely post-war.

Although the 1930s saw the beginning of the home-ownership boom, there were only about 3.5 million owner-occupied dwellings in Britain in 1945: about a quarter to a third of all households (Swenarton and Taylor, 1985). By 1990, however, the number had risen to nearly 15 million and two thirds of households owned their own homes. In just 45 years Britain has been transformed from a nation of tenants to a nation of home owners, and the great bulk of this change has taken place since the mid-1950s, when the Conservative council-house building programme was replaced by a switch in policy to a more explicit promotion of home ownership. As a result, mass home-ownership is a relatively recent phenomenon in Britain unlike other English-speaking countries.

The second factor has been the rapid growth of house prices in Britain since 1970. While house prices have also risen rapidly elsewhere in the 1980s, for example, in the USA and Canada and in parts of Europe thus increasing the importance of housing in net personal wealth in those countries, Britain is the only country to have experienced simultaneously a rapid growth of home ownership and rapid house-price inflation. As a result, we would argue that the importance of housing wealth in Britain has suddenly risen to prominence in a way that had not happened in other countries where mass home-ownership is a long-established phenomenon, or where, as in much of Western Europe, home ownership has not grown as rapidly as in Britain post-war and where house-price inflation has not been marked. Indeed, The Netherlands saw house prices fall by 30 per cent or more from the late 1970s to the early 1980s after a boom in 1976–8 (Priemus, 1987). The sudden discovery of housing wealth in Britain was followed in the 1980s by the equally sudden realization that the rise of mass home-ownership and wealth would be followed by a boom in housing inheritance.

There has thus been a set of circumstances in which the housing inheritance and wealth issue has arisen in Britain and we have suggested that these were unique to this country. In developing our conclusions to this book and the study that underpins it, we are conscious that we are reporting on a particular period in a particular country. We are not describing universal truths and in Britain we are likely to see a very different set of conditions unfolding over the next forty years. For example, the major period of growth in home ownership will have passed and the surge in inheritance will have begun to level off. Given the uniqueness of the period we are currently addressing, it makes the assessment of the future to which we now turn to as the core of this concluding chapter a complex task. We begin by considering future trends in home ownership, house prices and housing wealth.

We then move on to look specifically at future housing inheritance and its social distribution over the next thirty years. Set against this scenario will be a series of countervailing trends and, in the third and final section, we examine some of the ways in which the inheritance factor could be diminished. We conclude by returning to our overall theme, the nation of inheritors built upon the nation of home owners, and stress the need to recognize the complex interdependencies and tensions that lie at the heart of this situation.

Future trends in home ownership, housing prices and housing wealth

Central to any evaluation of the future of housing inheritance are likely trends in home ownership, house prices and housing wealth. It is currently estimated that housing accounts for almost half of personal wealth in Britain (net of mortgages). This is a very substantial proportion, and it has almost doubled from the figure in the mid-1960s. But will this proportion stablize or will it continue to increase? This is dependent on two factors, first, on the continuing growth of home ownership. This has risen rapidly in recent decades, and now stands at about two thirds of all households. While this rate of growth is unlikely to be continued, not least because home ownership is nearing what many commentators see as a maximum level of about 70–5 per cent of households, it is likely to go on rising for at least another ten or twenty years and it could go higher if more council houses are sold. A recent survey carried out for the Building Societies Association indicates that about 85 per cent of individuals express a desire to own their own homes, and this is highest in the younger age-groups (BMRB, 1989).

The second factor is whether house prices continue to rise faster than the price of other assets. This has been the case for the last 25 years and, as house prices keep closely in step with rising incomes, we see no reason why it is likely to cease now, although the rate of growth may be lower than in the past as a result of the falling number of people in the key first-time buyer age-groups. Reduced demand in this age-group may depress prices, but the number of people in the 30–50 age-group will continue rising for some time to come, and this may lead to a stronger demand for trading up and thus place upwards pressure on prices. Generally speaking, the more people earn, the higher the proportion of their income they spend on housing, and this is unlikely to change. The precise forecasting of house-price trends is fraught with difficulty since it rests on many other factors that are themselves hard to predict, e.g. interest rates, the Community Charge, wage levels, the outcome of the next general election, entry into the European monetary system and the integration of Eastern and Western Europe. Having said this, we see no reason why the underlying link between prices and incomes should be overturned and we would therefore expect continuing rises in house prices. In sum, we would therefore suggest that housing's share of personal wealth is likely to go on rising though probably at a slower rate than over the last 25 years and allowing for some fluctuations in the overall trend.

It should be noted that estimates of the share of housing in personal wealth are produced by the Inland Revenue on the basis of the data on estates passing at death. These, of course, are heavily biased towards the pattern of home ownership of a generation ago, and they considerably understate the share of housing in personal wealth at present. For this reason alone we can expect housing's share to continue to grow. Set against this are possible increases in the amount of wealth held as shares, although there have been recent suggestions that share ownership cannot be expected to grow rapidly while it receives such unfavourable tax treatment in comparison with home ownership (*Guardian*, 1990). Having said this, the recent drop in house prices in combination with new incentives for saving could produce a reduction in housing's share of personal wealth, at least temporarily. The absolute amount will, however, continue to rise reflecting the underlying growth in ownership levels still coming through.

The growth of home ownership and wealth has been linked with the redistribution of wealth away from the top 10 per cent of wealth owners towards the next 40 per cent. We can expect that as home ownership continues to grow, and as existing owners' equity increases, there may be further redistribution within the top 50 per cent and some slight redistribution towards the next 10 per cent, i.e. into the sixth decile of wealth owners. This is likely to be very small, however, as at any point in time there will always be a large number of recent first-time buyers who have substantial mortgages relative to the price of their houses. They may be home buyers but they have little or no housing wealth. The one third of tenant households will remain untouched by the extension of housing wealth. The distribution of housing wealth among home owners is also far from equal. There is a world of difference between those owners with housing equity measured in hundreds of thousands and those whose equity is measured in thousands. In certain respects all they have in common is their housing tenure. However, bearing in mind the dangers of overstating the case (see Saunders, 1990, and Forrest et al, 1990, for a critical analysis of the issue of capital gains), it is important to stress that most owners, regardless of class and regional location, do have an asset that can be sold (or even remortgaged) for more than they paid for it. In general terms, owners who spent more will accumulate more in absolute terms even though we recognize that, in relation to their income and their initial deposit, some of the purchasers of low-priced property may have done very well indeed.

In the 1980s the rise in house prices has been paralleled by a decline in personal-sector saving and a growth in personal-sector wealth. Households have also substantially increased their level of indebtedness, in part (it is thought) because of that increased wealth (UBS Phillips & Drew, 1989). As housing wealth increases there will be continuing pressure to utilize it both during the lifetime of the owner and by beneficiaries. This wealth, extracted in whatever way, is now becoming a factor of some considerable significance as a form of disposable income outside of the factors that normally control incomes. Over the next decades it is an issue governments will have to confront and we return to this later.

The future of housing inheritance

We showed in Chapter 3 that equity extraction from the housing market has increased sharply during the 1980s and we also point out that housing inheritance accounts for about 40 per cent of extraction when proceeds from sales of council and private-rented housing are excluded. The other 60 per cent consisted of other last-time sellers, and equity extracted by home owners trading down market or taking out a larger mortgage than required to purchase their new house and retaining some proceeds from the sale of their previous house (Holmans, 1986a; Lowe and Watson, 1989). These shares are not fixed, of course, and it is very likely that the importance of different forms of equity release have changed over time and will continue to change in the future. The removal of tax relief on 'home-improvement' loans was one such development that may have diminished extraction through this route and, as we hinted above, other restrictions could be introduced.

Although it has always been possible to move down market and release some equity, particularly on retirement, it is only since the house-price inflation of the early 1970s that an increasing number of home owners have begun to realize the possibility of releasing some equity through remortgaging. Until then it is likely that most equity was released via inheritance and it is only recently, with the liberalization of the mortgage finance market and the entry of major banks and specialist mortgage companies, that it has become possible to remortgage so easily. There has been a considerable expansion of schemes offering secured loans on property at only 1 or 2 percentage points above the normal mortgage interest rate. Definitive evidence in the form of detailed statistics is unfortunately unavailable. The *General Household Survey* (1983) looked at the issue in the early 1980s and it was apparent then that around 5 per cent of owners had remortgaged, though most used the money for house improvement.

A further aspect of equity extraction and one with particular significance to future patterns of housing inheritance is the range of mechanisms now available to elderly owners to 'draw down' some of the value of their property during their own lifetimes. Annuities and interest-only loans have become commonplace as devices for releasing cash for elderly householders to improve their property. More recently, we have seen the development of a range of home-income plans through which elderly households are able to supplement their annual income, though there do remain a number of problems with their use (see Wheeler, 1986, and Leather and Wheeler, 1988, for valuable reviews). The tax treatment still remains problematic and most recently the fall in the value of property has reduced the income likely to be made available by entering one of these schemes. These concerns are reflected in relatively low take up, despite substantial promotion, and this parallels experience in the USA. There the evidence suggests that elderly households tend to increase their housing equity by purchasing more expensive property rather than reducing it by cash extraction and that a lack of confidence and experience results in the elderly staying on in their homes without extracting equity (Scholen and Chen, 1980; Wise, 1985). Clearly this may change, but the conservative response of the elderly does reflect the fact that a dwelling is much more than a simple store of capital. Having said this, we would expect to find increased use of these different mechanisms over the next three decades.

The late 1970s and 1980s have also seen the development of a range of new housing options for the elderly, reflecting the growing market power of this age-group. All of these have implications for the equity already built up in property.

Indeed, they are specifically designed to take advantage of it. Private as opposed to public residential homes for the elderly have expanded rapidly in recent years. Although it is now possible to obtain State funding to enter these private homes where incomes are under a certain limit, it is likely that many residents were previous owners who have sold their homes to pay the high charges – averaging £250 per week in 1989. There has also been a considerable growth in sheltered housing for sale. There is a wide range of property available at prices that can often consume all the capital from the sale of the previous dwelling. There is also the question of the resale value of some sheltered housing. Standards are rising and tomorrow's elderly may be reluctant to occupy some of the more down-market schemes. If so, then the equity locked in them may be difficult to release. Either way, sheltered housing both for rent and sale is likely to erode the store of equity many households have built up prior to retirement. Survey evidence has shown that the 'new old' have a strong desire to benefit from the wealth accumulated in property (whether through their own efforts or via inheritance) during their working lives and that they plan to live out their retirement as affluently as possible (Vision, 1989).

Given all of the above it seems inevitable that the share, if not the absolute value, of housing equity going towards housing inheritance will fall. More equity release in life means that less will be available for inheritance after death. Of course, the continued growth of home ownership will act to counter this and it is to the issue of the number of estates containing house property that we now turn.

It will be recalled from Chapter 3 that, although the proportion of estates passing at death that included house property rose slightly from 46 per cent in the late 1960s to about 54 per cent in the mid-1980s, the number of estates containing house property did not increase substantially. In the most favourable calculation the number of estates increased by about 20 per cent but, otherwise, the number remained more or less stable throughout. This poses problems for the advocates of mass housing inheritance but, as we have argued earlier, the absence of growth was largely due to the fact that many of the currently dying elderly population were not home owners. The post-war growth of owner-occupation has not yet filtered though into inheritance and, therefore, has not yet shown up in the statistics. If and when it does, the number of finally dissolving elderly owner-occupier households is likely to double within the next thirty to forty years, as is shown in Chapter 4. There is, in other words, a substantial time lag between the growth of home ownership and the growth of housing inheritance. Over the next forty years we might reasonably expect the number of estates containing UK house property to rise to around 70 per cent.

The value of housing in estates passing at death rose sharply from 24 per cent of the total in the late 1960s to 40 per cent of the total in the mid-1980s. Contrary to popular preconceptions, this is almost entirely a product of the rise in house prices. Over this period they rose some 2.5 times faster than other assets present in estates. This proportion now seems to have stabilized at about 40 per cent and, even if it increases further, it is likely to be at a slower pace than previously. One reason for this may be the second-round effects of housing inheritance itself. As more people inherit and sell inherited property, so their financial assets increase and this, in turn, is likely to raise the proportion of financial assets in their own estates when they die. On the other hand, the expansion of home ownership down the social scale is likely to mean there will be more home owners whose only substantial asset is their house. When they die, their home will comprise a large proportion of their estate.

At present only about 150,000 estates per year include house property. On the assumption that the average number of major beneficiaries is two, this suggests that about 300,000 individuals inherit a share of house property each year. This is only about 0.7 per cent of the population aged 18 years or over and about 1.4 per cent of households, assuming each beneficiary lives in a separate household. If the number of major beneficiaries is nearer three, as our survey suggested, the numbers rise to 450,000 individuals and 2 per cent of households each year. This may not seem a large figure but, by the end of a 10-year period, perhaps one fifth of households could contain someone who had inherited a share of house property. This figure is larger than might be supposed because of the sharing of estates. But the figures are inflated because of the assumption that all beneficiaries live in separate households and that each beneficiary inherits only once. In reality, because of the tendency for children of home owners to marry the children of other home owners and for the children of tenants to marry the children of tenants, many households will inherit house property more than once and some will never inherit house property at all. As a result, the number of inheriting persons and households will be lower than the crude figures above would suggest. Taken in combination with our earlier comments about the lower than expected conversion of high home-ownership into high house-property inheritance, we can see that the process is more muted than might at first be thought.

Although housing inheritance may not be as widespread in the future as some would believe, it will still have a range of important implications. In Chapter 7 we discussed a range of theses with respect to the housing and finance markets and our purpose here is to review these again briefly in relation to future levels of inheritance. With respect to first-time buyers, there is little evidence at present that a large amount of assistance passes to them and, despite current difficulties, we do not envisage this situation changing dramatically in the future unless a very different set of circumstances prevails. As now, individuals will be helped, but the very nature of the house-price–income relationship should always mean that most first-time buyers can enter the market without major assistance. In our view, assistance was more likely in the past than the future. We would expect to see a growth in second-home purchase and in financial investment as a consequence of inheritance. These are commensurate with the stage in the life-cycle of beneficiaries. Trading up may be an option some will consider but this will depend heavily on the future state of the market. If the era of sharp increases in property values has passed, the attractions of ever-larger properties may diminish. At the same time, the lifestyle of the next century may place a great premium on space and trading up may be one way to achieve this.

In general we would expect housing responses to be similar to those today. It is when we turn to the finance market that there seems to be a greater potential for change. At present, much of the money realized passes back into the building societies. These institutions are themselves undergoing fundamental change and we can expect a much more targeted approach by them to the large sums of money released via inheritance. It is likely that this will become a very competitive market with a range of institutions vying for this business. Housing may no longer be the ultimate destination as at present and this would seem to offer considerable potential to companies that invest in a range of markets. Investors will probably remain cautious in their approach and may want relatively easy access to at least a portion of their inheritance.

Our survey revealed the limited range of uses to which inheritance is now put. It indicated a considerable conservatism that could well slow the response to new products aimed at this market. It would also suggest that the government may face particular difficulties if it tried to direct the use of housing inheritance. A home of one's own seems also to connect to the idea of an inheritance of one's own and the government could find a deep vein of resistance in this area. Equally, there is little to suggest at present that many households want to go down the path of paying for education or health from their inheritance. They could be forced into it but this may rebound on the government that took this action. As we argue elsewhere in this chapter, incentive schemes are much more likely to succeed because the choice remains with the user. To conclude this brief discussion on the future implications of inheritance, there is little evidence to suggest fundamental changes from current behaviour. Much rests on the capacity of the markets concerned to produce the products and services likely to wean the beneficiary away from the conservative habits practiced at present.

The social distribution of housing inheritance

This brings us to a discussion of the social distribution of housing inheritance and the ways that may develop in future years. We argued in Chapter 6 that, at present, housing inheritance is not the great equalizer some writers seem to have suggested. On the contrary, the current distribution of housing inheritance is heavily skewed towards owner-occupiers, and the incidence of inheritance was much higher among owners and the higher social classes than it was among council tenants and the lower social classes. This was also evident in our case studies presented in Chapter 8, though as we pointed out, they are a self-selected group. We argued that the distribution of inheritance was primarily because of two factors. First, it was a product of the social distribution of home ownership a generation ago (which was largely but not entirely restricted to the middle classes – the North West and Wales being examples of two areas where working-class home ownership has a long history) and, second, it was because the children of home owners are themselves more likely to be owners than are the children of tenants. But, just as the current uneven distribution of house inheritance reflects the social distribution of home ownership a generation ago, the extension of this tenure across all social classes over the last thirty years and its further extension in the next decade means that housing inheritance in the future will be much more widely spread than at present. Home ownership is now the most heterogeneous tenure in social-class terms and this, in conjunction with a less rigid class structure, means that the benefits of housing inheritance should be enjoyed by a bigger proportion of the total population. This will not mean that all will enjoy equal benefits. Some will inherit a low-value property, others a high-value one. Some will share the inheritance with several relatives, others with none. The children of home owners are still more likely to marry the children of other owners and thus some households will enjoy more than one inheritance while others will get none.

The situation in thirty years is likely to be one where a substantial majority of individuals and households stand to inherit house property at some stage of their lives, and a considerable number of households will inherit twice. But, on the other hand, there will be a significant minority of households – between 10 per cent and 30 per cent who are unlikely to inherit house property from parents and probably not from anyone else. Even if all local-authority housing was given away, we would probably still have around 12 per cent of the population renting and unlikely to benefit from inheritance. It is therefore a problem that is unlikely to go away. Arguably it is possible to develop policies to extend owner-occupation that might reduce this inequality (see Saunders, 1990, Chapter 6), but it probably cannot be eradicated. We are therefore likely to move from the situation thirty years ago where a small minority of people – generally the children of landlords – would inherit house property, to a situation in another forty years' time where the majority of the population are likely to inherit. Housing inheritance will therefore be widely spread but whether it will be possible to justify a label, such as 'a nation of inheritors', is more doubtful. Moreover, as we have sought to argue above, we should not automatically assume that the spread of housing inheritance will bring greater equality. People will inherit in very different ways and do very different things with their inheritance. It is the outcome of these events that will really affect the distribution of income and wealth rather than the simple presence or absence of property inheritance.

Countervailing trends

The preceding discussion assumes that housing inheritance will grow in line with our projections. But this makes the assumption that other things remain equal. This is doubtful to say the least. As we have indicated already, there are a number of countervailing tendencies that become stronger as property inheritance grows in size and significance. The first of these is what has been termed 'premature equity extraction'. Even today only 40 per cent of home owners' equity is released through inheritance. The remaining 60 per cent is released through a variety of means including moving down market, remortgaging or moving to areas where equivalent or better property is cheaper. This proportion could easily increase. The financial institutions have begun to realize the enormous amount of wealth 'locked up' in peoples homes and they are keen to unlock some of it. House owners are being encouraged to borrow against their property to buy boats, second homes, holidays, health care and education, with a view to this loan being repaid out of income but secured against their property.

It is difficult to speculate about the extent to which premature equity extraction by home owners in their middle life will grow. Some of the equity may be put into alternative and better investments that will add to estates rather than diminish them. However, there is a growing undercurrent of right-wing opinion that equity could be taken out to meet the costs of health care and one can see the temptation to take advantage of this untapped wealth. It would be ironic indeed if the Conservative party, the party of home owners, was to move in the direction of forcing owners to realize equity in their homes. While such ideas were clearly very influenced by the boom in the housing market, it should not be thought they have no relevance today. Despite price falls, the level of equity remains very high. Indeed, because total equity withdrawal from the housing market has increased sharply over the decade, it has become a significant part of total personal disposable income (including inheritances it stood at around 10 per cent of disposable income in 1988 – *Barings Review*, 1989). Such additional income undermines efforts to restrain consumer spending via wage curbs, though higher interest rates may force households to utilize the income to service existing debt. What it does indicate is that for a considerable number of households wages are only one source of their total disposable income and that governments will have an ever-more complex task in seeking to regulate their behaviour in line with macro-economic targets. This could result in a tighter policy on inheritance and on equity extraction in general.

Earlier we discussed equity extraction by the elderly home-owners themselves and this certainly remains one of the most potent sources of leakage from accumulated housing wealth. Until around fifteen years ago, most elderly owners had little option but to leave their homes to their beneficiaries even if they had to spend their old age in poverty. The mechanisms for equity release simply did not exist. Indeed, even letting out spare space was a option most did not take up yet, elsewhere (e.g. in the USA), this has been a commonplace solution. The elderly home-owner in Britain was 'capital rich but income poor'. Today, however, a variety of possibilities exist, including home-income plans, home-equity release schemes and annuity loans, as well as a range of specialist housing specifically marketed at the elderly home-owner. For those needing or wanting care, there are private residential homes for which they must pay. The costs are often very high (reflecting the level of care provided) and residents will need to sell up their property to live there. With costs in 1990 running at £8,000 to £15,000 a year per person, it would not take many years to eat up the entire housing equity anyone may have realized. There are also sheltered-housing developments that through design and/or by the provision of alarm systems and/or wardens are intended to meet the needs of the elderly. Some now go so far as to incorporate the spectrum of needs within the same complex. The financial arrangements vary but, typically, residents are assumed to be applying the cash from a previous property. This is often a critical factor in keeping the annual costs of their new home in line with their income.

The increase in house prices over the last two decades has resulted in a rise in the proportion of the price covered by a mortgage (for first-time buyers). This increase in indebtedness might be thought to diminish the equity in housing but, in reality, most households move and, taking advantage of house-price inflation, they buy a larger property though often with a proportionately smaller mortgage. Thus over time the level of outstanding debt on a property tends to fall in relation to its current price. Certainly, mortgage terms have become longer as a means of spreading debt and reducing monthly payments, but this does not appear to have resulted in any substantial erosion of the equity left to beneficiaries. Generational mortgages that require the beneficiaries rather than the original mortgage holder to repay the debt have been introduced in Japan in response to very high house prices. Clearly this device provides a good way of reducing mortgage costs during the lifetime of the benefactor and, with price inflation, should mean that beneficiaries can clear the debt and still realize the equity. While it is very unlikely such devices would be introduced in the UK it demonstrates the point that new approaches to mortgaging could be developed that might have an impact on equity transfer.

This raises the question of a longer-term shift in attitudes to property and property inheritance. For the current generation of the elderly, there is still a very strong desire to pass on property to children, although there is some evidence this is weakening. They are very conscious of the material advances made in their own lifetimes and concerned to consolidate that position for their successors. However, it is possible that succeeding generations will not take the same view. If the material comfort of children is visibly secure, parents may themselves feel under less pressure to pass on the full value of their estate. Moreover, their children may encourage their parents to make fuller use of their assets during their lifetime. Any such change in attitudes will not be universal. It will rest upon the varied circumstances of individual households. In making this point it is important not to lose sight of the way households and families have changed. The nuclear family of two adults and two children is no longer dominant. Single-person households with or without children are equally important and this may have important implications for bequeathing behaviour in the future. For many households there will be no immediate successors and that must influence their behaviour.

Attitudes and behaviour are shaped within a context that is not of an individual household's making. The government has the capacity to alter the taxation regime to produce a different response than at present. It might also take the view that the 'unearned increment' represented by housing equity should be utilized during the benefactor's lifetime or not passed on in full to the beneficiary. We have already mentioned the interest expressed regarding the use of equity to meet health-care costs. As the size of the retired population grows in relation to the workforce, so the pressures to 'draw down' some of that stored wealth may increase. Similarly, there have been suggestions that some form of taxation should be introduced on the proceeds of the sale of property. In the USA such proceeds are eligible for taxation unless the cash realized is put back into the next property. Such schemes could be introduced as could a more punitive regime regarding the taxation of estates. All of these possibilities lie within the remit of a government and as circumstance change and develop over the next decades, it is possible more will be done to confront this new situation. Mention has been made of the macro-economic effects of the spending arising from equity extraction in general and this may become a matter of greater concern with respect to the overall management of the economy. If so, it might trigger some of the developments we mention above.

Any moves to restrict the financial benefits of home ownership would, of course, be highly contentious in political terms. The withdrawal or restriction of mortgage tax relief has remained on the agenda and it is conceivable that a package of reforms could be introduced that also addressed the housing-equity question. The politics of this would be very complex and any changes would probably have to be staged over a long period of time. However, it might be possible to introduce policy initiatives into the area of housing equity by means of the provision of incentives to utilize the accumulated wealth. This may be viewed more positively than direct taxation and therefore have greater political appeal. It is our view that there may be considerable change in this area in future years. For reasons of macro-economic management, the functioning of the housing market, the pressures on public spending and the issue of inequality, we believe it is possible that new policies will be introduced regarding housing wealth.

In the short term our attention is focused on the problems of the existing housing market and the possibilities or otherwise of extending home ownership to 70 per cent or more of the population. While inheritance has been highlighted as a major issue today, we have shown in this book that, in reality, its full potential will only be realized in the next three decades (assuming all else remains equal). In other words, only when the first goal of achieving and sustaining a nation of home owners is realized can we really expect to understand and confront the objective of creating a nation of inheritors. As this book makes very apparent, there is much that could happen to confound the achievement of this second goal.

REFERENCES AND BIBLIOGRAPHY

Amex Bank Review (1990) 26 February, Vol. 17, no. 2, pp. 3–4.

Atkinson, A. B. (1971) The distribution of wealth and the individual life cycle, *Oxford Economic Papers* (NS), Vol. 23, pp. 239–54.

Atkinson, A. B. (1972) *Unequal Shares*, Penguin Books, Harmondsworth.

Atkinson, A. B. (1983) *The Economics of Inequality* 2/e, Clarendon Press.

Atkinson, R. (1989) *Mortgage Interest Relief: Time for Abolition*, Bow Paper Publications, London.

— Badcock, B. (1989) Homeownership and the accumulation of real wealth, *Space and Society*, Vol. 7, no. 1, pp. 69–91.

Ball, M. (1976) Owner occupation, in M. Edwards, F. Gray, S. Merrett and J. Swann (eds.) *Housing and Class in Britain*, Political Economy of Housing Workshop, London.

Ball, M. (1988) The international restructuring of housing production, in M. Ball, M. Harloe, and M. Martens (eds.) *Housing and Social Change in Europe and the USA*, Routledge, London.

Bank of England (1985), The housing finance market: recent growth in perspective, *Bank of England Quarterly Bulletin*, pp. 80–91. March.

Barings Review (1989) October, no. 28, pp. 1–4, 9.

Blinder, A. S. (1973) A model of inherited wealth, *Quarterly Journal of Economics*, Vol. 87, pp. 608–26.

BMRB (1989) *Housing and Saving*, Building Societies Association, London.

Boleat, M. (1986) *The Building Society Industry*, Allen & Unwin, London.

Boleat, M. and Coles, A. (1987) *The Mortgage Market*, Allen & Unwin, London.

Building Societies Association (1986) Home improvements, *BSA Bulletin*, no. 48, pp. 6–8.

Building Societies Association (1987) *Building Society News*, Vol. 7, no. 4.

Building Societies Association (1988) *BSA Bulletin*, no. 55, pp. ??–?.

Building Societies Association (1989) *Housing in Britain*.

Chen, A. and Jensen, H. (1986) The home equity resource: will older homeowners use it?, *Journal of Housing for the Elderly*, Vol. 4, pp. 5–20.

Coles, A. (1989a) Risk and the Future of the Mortgage Market, *Housing Finance*, no. 4, p. 8

Coles, A. (1989b) The home improvement market, *Housing Finance*, 3 July, pp. 24–6.

Congdon, T. (1982) *The Coming Boom in Housing Credit*, L. Messell & Co., London, June.

Cooper, S. (1985) *Public Housing and Private Property*, Gower, Aldershot.

Counsell, G. (1988) The property lottery, *The Independent*, 3 June.

Davis, E. P. and Saville, I. D. (1982) Mortgage lending and the housing market, *Bank of England Quarterly Bulletin*, pp. 390–8, September.

Department of the Environment (1977) *Housing Policy: Technical Volume* (Part I), HMSO, London.

Department of the Environment (1987) *1985 Based Estimates of Numbers of Households in England, the Regions, Counties, Metropolitan Districts and London Boroughs 1985–2001*, Government Statistical Service, London.

Diamond Commission (1975) *Royal Commission on the Distribution of Income and Wealth: Initial Report on the Standing Conference* (report no. 1) Cmnd 6171, HMSO, London.

Diamond Commission (1977) *Royal Commission on the Distribution of Income and Wealth: Third Report on the Standing Conference* (report no. 5), Cmnd 6999, HMSO, London.

Dicks, M. (1988) The demographics of housing demand: household formation and the growth of owner-occupation, *Bank of England Discussion Paper*, no. 32, London.

Downs, A. (1981) Too much capital for housing?, *The Brookings Bulletin*, Vol. 17, no. 1, pp. 1–5.

Drayson, S. J. (1985) The housing finance market: recent growth in perspective, *Bank of England Quarterly Review*, pp. 80–91.

Duncan, A. (1981) Do house prices rise that much? A comparison of Britain and Europe, *Urban and Regional Studies* (W.P. 70), University of Sussex.

Dupis, A. (1989) Consumption sectors: a comparative study of housing experiences in New Zealand and Britain, 1840–1988 (unpublished MA thesis, Department of Sociology, University of Canterbury, New Zealand).

The Economist, (1988a) Growing rich again, 9 April, pp. 13–14.

The Economist, (1988b) Through the roof, 21 May, p. 41.

Evandrou, M. and Victor, C. (1988) *Differentiation in Late Life: Social Class and Housing Tenure Cleavages* (Welfare State Programme WSP 30), Suntory Toyota International Centre for Economics and Related Disciplines, London School of Economics.

Eversley, D. and Kollmann, W. (1982) *Population Change and Social Planning*, Edward Arnold, London.

Farmer, M. K. and Barrell, R. (1981) Entrepreneurship and government policy: the case of the housing market, *Journal of Public Policy*, Vol. 1, no. 3, pp. 307–32.

Fijalkowski-Bereday, G. Z. (1950) The equalizing effects of the death duties, *Oxford Economic Papers* (NS), Vol. 2, pp. 176–96.

Foley, P. (1986) House price boom or bust, *Lloyds Bank Economic Bulletin*, Vol. 93, pp. 1–4.

Forrest, R. and Murie, A. (1987) The affluent home owner: labour market position and the shaping of housing histories, in N. Thrift and P. Williams (eds.) *Class and Space*, Routledge, London.

Forrest, R. and Murie, A. (1989) Differential accumulation: wealth inheritance and housing policy reconsidered, *Policy and Politics*, Vol. 17, no. 1, pp. 25–39.

Forrest, R., Murie, A. and Williams, P. (1990) *Home Ownership: Differentiation and Fragmentation*, Unwin Hyman, London.

Gibbs Report (1984) *Housing Finance into the 1990s: Report of a Working Group under the Chairmanship of Mr Michael Gibbs*, Building Societies Association, London.

Guardian (1990) 20 April, p. 12.

Halifax Building Society (1989) Press Release, 27 December.

Halifax Building Society (1990) Press Release, 10 April.

Hamnett, C. (1984) Housing the two nations: socio-tenurial polarisation in England and Wales, *Urban Studies*, Vol. 21, no. 3, pp. 389–405.

Hamnett, C. (1985) The unjust legacy, *New Society*, 23 August, p. 277.

Hamnett, C. (1986a) Making money from home ownership, *New Society* 27 June, pp. 18.

Hamnett, C. (1986b) How much lending leaks into luxuries?, *Guardian*, 17 September, p. 25.

Hamnett, C. (1988) Regional variations in house prices and house price inflation in Britain 1969–1988, *Royal Bank of Scotland Review*, no. 159, pp. 28–40.

Hamnett, C. (1989a) Regional variations in house prices and house price inflation in Britain, 1969–1989, *Journal of Valuation*, Vol. 7, no. 4.

Hamnett, C. (1989b) The political geography of housing in contemporary Britain in J. Mohan (ed.) *The Political Geography of Contemporary Britain*, Macmillan, London.

Hamnett, C., Harmer, M. and Williams, P. (1989) *Housing Inheritance: A National Survey of its Scale and Impact*, Housing Research Foundation, London, pp. 342–60.

Hansard (1894) Finance Bill, 7 May, clms. 519–22.

Hansard (1909) Vol. 4, clm. 548.

Hansard (1946) Vol. 421, clm. 1836.

Harbury, C. D. (1962) Inheritance and the distribution of personal wealth in Britain, *Economic Journal*, Vol. 72, pp. 854–68.

Harbury, C. D. and Hitchins, D. M. (1976) The inheritances of top wealth leavers: some further evidence, *Economic Journal*, Vol. 86, pp. 321-6.

Harbury, C. D. and Hitchins, D. M. (1977) Women, wealth and inheritance, *Economic Journal*, Vol. 87, pp. 124-31.

Harbury, C. D. and McMahon, P. C. (1973) Inheritance and the characteristics of top wealth leavers in Britain, *Economic Journal*, Vol. 83, pp 810–33.

Harmer, M. and Hamnett, C. (1990) Regional variations in housing inheritance in Britain, *Area*, Vol. 22, no. 1, pp. 1–15.

Harre, R. (1979) *Social Being*, Blackwell, Oxford.

Harris. R. and Hamnett, C. (1987) The myth of the Promised Land: the social diffusion of home ownership in Britain and North America, *Annals of the Association of American Geographers*, Vol. 77, no. 2, pp. 173–90.

Heseltine, M. (1979) in Hansard, Vol. 967, 17 May.

Hills, J. (1989) *Distributional Effects of Housing Subsidies in the United Kingdom*, Welfare State Programme (WSP 44), Suntory Toyota International Centre for Economics and Related Disciplines, London School of Economics.

Hinton, C. (1989) *Using Your Home as Capital*, Age Concern, London (revised edn.).

Hogg, S. (1987) A nation of inheritors, *The Independent*, 30 November.

H.M. Treasury (1990) Supplementary analyses and index in *The Government's Expenditure Plans 1990-91 to 1992-93* (Cmnd 1021), HMSO, London.

Holmans, A. (1983) Demography and housing in Britain: recent developments and aspects for research (paper presented at the ESRC Housing Conference, Bristol).

Holmans, A. (1986a) *Flows of Funds Associated with House Purchase for Owner Occupation in the United Kingdom 1977–1984 and Equity Withdrawal from House Purchase Finance* (Government Economic Service Working Paper no. 92), Departments of the Environment and Transport, London.

Holmans, A. (1986b) Owner occupied house property in England: its market value in 1977 analysed according to the marital status, sex and age of the owners (mimeo), Department of the Environment, London.

Holmans, A. (1990) *House Prices: Changes Through Time at National and Sub-National Level* (Government Economic Service Working Paper no. 110), Department of the Environment, London.

Holmans, A., Nandy, S. and Brown, A. C. (1987) Household Formation and Dissolution and Housing Tenure: A longitudinal perspective, *Social Trends*, Vol. 17, pp. 20–8.

Horsman, E. G. (1978) Inheritance in England and Wales: the evidence provided by wills, *Oxford Economic Papers* (NS), Vol. 30, pp. 409–22.

Inland Revenue (1857) *First Annual Report*, HMSO, London.

Inland Revenue (1905) *48th Annual Report* (Cd 2633), HMSO, London.

Inland Revenue (1920) *63rd Annual Report* (Cmd 1083), HMSO, London.

Inland Revenue (1950) *92nd Annual Report* (Cmd 8052), HMSO, London.

Inland Revenue (1984) *Inland Revenue Statistics, 1984*, HMSO, London.

Inland Revenue (1987) *Inland Revenue Statistics, 1986*, HMSO, London.

Inland Revenue (1989) *Inland Revenue Statistics, 1988*, HMSO, London.

Inland Revenue (1990) *Inland Revenue Statistics, 1989*, HMSO, London.

Jenkins, S. P. and Maynard, A. K. (1983) Intergenerational continuities in housing, *Urban Studies*, Vol. 20, pp. 431–8.

Kay, J. A. and King, M. A. (1986) *The British Tax System*, Oxford University Press (fourth edn.).

Kemeny, J. and Thomas, A. (1983) Capital leakage from owner occupied housing, *Policy and Politics*. Vol. 12, no. 1, pp. 13–30.

Kendig, H. (1984) Housing tenure and generational equity, *Ageing and Society*, Vol. 4, no. 3, pp. 249–72.

Kilroy, B. (1979) Housing finance: why so privileged?, *Lloyds Bank Review*, no. 133, pp. 37–52, June.

Kleinman, M. and Whitehead, C. (1988) British housing since 1979: has the system changed?, *Housing Studies*, Vol. 3, no. 1, pp. 3–19.

Lawson, N. (1987) Mansion House Speech, November.

Leather, P. (1987) Home income plan survey (mimeo), School of Advanced Urban Studies, University of Bristol.

Leather, P. (1990) The potential and implications of home equity release in old age, *Housing Studies*, Vol. 5, no. 1, pp. 3–13.

Leather, P. and Wheeler, R. (1988) *Making Use of Home Equity in Old Age*, Building Societies Association, London.

Leigh Pemberton, R. (1979) Banks, building societies and personal savings, *National Westminster Bank Quarterly Review*, pp. 2–10, May.

Lewis, J. and Townsend, A. (1989) *The North–South Divide: Regional Change in Britain in the 1980s*, Paul Chapman, London.

Lowe, S. (1987) New patterns of wealth: the growth of owner occupation, in R. Walker and G. Parker (eds.) *Money Matters*, Sage, London.

Lowe, S. (1988) The consequences of equity withdrawal from the housing market for living standards (mimeo), International Housing Research Conference, Amsterdam, June.

Lowe, S., and Watson, S. (1989a) Equity withdrawal from the housing market: a re-appraisal (mimeo), British Sociological Association, Sociology, Environment and Architecture Study Group, February.

Lowe, S. (1989b) *From First-Time Buyers to Last-Time Sellers*, Department of Social Policy and Social Work, University of York.

Mackintosh, S., Leather, P. and Means, R. (1990) *The Housing Finance Implications of an Ageing Society*, School for Advanced Urban Studies, University of Bristol.

McDowell, L. (1982) Housing deprivation in longitudinal analysis, *Area*, Vol. 14, no. 2, pp. 144–50.

Mintel (1987) *New Wealth and the Individual* (Special Report), London.

Morgan Grenfell Economic Review (1987) Housing inheritance and wealth, no. 45, November.

Meullbauer, J. and Murphy, A. (1988) *UK House Prices and Migration: Economic and Investment Implications*, Shearson Lehman Hutton, London.

Munro, M. (1988) Housing wealth and inheritance, *Journal of Social Policy*, Vol. 17, no. 4, pp. 417–36.

Murie, A. and Forrest, R. (1980) Wealth, inheritance and housing policy, *Policy and Politics*, Vol. 8, no. 1, pp. 1–19.

Nationwide Building Society (1985) *House Prices over the Last Thirty Years*, London, April.

Nationwide Building Society (1986) *Housing as an Investment*, London, April.

Nationwide Building Society (1987) *House Prices: The North–South Divide*, London, April.

NEDO (1987) *Construction Forecasts 1987, 1988, 1989*, HMSO, London.

OPCS (various years) *General Household Survey*, HMSO, London.

OPCS (1987) *Population Projections 1985–2025*, no. 15, London, p. 2.

OPCS (1989) *Population Trends*, no. 55, p. 59, HMSO, London.

Oulton, N. (1976) Inheritance and the distribution of wealth, *Oxford Economic Papers*,

(NS), Vol. 28, pp. 86–101.

Pahl, R. (1975) *Whose City?*, Penguin Books, Harmondsworth.

Pawley, M. (1985) Playing reverse monopoly with houses. *Guardian*, 26 June.

Priemus, H. (1987) Economics and demographic stagnation: housing and housing policy. *Housing Studies*, Vol. 2, no. 1, pp. 19–29.

Pryor F. L. (1973) Simulation of the impact of social and economic institutions on the size distribution of income and wealth, *American Economic Journal*, Vol 63.

Roof (1990) Interview with Mark Boleat, March, pp. 23–5.

Royal Commission on the Distribution of Income and Wealth (1975) *Initial Report on the Standing Conference* (Report no. 1) (Cmnd 6171), HMSO, London.

Royal Commission on the Distribution of Income and wealth (1977) *Third Report on the Standing Conference* (Report no. 5) (Cmnd 6999), HMSO, London.

Rubinstein, W. D. (1986) *Wealth and Inequality in Britain*, Faber & Faber, London.

Russell, B. (1984) *A History of Western Philosophy*, Counterpoint, London.

Sandford, C. T. (1967) Taxing inheritance and capital gains (Hobart Paper 32), Institute of Economic Affairs, London.

Sandford, C. T. (1971) *Taxing Personal Wealth*, Allen & Unwin, London.

Saunders, P. (1978) Domestic property and social class, *International Journal of Urban and Regional Research*.

Saunders, P. (1986) Comment on Dunleavy and Preteceille, *Society and Space*, Vol. 4, pp. 155–63.

Saunders, P. (1988) The sociology of consumption: a new research agenda, in P. Otnes (ed.) *The Sociology of Consumption*, Solum Forlag, Oslo.

Saunders, P. (1990) *A Nation of Home Owners*, Unwin Hyman, London.

Saunders, P. and Harris, C. (1987) Biting the nipple: consumer preferences and state welfare, Urban and Regional Studies Working Paper, University of Kent.

Saunders, P. and Harris, C. (1988) Home ownership and capital gains, Urban and Regional Studies Working Paper no. 64, University of Sussex.

Sayer A. and Morgan, K. (1985) A modern industry in a declining region: links between theory, method and policy in Massey, D. and Meegan, R. (eds.) *Politics and Method*, Methuen, London.

Scholen, K. and Chen, Y. P. (1980) *Unlocking Home Equity for the Elderly*, Ballinger, Cambridge, Mass.

Spencer, P. (1987) *UK House Prices: Not an Inflation Signal*, Economic Series, Credit Suisse First Boston, September.

Sternlieb, G. and Hughes, J. W. (1978) The post-shelter society, *The Public Interest*, pp. 39–47.

Stow Report (1979) *Mortgage Finance in the 1980s: Report of a Working Party under the Chairmanship of Mr Ralph Stow*, Building Societies Association, London.

The Sunday Times (1988) 30 October.

Swenarton, M. and Taylor, S. (1985) The scale and nature of the growth of owner occupation in Britain between the wars, *Economic History Review*, no. 38, pp. 373–92.

Tait, A. A. (1960) Death duties in Britain, *Public Finance*, Vol. 15, pp. 346–65.

Thatcher, M. (1979) Hansard, Vol. 967, Cols 79–80, 15 May.

Thorns, D. (1982) Industrial restructuring and change in the labour and property markets in Britain, *Environment and Planning A*, Vol. 14, pp. 745–65.

Todd, J. E. and Jones, L. M. (1972) *Matrimonial Property*, HMSO, London.

Tory Reform Group (1979) *An End to the Council Landlord*. TRG, London.

UBS Phillips & Drew (1989) UK Economics, *Economic Briefing*, no. 213.

Vision (1989) *Towards 2000*, winter, pp. 34–9 (published for the Halifax Building Society), London.

Walker, P. (1989) British economy in the 1990s (Westminster Lecture), 10 April.

Wedgwood, J. (1929) *The Economics of Inheritance*, Routledge & Sons, London.

Whalley, J. (1974) Estate duty as a 'voluntary' tax: evidence from stamp duty statistics, *Economic Journal*, Vol. 84, pp. 638–44.

Wheeler, R. (1986) *The Needs of Elderly Owner Occupiers: A Discussion Paper*, Building Societies Association, London.
Whitehead, C. (1979) Why owner-occupation?, *CES Review*, no. 6, Centre for Environmental Studies.
Wise, D. (1985) *The Economics of Ageing*, University of Chicago Press, Chicago, Ill.

INDEX

account duty 143, 144
advantage 'informally inherited' 80
age: of beneficiaries 100; at death 71; and
    home ownership 70; and housing
    inheritance 113, 138
ageing society, social provision for 9; see
    also elderly people
Amex Bank Review 5, 151
annuities 155, 160
Asquith, H.H. 145
assets: composition at death 58-61, 63-4;
    relative importance 40-1; relative
    prices 153
Atkinson, A.B. 39, 76, 78
Atkinson, R. 7
Australia home ownership in 11, 152

Badcock, B. 31, 33
Ball, M. 30
Bank of England Quarterly Bulletin 45, 47,
    48-9, 50-1
Bank of Scotland equity-release
    scheme 43-5
banks: equity release schemes 43-5;
    mortgage lending 43
Barclays Bank equity-release scheme 45
Barings Review 160
Barrell, R. 32
beneficiaries: age 100; asset-rich, income
    poor 131; case studies 128-39;
    expenditure 116-18; as home-owners
    already 4, 70, 100-1, 129; numbers 97,
    157; regional distribution 101-2; social
    class 103-4; studying, problems
    of 97-8; tenure 103-4; use of
    inheritance 112, 113, 114, 115-19, 127
bequeathing: to charity 77, 81; of housing

wealth 92-4; laws and customs 77; and
    marital status 82-3, 89-91; patterns of
    79-84, 87-92; and sex 83-4, 88-9, 91;
    and trust funds 81
birth rate, low 65, 70
Blinder, A.S. 79
BMRB 75, 153
Boleat, Mark 8
Bow Group 7
Britain, see United Kingdom
Building Societies Association 11, 19, 26,
    33, 122, 124, 152, 153
building societies: and equity release 158;
    investment in 123, 124-5; traditional
    dominance 43

Canada: home ownership in 11, 152; house
    prices 152
capital accumulation: measurement
    of 31-2; sources of 36-8
capital gains, gross 31-2
capital gains tax 7; exemption from 30, 36,
    37; and higher prices 36-7
capital investment, housing wealth and 3
capital leakage 45, 63; measurement
    of 48-51
capital transfer tax, rates of 148
case studies 129-39; methodology 128-9;
    value of 127-8
Chamberlain, Austen 146
charitable bequests 77, 81
Chen, Y.P. 8, 155
children: housing inheritance used for 138;
    inheritance by 81, 82, 83, 84, 87-8, 91,
    94, 100, 104; number of 66; tenure, and
    parental tenure 106
choice 2, 9; government emphasis on 9;

paying for 9, 113
Churchill, Winston 146
'Code Napoleon' 77
Coles, A. 75
Congdon, T. 45
Conservative Party: and elderly home-
    owners 8; and home ownership 8, 152;
    and housing equity release 160; and
    inheritance 2, 96; and tax
    concessions 7
consumption cleavages 113
Cooper, S. 1
council tenants 2; future tenure 109–10;
    marginalisation 3–4; right-to-buy
    scheme 6, 8, 32, 74–5
Counsell, G. 26–7
Cripps, Sir Stafford 147
Currie, Edwina 113
cyclical house-price inflation 26–7, 29–30

Dalton, Hugh 147
Davis, E.P. 45–7
death: age at 71; and housing wealth 4, 5;
    rate, rising 65, 70
death duties: decline 147–9; development
    of 141–4; and distribution of
    wealth 145, 147, 149; and post-war
    settlement 147; reforms 144–5; as
    revenue producers 147; and social
    reform 145–6; as war tax 141, 146; see
    also tax concessions
debt, mortgage 160–1
demographic change 6; inheritance
    and 65–6
Diamond Commission (1975), see Royal
    Commission on the Distribution of
    Income and Wealth (1975)
distribution of housing inheritance,
    future 158–9
distribution of wealth: death duties
    and 145, 147, 149; housing inheritance
    and 39–40, 96–7; from large
    estates 82–3
divorce: and housing careers 69; and
    inheritance 69–70; owner-
    occupiers 69–70; and trading
    down 69–70; trends in 66
Dover, house prices 20
Down, County, house-prices 20
Downs, A. 12, 45
Drayson, S.J. 47
Duncan, A. 12, 31
Dupuis, A. 32

earnings, see incomes

East Anglia: average house-price
    inflation 24, 25, 26, 27; house
    prices 13, 20, 21, 23; housing
    inheritance in 102, 104, 105;
    inheritance use 119, 120; value of
    housing inheritance 103
East Midlands: average house-price
    inflation 24, 25, 26, 27; house
    prices 21, 22; housing inheritance in
    102, 104, 105; value of housing
    inheritance 103
economic conditions and inheritance 2,
    78–9
Economist, The 4, 34, 96, 113
Eden, Anthony 96, 110
Edinburgh, house prices 20
elderly people: equity release 8, 9, 110–11,
    114, 139, 155, 160; households,
    increase 67, 68, 69: housing
    options 155–6; housing wealth and
    155–6; increase in 6, 8, 9, 65, 69, 70;
    inheritance by 129, 130, 131; private
    residential homes 156, 160; sheltered
    housing 156, 160
England: estates containing housing 63;
    households, by age of head 67, 68;
    households, type 67, 68, 69; population
    changes 67
England and Wales: ageing population 6;
    charitable bequests 77; households
    decline 6
Environment, Department of 106
equity, see housing equity
estate duty 146, 147; and inheritance 81,
    82; exemptions 147; 'temporary' 144
estates: asset composition 58–61, 63–4;
    housing wealth in 6, 92; increase in 65,
    70; large 81, 82–3, 84; number
    containing housing 55–7, 58; size
    distribution 54–5; size and
    gender 89–91, 92–3; size, and value of
    housing 60, 61, 64; small 81, 82; value
    of housing in 57–8, 59, 60–1, 63, 156–7

families, changing composition 161
family size: decline in 66; and
    inheritance 78, 114; and poverty 78
Farmer, M.K. 32
fertility and social class 79
Fife, house-prices 20
Fijalkowski-Bereday, G.Z. 87
financial market: and financial
    investment 118, 119, 123, 125; and
    housing inheritance 123–5, 158
Financial Times index 32

first-time buyers: assistance 157; debt 160–1; reduced demand 153
Foley, P. 26
Forrest, R. 4, 96, 110, 114

Galsworthy, John 43
gender: and bequeathing patterns 83–4, 88–9; and estate size 89–91, 92–3
General Household Survey 70, 155
generational mortgages 161
Gibbs Report (1984) 124
Gladstone, W.E. 142, 143, 145
Glasgow: commissary records 92–3; house prices 20

Halifax Building Society 5, 13, 20, 27, 151
Hamnett, C. 9, 11, 19, 108, 125, 152
Hansard 144, 145, 147
Harbury, C.D. 79, 80
Harre, R. 127
Harris, C. 38, 114
Harris, R. 11, 152
Harrogate, house prices 20
health care privatization 139, 160, 161
Heseltine, M. 30–1
Hitchins, D.M. 80
Hogg, S. 96
Holmans, A. 5, 49–51, 65, 66, 69, 121, 122, 125, 151, 155
home improvement expenditure 118, 120, 122, 123, 157; and taxation 7, 43, 155
home ownership: and age 70; attitudes to 150–1; benefits of 3; compared to saving 12; as dominant tenure 1, 2, 4, 11, 39, 42, 151–4; future trends 70–5, 153, 154; and housing inheritance growth 156; incidence of 9; as investment 1, 11–12, 150–1; parental influence on 106; political implications of 2; promotion of 7; scale of equity extraction 47–8; social class and 4, 107–8; as source of wealth 6, 12, 30
home-equity plans, see housing equity
home-income plans, see housing equity
Horsman, E.G. 80–1, 84, 86, 87
house prices: cyclical inflation 26–7, 29–30; earnings compared to 5; fluctuation 5, 12–13, 151; and income, ratio 5, 13–19, 38, 151, 153; and inflation 13, and mortgage, ratio 151; north-south divide 26–7; rapid growth 11, 152; real 13, 31; regional differences 5, 19–29; rising 2, 3, 5, 152; slump 151; and tax concessions 8; trends 125, 126, 153
housing associations, right-to-buy scheme 8
housing careers, divorce and 69
housing equity: accumulation 30–1; analysis of extraction 48–51; appreciation, regional variation 34, 35; definition vii; as disposable income 160; growth 5; implied 35; premature extraction 43, 159–60; use of 8; withdrawal, compared to net cash withdrawal 51, 52
housing equity release 5, 7, 43–5, 123, 125, 126, 154–5, 159, 160; defined 48, 49, 50; by elderly 89, 110–11, 114, 139, 155, 160; from housing market 42–7; inheritance and 63; politics of 162; premature 43, 159–60; scale of extraction 47–8
housing inheritance: age and 113, 138; analysis 53–4; attitudes, changing 161; benefits of 96; case studies 128–39; and cross-regional flows of funds 121; and demographic trends 65–6; differential values 110; and distribution of wealth 96–7; divorce and 69–70; effects of 113–14, 115, 119–20; in equity extraction 51, 63; factors affecting 11; financial market and 123–5; future of 70–5, 154–8; future distribution 108–10, 158–9; generational bias 100; growth, home ownership and 156; by home-owners 4, 70, 100–1, 129; and housing equity release 154–5; impacts on housing market 114–15, 120–3; importance in UK 151–3; inequality and 95, 96–7, 99–100, 103, 107, 110, 112, 114; parental tenure in 107; regional flows 102–3; regional inequality and 96–7, 103; regional variation 101–2; sale of 115–16; social class and 95–6, 101, 103, 107–8, 110; social division and 8–9; as surplus wealth 138; uses 112, 113, 114, 115–19, 120, 127; value of 103
house purchase as investment 30–1
house sales, taxation on 161
house types, regional differences 20
households: as beneficiaries 98–9, 157, 159; changing composition 6, 67–9, 161; elderly, increase 67, 68, 69; formation rates 66, 67–9; married-couple 67; one-parent 67; retired people 67, 68, 69
housing: excess of supply 74; importance in inheritance 51

housing market, equity extraction
    from 42-7, 154-5; gluts 113; and
    housing inheritance 114-15, 120-3; net
    cash withdrawal 47, 48. transactors 49
housing wealth 6; bequeathing 92-4; and
    capital investment 3; death and 4, 5; in
    distribution of wealth 39-40; and
    elderly 155-6; factors affecting 11;
    future trends 153, 154; growth 39-42;
    inflation and 3, 5; real or fictitious 3;
    sudden importance of 4, 152
Hughes, J.W. 12

implied equity 35
incomes: growth 16; and house prices,
    ratio 5, 13-19, 38, 151, 153; net rises
    in 38
inequality: housing inheritance and 95,
    96-7, 99-100, 103, 107, 110, 112, 114,
    159; inheritance and 76-8, 79, 95,
    99-100, 112
inflation and housing wealth 3, 5, 13, 32
inheritance: and charitable bequests 77; by
    children 66, 81, 82, 83, 84, 87-8, 91, 94,
    100, 104; customs 129; and dependence
    on State 9; distribution of wealth
    and 76-9; economic conditions
    and 78-9; effects of 2, 79; family size
    and 78; housing, importance in 51; and
    inequality 76-8, 79, 95, 99-100, 112;
    laws and customs 77; longevity and 6;
    marriage customs and 78; process,
    nature of 103; rates of 148; by
    relatives 81, 82, 83, 84, 142, 145; social
    conditions and 78-9; as social
    mechanism 76; by spouse 66, 69, 81,
    82, 83, 84, 87-8, 91, 93; studies
    of 76-85
inheritance tax 7, 77; concessions 6,
    138-9, 141, 147-9; consanguinity
    rules 142; and government 141
inheritors, see beneficiaries
Inland Revenue 36, 53-4, 57, 63, 84, 89, 91,
    97, 99-100, 105, 141, 142, 145, 146, 147
interest-only loans 155

Japan, generational mortgages 161
Jenkins, S.P. 106
Jones, L.M. 91

Kay, J.A. 7
Kemeny, J. 45, 48
Kendig, H. 152
Kilroy, B. 45
King, M.A. 7

Labour party: and death duties 147; and
    inequality 81
labour-market conditions, owner-occupied
    market and 19
last-time sales, and equity release 5, 50, 51,
    53
law, inheritance in 77
Lawson, Nigel 7, 96, 110
Leather, P. 9, 155
legacy duty 141-2, 143, 144, 146, 147
Leigh Pemberton, R. 45
Liberal party and death duties 145, 149
Lloyd George, David 77, 145-6, 149
London: average house-price inflation 24,
    25, 26, 27; compared to regions 23, 24,
    27-9; and cyclical price inflation 29-30;
    house prices 5, 20, 21, 23, 26, 27;
    house-price fluctuation 12-13; housing
    equity appreciation 34, 35, 36; housing
    inheritance in 102, 104, 105; income-
    prices ratio 17; inheritance use 119,
    120; property types 20; public
    housing 5; semi-detached house-
    prices 20; wills study 85-92, 98
longevity: increased 6, 65, 69, 70; and
    inheritance 6; women 89, 91
Lowe, S. 48, 51, 113, 114, 115, 155

McDowell, L. 106
Mackintosh, S. 9
Macleod, Iain 2
McMahon, P.C. 80
Margate, house prices 20
marital status and bequeathing patterns 67,
    82-3, 89-91, 93-4, 134
marriage: customs and inheritance 78;
    rates 67, 69; trends in 66
Maynard, A.K. 106
Means, R. 9
men, housing wealth bequeathed 92-3;
    longevity 69
Meullbauer, J. 42
Midland Bank equity-release scheme 45
Midlands: average house-price
    inflation 27; property types 20; static
    house prices 19; use of inheritance 119,
    120
Mintel 97, 100, 113, 127
moderate wealth leavers, and housing
    wealth 85, 92
Morgan Grenfell Economic Review 2-3,
    53-4, 57, 74, 96, 97, 113, 115, 119, 127
Morgan, K. 128
mortgage debt 160-1
mortgage and house price, ratio 151

mortgage interest rates: high 5, 7; negative 30, 36
mortgage lending: for consumption 45-7, 48; as equity release 45-7; structural change 43
mortgage markets, transactors in 49
mortgage-interest tax relief (MINTR) 30, 36-7; and higher prices 36-7; withdrawal 7, 162
mortgages, generational 161
Munro, M. 92-3, 113
Murie, A. 4, 96, 110, 114
Murphy, A. 42

Nandy, S. 66, 69
Nat West equity-release scheme 45
Nationwide Building Society 13, 20, 27, 32, 125
'net cash withdrawal' 47, 48-51; compared with equity withdrawal 51, 52
Netherlands, house prices 152
New Zealand, home ownership in 152
NOP survey 98, 99
North West region: average house-price inflation 24, 25, 26, 27; house prices 21, 22; housing inheritance in 102, 103, 104, 105
Northern Ireland: assets, relative importance 63; average house-price inflation 24, 25; estates containing housing 63; house prices 21, 22, 63; population changes 67
Northern region: average house-price inflation 24, 25, 26, 27; house prices 5, 20, 21, 23; housing inheritance in 102, 104, 105; inheritance use 119, 120; static house prices 19; value of housing inheritance 103

one-parent households, increase 67
OPCS 71, 72, 121
Oulton, N. 79
owner-occupied sector: and labour-market conditions 19; rapid expansion 11; value of 41
owner-occupiers: divorce 69-70; moving, and equity withdrawal 49, 50, 51, 53
ownership, see home ownership; property

Pahl, R. 12
parents: home-owning, increase 70; social class 103-7; tenure 104, 106
Pawley, M. 47, 48
pensions, death duties and 145
personal wealth: distribution of 39-40; growth in 154; housing in 5-6, 11,

39-42, 153-4; patterns 5-6
population: changes in 66-7; slow aggregate increase 65, 70
poverty: family size and 78; and public housing 4
premature equity extraction 43, 159-60
Priemus, H. 152
private rented sector, decline 3, 123
probate duty origins 141, 142, 143, 144
probate records, as data source 79-80
probate valuation, exact 85
property: attitudes, changing 161; confidence in 2; inheritance value 2-3; see also housing
Pryor, F.L. 79
public housing: rapid increase 11; residualisation 3-4; right-to-buy scheme 8

regional house prices: and London's 23, 24; inflation rates 24, 25
regional inequality, and housing inheritance 96-7, 103
regional variation: in estates containing housing 62-3; in house prices 19-29; housing equity appreciation 34, 35; housing inheritance 101-2; in inheritance use 119, 120; rates of price inflation 19, 24, 25, 26-9; in tenure 102
relatives, inheritance by 81, 82, 83, 84, 142, 145
remarriage: rates 69; trends in 66, 69
remortgaging 50; and equity release 7, 42, 43, 155; in situ 42, 49
rental sector: erosion 123; growth 120, 122
'rents into mortgages' scheme 8
repossession, risk of 45
residential homes, private 156, 160
residential property: number of estates containing 55-7, 58; in personal wealth 40-2; value in estates 57-8; see also housing
retired people, households 67, 68, 69
rich people: beneficiaries of 80; and housing wealth 85
Roof magazine 8
Royal Bank of Scotland equity-release scheme 45
Royal Commission on the Distribution of Income and Wealth (1975) (Diamond Commission) 11, 39, 81-4, 87, 89, 105
Rubinstein, W.D. 108, 149
Russell, B. 141

Sandford, C.T. 143, 146, 147
Saunders, P. 3, 30, 32, 33, 36, 37, 38, 95,

97, 103, 107, 110, 114, 159
Saville, I.D. 45–7
savings: enforced 36, 37; growth in 154; home ownership compared to 12
Sayer, A. 128
Scholen, K. 8, 155
Scotland: assets, relative importance 63; average house-price inflation 24, 25, 26, 27; estates containing housing 63; home ownership in 102; house prices 21, 22; housing inheritance in 101, 102, 103; owner-occupation 63, 102; parental home ownership 106; population changes 67; 'rents into mortgages' scheme 8; Sasine records 92; tenure, dominant 102
second homes 120, 122, 123, 157
semi-detached houses, regional price variations 20, 22
share ownership 154
Shaw, George Bernard 43
sheltered housing 156, 160; resale 156
sitting-tenant council buyers 32, 33
Snowden, Philip 146
social class: divisions, weakening 97, 110; and home ownership 107–8; and housing inheritance 95–6, 101, 103, 107–8, 110; parental 103–7
social conditions and inheritance 78–9
social division and inheritance 8–9
social reform, death duties and 145–6
Somerset House 97
South East region: average house-price inflation 19, 24, 25, 26, 27; cyclical price inflation 26–7, 29–30; house-price fluctuation 13, 20, 21, 23; house-price slump 151; housing equity appreciation 34, 35, 36; housing inheritance in 101–2, 103; income-prices ratio 17; inheritance use 119, 120; parental home-ownership 106; property types 20; regional flow of inheritance 102, 103; tenure, dominant 102; value of housing inheritance 103
South West region: average house-price inflation 24, 25, 26, 27; house prices 13, 20, 21, 23; inheritance in 102, 104, 105
South Yorkshire, house prices 20
Spencer, P. 33, 36
spinsters, estate size 91
spouses: and death duties 147; inheritance by 66, 69, 81, 82, 83, 84, 87–8, 91, 93
Sternlieb, G. 12

Stockport, house prices 20
Stow Report (1979) 124
succession duty 142, 143, 144, 146, 147
Swenarton, M. 152

Tait, A.A. 147
tax concessions 30; inheritance and 138–9, 141, 147–9; as subsidy 36–8; see also mortgage interest tax relief (MINTR)
taxation: and inheritance 77; and home ownership 6–7; on house sales 161
Taylor, S. 152
tenure: changing, and equity release 7; dominant form 1, 3, 4, 151–2; and equity release 5, 7; parental 104, 106; regional differences in 102
testators: characteristics of 103–7; inherited wealth 79–80
Thatcher, Margaret 2, 7, 96
Thomas, A. 45, 48
Thorns, D. 19, 33
Todd, J.E. 91
Tory Reform Group 8
trading down: divorce and 69–70; and equity release 42
trading up, on inheritance 120, 122, 123, 153, 157
Trollope, Anthony 43
trust funds 81
Trustee Savings Bank equity-release scheme 45

UBS Phillips & Drew 154
United Kingdom: average house prices 12–13, 21, 22, 23; average house-price inflation 24, 25; death duties 141–9; demographic changes 6, 65, 66–7, 70; estates containing housing 55–7; home ownership in 11, 151–2; household-formation rates 6, 67; housing inheritance in 102, 104, 105, 151–3; housing in personal wealth 11; housing wealth, sudden 152; inheritance studies 76–85; as nation of inheritors 57, 64, 96, 110, 159; population estimates 6; as property-owning democracy 96, 110; public housing 3, 11; taxation of home-ownership 6; taxation of inheritance 141, 147
United States: home ownership in 11, 152; house prices 152; as 'post-shelter' society 12

Vision (1989) 156

Wales: average house-price inflation 24, 25, 26, 27; estates containing housing 63; house prices 21, 22; households, type 67, 68, 69; housing inheritance in 102, 104, 105; population changes 67; 'rents into mortgages' scheme 8

Walker, Peter 1–2, 8

Watson, S. 48, 51, 155

wealth: inherited and then bequeathed 79–80; see also distribution of; housing wealth; personal wealth

Wedgwood, Josiah 76–8, 79

West Midlands: average house-price inflation 24, 25, 26, 27; house prices 21, 22; housing inheritance in 102, 104, 105

Whalley, J. 82, 149

Wheeler, R. 155

Whitehead, C. 30

widowed people. bequeathing patterns 81, 82

widows, estate size 91

William III, King of England 141

Williams, P. 4

wills: clarity 86; surveyed 79–94; see also bequeathing

Wise, D. 8, 155

women: bequeathing patterns 83–4, 88–9, 91; as home-owners 93; housing wealth bequeathed 92–3; longevity 69, 89, 91; size of estate 89–91; sources of wealth 80

working class: attitudes to wealth 114; buyers 32, 33

working population, decline 65, 70

York, house prices 20

Yorkshire and Humberside: average house-price inflation 24, 25, 26, 27; house prices 20, 21, 23; housing inheritance in 102

young inheritors 133–4